MORE THAN YOU WANTED TO KNOW

MORE THAN YOU WANTED TO KNOW

THE FAILURE OF MANDATED DISCLOSURE

Omri Ben-Shahar
Carl E. Schneider

Princeton University Press
Princeton and Oxford

Published by Princeton University Press, 41 William Street, Princeton, New Jersey 08540

In the United Kingdom: Princeton University Press, 6 Oxford Street, Woodstock, Oxfordshire OX20 1TW

press.princeton.edu

Jacket art © JosA Carlos Pires Pereira/Getty Images. Jacket design by Marcella Engel Roberts. Jacket front cover by Wanda España.

Library of Congress Cataloging-in-Publication Data

Ben-Shahar, Omri, author.
More than you wanted to know : the failure of mandated disclosure /
    Omri Ben-Shahar, Carl E. Schneider.
        pages cm
Includes bibliographical references and index.
ISBN 978-0-691-16170-9 (hardcover)
1. Disclosure of information—Law and legislation—United States.
    2. Consumer protection—Law and legislation—United States.
    3. Decision making—United States. I. Schneider, Carl, 1948– author. II. Title.
KF1609.B46 2014
346.7302'1—dc23
2013034453

British Library Cataloging-in-Publication Data is available

This book has been composed in Minion Pro

Printed on acid-free paper. ∞

Printed in the United States of America

10 9 8 7 6 5 4 3 2 1

To Sarah—

Who sets no terms or conditions

—Omri Ben-Shahar

To Joan—

"Oh ye gods, render me worthy of this noble wife."

—Carl E. Schneider

CONTENTS

PREFACE

This book began at lunch. We were casually discussing our research, which we had thought must be far apart. What could two scholars, one of law-and-economics and private law (Ben-Shahar) and the other of health law and bioethics (Schneider) have in common? To our surprise and pleasure we realized we were pursing the same core thesis. Ben-Shahar had just published an article, titled "The Myth of Opportunity to Read in Contract Law," arguing that advance disclosure of fine print to consumers is pointless. Schneider's book *The Practice of Autonomy* had argued that informed consent has failed to improve patients' medical decisions. As lunch progressed we discovered that we shared a fundamental skepticism about two different aspects of the same method of regulation—mandated disclosure. And we soon realized that both the structure of the arguments we were developing and the kinds of empirical support we were recruiting had many similarities.

In the spring of 2008, we decided to write an article making our joint case against mandated disclosure in our two areas—consumer law and health law. To write it, we searched electronically for all the disclosure statutes in three states (Illinois, Michigan, and California). We were startled to find that disclosures were mandated almost wherever we looked. There were hundreds of statutes, regulations, and rulings mandating countless disclosures, all trying to do the same thing: give lay people information to help them make better decisions as consumers, cardholders, patients, employees, tenants, policyholders, travelers, and citizens. It was that revelation—the ubiquity of mandated disclosure—that set us on the course to this book.

Numerous academics have contributed to our thinking about our topic. We acknowledge in the footnotes the writings of hundreds of researchers who have spent their careers examining disclosures of many kinds. In addition, we have presented versions of the manuscript to our colleagues at Chicago and Michigan and to workshops at NYU, UCLA, the universities of Pennsylvania and Washington, Tel-Aviv and Vanderbilt Universities, Academia Sinica in Taipei, and Universitat de València. Special thanks for extended discussions and comments are due to Ryan Calo, Sarah Clarke, Richard Craswell, Bob Hillman, Florencia Marotta-Wurgler, Chuck Myers, Ariel Porat, Joan Schneider, and Doron Teichman. Ben-Shahar acknowledges the invaluable critique and feedback from his long time academic collaborator and friend, Oren Bar-Gill.

PART I

THE UBIQUITY OF MANDATED DISCLOSURE

CHAPTER 1

INTRODUCTION

Publicity is justly commended as a remedy for social and industrial diseases. Sunlight is said to be the best of disinfectants; electric light the most efficient policeman. And publicity . . . must, in the impending struggle, be utilized in many ways as a continuous remedial measure.

—Louis Brandeis, *Other People's Money*

"Mandated disclosure" may be the most common and least successful regulatory technique in American law. It aspires to help people making unfamiliar and complex decisions while dealing with specialists by requiring the latter (disclosers) to give the former (disclosees) information so that disclosees choose sensibly and disclosers do not abuse their position.

For example: You are mortgaging your new house. Or considering prostate-cancer surgery. Or buying software on line. Or being questioned by the police. You've never faced your choice before. It turns on much you do not understand. The specialists you're dealing with—lenders, doctors, vendors, and police—understand it well. Mandated disclosure requires the specialists to tell you what you must know to choose well. Thus truth-in-lending laws oblige your lender to describe its credit terms. Informed-consent doctrine obliges your doctor to describe treatments for prostate cancer. Contract law obliges your vendor to reveal terms like warranties and mandatory arbitration. *Miranda* obliges the police to recite your rights. Thus informed, you are supposed to understand your choices well enough to make sound decisions about your credit, your cancer, your computer, or your confession.

3

Mandated disclosure has been the principal regulatory answer to some of the principal policy questions of recent decades. A core response to financial crisis is to ratchet up (already considerable) disclosure mandates. Much health-care reform requires that patients be told about health plans, insurance, doctors, hospitals, treatments, and costs so that they can choose thoughtfully and thriftily. Much Internet commerce is regulated by disclosure mandates. So are many kinds of privacy. Several constitutional rights are guarded through disclosures like the *Miranda* warning. Campaign-finance regulation is now largely about disclosure.

These are just a few peaks in a mountain range. Undisclosed contract terms are generally unenforceable—hence fine print. So every "I agree" clicked, every dotted line signed is a disclosure moment. Vast stretches of consumer-protection law mandate disclosures. Mortgages, savings accounts, checking accounts, retirement accounts, credit cards, pawnshops, and rent-to-own plans are subject to disclosure mandates. Health law abounds in disclosures—in informed consent, drug labeling, research regulation, health insurance, living wills, and medical privacy. Mandated disclosures adorn food labels, travel tickets, leases, copyright warnings, time-share agreements, house sales, store return policies, school enrollment and graduation data, college crime reports, flight-safety announcements, parking-garage stubs, product and environmental hazards, and car and home repairs.

Nevertheless, mandated disclosure is a Lorelei, luring lawmakers onto the rocks of regulatory failure. This book hopes to silence its siren song. First, by identifying mandated disclosure as a distinctive regulatory method. Second, by describing its almost incontinent use. Third, by showing that it routinely fails to achieve its goals. Fourth, by explaining why it fails and cannot be fixed.

Mandated disclosure is alluring because it addresses a real problem: Modernity showers you with unfamiliar and complex decisions. Knowing little, you depend on specialists. Only a few decades ago, you made fewer choices about fewer things. You got a black telephone from AT&T. You got a mortgage from the First Local Bank, which offered only a few kinds of mortgages on quite limiting conditions. You got (often) the medical treatment your doctor thought you needed. You got a pension only if you worked many years for one company, and you got the pension the company designed.

Today, phones come in landline, cell, and VOIP versions from many manufacturers making many models for many service providers offering many plans. National lenders proffer mortgages in a medley of forms with a cornucopia of conditions. Your doctor must describe the various treatments for your ills and their effects. Pensions are portable, come in numberless forms, and may let you choose among thousands of securities.

This is largely excellent news: You have not just more, but often better, choices. Yet proliferating choice requires increasingly elaborate and arcane knowledge. So mandated disclosure addresses the problem of a world in which nonspecialists must make choices requiring specialist knowledge. Its solution is alluringly simple: if people face unfamiliar and complex decisions, give them information until the decision is familiar and comprehensible. Don't people want to make decisions for themselves, want to make them well, and try to do so? Isn't more information axiomatically better than less? Won't people gratefully take and earnestly use information they are offered?

Mandated disclosure is alluring because it resonates with two fundamental American ideologies. The first is the free-market principle. Markets work best when buyers are informed; disclosures inform them. Buyers fear sellers' rapacity and the perils of caveat emptor; disclosures protect them without distorting markets by specifying prices, quality, and terms. The second ideology is the autonomy principle. People are entitled as a matter of moral right and of practical policy to make the decisions that shape their lives. Disclosures equip them to do so.

Mandated disclosure is alluring because it seems to regulate lightly. Direct regulation of economic behavior—imposing safety and quality standards or restricting sales of products or services—can be clumsy and costly; can reduce freedom, innovation, and efficiency; can inspire burdensome bureaucracy and regulations. Mandated disclosure lets sellers sell and buyers buy, as long as buyers know what sellers are selling.

Mandated disclosure is alluring because it is relatively easy to enact. With its ecumenical ideology and apparent modesty, it provokes relatively slight political opposition. Regulated entities often prefer it to more intrusive techniques, and lawmakers know it costs the fisc peanuts.

Mandated disclosure is alluring because its failures are little noticed and soothingly explained. It has been too little recognized as a regulatory technique, and most lawmakers and many commentators do not realize that it is a method with standard characteristics and consequences that has been intensively and extensively tried. So a mandate's failures can readily be attributed to the particular way it was implemented to respond to a particular social problem rather than to defects of the regulatory form: a mandate fails because it was too narrow, disclosures were unnoticed, or forms were obscure. Mandated disclosure is a god that cannot fail.

Finally, mandated disclosure is alluring because even if it does little evident good, it does little obvious harm. If disclosures seem to burden anyone, it is the sophisticated parties to transactions who already have information and may have a moral duty to disseminate it.

So alluring is mandated disclosure—so plainly does it seem to be good regulation—that many lawmakers that enact it and commentators who urge it simply assume that its benefits exceed its costs. Some sophisticated lawmakers and commentators have begun to see it as a distinctive regulatory method. But while they acknowledge its failures, they assume that care, ingenuity, and effort can fix them. We need a term for the lawmakers and commentators who, implicitly or explicitly, favor the method. "Disclosurite" seems direct and descriptive. It includes people and institutions with varying views and faith, for it is a generalization as, say, "environmentalist" is. But it is a useful generalization because so many lawmakers and commentators embrace some version of mandated disclosure.

Mandated disclosure is alluring, but it routinely fails to achieve its ambitious goals. It is not doomed to fail, but empirical studies rarely report that disclosures lead disclosees to good decisions. For example, Lauren Willis concludes that "disclosures currently mandated by federal law for home loans neither effectively facilitate price shopping, nor do they result in good deliberate decision making about risk."[1] The National Research Council acknowledges that "[d]espite decades of research" there has been "little progress" toward "achieving informed consent."[2] More broadly, Winston's review of the empirical evidence on "federal and state information policies, including but not limited to disclosure policies, suggests that they have not made consumers significantly better informed and safer."[3]

Mandated disclosure's failure is as plausible as its success. Who has not derided disclosures as "fine print"? Who has not joked—ruefully or resentfully—about clicking "I agree" without reading the terms? Who has not competed to tell the most damning disclosure story? The mortgage closing, the car-rental counter, and the pharmacy checkout have become iconic moments when we all have declined to read disclosures, have failed to understand them when we tried to read them, and signed anyway.

The reason is that mandated disclosure is ill suited to its ends. Exactly because the choices for which it seeks to prepare disclosees are unfamiliar, complex, and ordinarily managed by specialists, novices cannot master them with the disclosures that lawmakers usually mandate. Consider the arcana the Federal Reserve Board thinks consumers should understand to select adjustable-rate mortgages: "indexes, margins, discounts, caps on rates and payments, negative amortization, payment options, and recasting (recalculating) your loan."[4] Similarly, to *begin* evaluating prostate-cancer treatments, you must understand the various therapies, why it may be best to reject them, and what their side effects are. When so much must be explained, mere disclosures rarely equip people for a well-considered decision.

Mandated disclosure fails because it depends on a long chain of fragile links. It works only if three actors—lawmakers, disclosers, and disclosees—play demanding parts deftly. Rarely can each actor meet all the part's demands. Lawmakers must correctly conclude that a problem needs a regulatory solution and that disclosure is a good one. They must correctly gauge what disclosure to mandate. They must articulate the mandate correctly and comprehensibly. Each step is hard; managing all four is uncommon, especially under the pressure that often drives lawmakers. Disclosers also face challenges. Even under the sweetly optimistic assumption that disclosers truly try to obey mandates, they must read, understand, and heed the mandate, create or assemble data, and explain them effectively.

But the lawmaker's and discloser's roles look blessedly simple next to the disclosee's. Suppose that people really make decisions the way that disclosurites imagine—that they want to make them and that they want to assemble the relevant information, identify the possible outcomes, assess their own preferences, and determine which choice best serves those preferences. Disclosees would still need to *understand* disclosures. But even experts can struggle. Elizabeth Warren, former special advisor for the Consumer Financial Protection Bureau, said of a credit-card disclosure: "I teach contract law at Harvard, and I can't understand half of what it says."

In truth, many people cannot read most disclosures. Over forty million adults are functionally illiterate; another fifty million are only marginally literate. In one study, 40 percent of the patients could not read instructions for taking pills on an empty stomach. Innumeracy is worse. In a test of *basic* numeracy, only 16 percent could answer three (*really*) simple questions (like, how much is 1 percent of $1000?). Yet financial- and medical-privacy notices are generally written at a college level, and only a tiny percent of the population can understand ordinary contractual language. (Even eBay's users' contract—a document written in lay language—contains sentences like this: "When you give us content, you grant us a non-exclusive, worldwide, perpetual, irrevocable, royalty-free, sublicensable (through multiple tiers) right to exercise the copyright, publicity, and database rights (but no other rights) you have in the content, in any media known now or in the future."[5])

Disclosurites count on simpler and better disclosure—"targeted transparency" and "smart disclosure" and "behaviorally informed" reform and "heightened" and "meaningful" disclosures tested in labs. But disclosures are unreadable and unread because you can't describe complexity simply. The problem is not just illiteracy and innumeracy. It is also the "quantity question," which comprises the "overload" problem and the "accumulation" problem. The overload problem arises when a disclosure is too copious and complex to handle. The accumulation problem arises because disclosees daily confront so many disclosures and yearly confront so many consequential disclosures that they cannot attend to (much less master) more than a few. Disclosures, recall, should prepare people for unfamiliar and complex decisions. Decisions are complex because so much must be learned well and used capably. But it is hard to organize and present masses of information cogently. It is hard to remember, interpret, and apply even cogent presentations. Unfamiliarity exacerbates these problems: the less you know about a choice, the more you must learn.

The disclosurite demand for simplification is in tension with the disclosurite goal of thorough information. How might you simplify? If you disclose less, disclosees can learn less. If people have a right to know how private data are used, how can a Web site tell them less than the full truth? If patients' consent to prostate-cancer treatment is to be "informed," how do you delete information? What information should a physician omit? A treatment option? A side effect? A description of the side effect? An estimate of a side effect's likelihood? A review of the factors affecting the risk of a side effect?

Or do you simplify by summarizing? Scores summarizing information, like a loan's APR, can sometimes be devised. But can that score both describe problems accurately and be understood and used by the naïve? Such problems afflict even the APR, on which lawmakers and scholars have labored for decades. The disclosurite poster child has been restaurant hygiene grades: A, B, or C. But it turns out that much is omitted or distorted in those grades and that their success is dubious.

Disclosurites also swear by simple language. But specialized words summarize complex ideas. Explanations are shorter if "brachytherapy" replaces "a form of radiotherapy where a radiation source is placed inside or next to the area requiring treatment." But because disclosees are nonspecialists, these are the very terms they don't know.

Even if simple words and ideas could efficiently describe unfamiliar and complex issues, novices lack the background to understand those issues. For example, you can't evaluate the arguments against PSA screening if, as many men do, you conflate screening and prevention. Worse, to use information adeptly you need skills in processing and evaluating it that come from practice, not disclosure. As Iyengar puts it, "When we learn, through study and practice, to simplify, prioritize, and categorize elements and to recognize patterns," we can "create order in seeming chaos."[6]

We have been assuming that people want to make decisions and to make them in the disclosurite way. But many people avoid making decisions. Patients take their doctor's advice instead of reasoning to their own conclusion; employees duck retirement planning. This may be imprudent, but people are not deciding machines. Their family, friends, work, play, and prayer more than fill their lives. Mastering just one complex and unfamiliar choice is a struggle and a distraction; taking on even a trickle of the flood of disclosures can mean drowning.

Furthermore, many people make decisions with scant information and slight deliberation. They overlook, skip, or skim disclosures. Far from gathering information, people strip it away to make choices manageable. Thus many women base their choice of breast cancer treatment on a single factor. Furthermore, experience teaches people how little they may gain from studying disclosures and how little they may lose by ignoring them. In short, people often calculate that a well-informed decision's benefits poorly justify its costs.

After all, our eyeballs are daily drenched with disclosures old, revised, and new: online, in the mail, in doctors' offices, and at Best Buy; in inserts, boxes, and shrink-wraps; on the back of bills and the front of order forms. Disclosure is a ritual to be endured: patients are "consented," borrowers sign their way through closings, smartphone users "accept" terms, and Internet users are informed of privacy policies through linked scrolls. How can we not filter the white noise of disclosure? Lawmakers then turn up the volume to get our attention, and we close our ears to the din.

In short, mandated disclosure seems plausible only on logically reasonable but humanly false assumptions. When buying software on line, how many people click to read the terms of sale, much less read them, much less try to understand them, much less succeed? In one study only one or two shoppers in a thousand spent even one second on the terms page. At a mortgage closing how many people even skim the stack of documents they sign, much less understand them? Surely nobody, since for a simple fixed-rate mortgage that pile can include one hundred pages with forty-eight separate disclosures requiring fifty-four signatures. How many men with prostate cancer try to decipher their prospects of cure and of side effects with each of the principal treatments, much less learn and remember enough to use the data? Nearly nobody, since patients do not read, understand, and remember *much* simpler medical information. How many people given the *Miranda* warning understand its implications? Yale faculty members and graduate students did not. How many people realize they received their bank's data-collection disclosure, much less read it? One Web site's disclosure offered $100 to anyone noticing it; it kept its $100.

Even if unfamiliar and complex choices could be simply presented, the dynamics of lawmaking would discourage it. Those dynamics drive lawmakers toward ever more and ever broader mandates. Chapter 2 will describe the consumer-credit disclosure that morphed from one short page to a long, two-sided "bed sheet" of disclosures jostling for attention. The terms of iTunes now stretch thirty-two feet in tiny font. Under regulators' intensive supervision, consent forms in human-subject research have swollen steadily. Each scandal in which information (if properly used) *might* have prevented disaster provokes more mandates. Each disclosure that seems to be working is extended further. (If listing the calories on a can of beans worked, why not add fat and sodium? The country of origin? Genetic modifications?) Furthermore, in our system several lawmakers can issue mandates in one jurisdiction. A single loan can be subject to a battery of disclosures mandated by federal, state, and local legislatures, agencies, and courts. Disclosure is a ratchet, expanding easily, contracting rarely.

Mandated disclosure's unreliability might not matter were it harmless. Mandates look free because they cost government little, because disclosure is rarely a line item in a discloser's books, and because disclosees do not realize that they pay its costs. Even if the administrative costs of one mandate are modest, the aggregate cost of thousands of mandates is not. And mandates can do harm. Not least, bad law drives out good: mandates spare lawmakers the struggle of enacting better but less popular reforms. Disclosures can be inequitable: complex instructions may sometimes help the affluent and sophisticated but be useless for the poor and naive. Since all disclosees ultimately pay for disclosures, the poor subsidize the rich. Mandated disclosures can crowd out more useful information (time spent "consenting" patients cannot be spent treating them). Disclosures can shield disclosers from other regulation, like tort liability or antifraud and deception statutes. And complying with mandates can take time and effort that is little noticed but quite damaging (like disclosures to research subjects, which have become so detailed and disruptive that valuable research is slowed, damaged, and even stopped).

In sum, not only does the empirical evidence show that mandated disclosure regularly fails, failure is inherent in it. First, mandated disclosure rests on false assumptions about how people live, think, and act. Second, it rests on false assumptions about how well information improves decisions. Third, its success requires a chain of demands on lawmakers, disclosers, and disclosees too numerous and onerous to be met often.

Mandated disclosure is a regulatory response to the problems of non-specialists facing unfamiliar and complex decisions. It is broadly, almost indiscriminately, used. But it fails to achieve its goals because unfamiliar and complex decisions are much harder than disclosurite ideology assumes. Giving consumers information about such decisions cannot equip them to make the truly informed decisions that disclosurites desire. Mandated disclosure is a fundamental failure that cannot be fundamentally fixed.

We are often asked how to replace mandated disclosure. We first reply that even if lawmakers don't know what works, at least they can know what fails, and what fails should be abandoned. Second, "what would you do instead?" is the wrong question if it suggests that another panacea should be contrived, that *any* regulatory technique can do everything asked of disclosure. Nothing can be so variously effective. So commentators and lawmakers must acknowledge the limits of their tools and undertake the intellectual and political challenge of tailoring solutions to problems. This is a counsel of realism but not despair.

For one thing, people are less foolish than disclosurism assumes. *Many* disclosures fail because they are not wanted or needed. *Much* that is disclosed people sensibly ignore. They rightly calculate that reading an end-users license agreement won't change their minds. They reasonably prefer working with their doctor toward a good decision to using disclosures to make their own choice. They sensibly suppose that while a disclosure might improve a decision, the improvement is too improbable and imperceptible to justify the time and effort. And they correctly rely on government and the market to reduce the risks of leaving disclosures unstudied.

In addition, people ignore disclosures because they can get information—sometimes better information—elsewhere. For example, people commonly prefer advice to data. Mandates require listing a company's contract terms; Amazon's ratings and Yelp reviews tell you whether people liked what they bought. Many enterprises—from Consumer's Reports to Standard & Poor's—collect and offer information tailored to their clients.

How could a regulatory technique be so common and yet so bad? Mandated disclosure asks the wrong question, "What information do people need to make good decisions?" That is an important question to which a rich and fascinating literature has begun to find answers. But it is the wrong question because for lawmakers the relevant issue is whether this kind of regulation does more good than harm. Does requiring the sophisticated party in a transaction to give the naïve party information about an unfamiliar and complex decision work? The evidence of many decades in many fields shows that mandated disclosure persistently fails to achieve its purposes, cannot be fixed, and too often causes harm. Lawmakers should stop using it, commentators should stop proposing it, and interest groups should stop advocating it unless they can convincingly show that this time it *really* is different.

CHAPTER 2

COMPLEX DECISIONS, COMPLEX DISCLOSURES

[H]ow intricate a work then have they who are gone to consult which of these sicknesses of mine is, and then which of these fevers, and then what it would do, and then how it may be countermined.

—John Donne, *Devotions Upon Emergent Occasions*

Chapter 1 introduced mandated disclosure as a distinctive regulatory technique used in an impressive range of areas. It argued that while some disclosures may sometimes help some people, mandated disclosure poorly serves its goal of leading disclosees to make good decisions about unfamiliar and complex choices in interactions with knowledgeable parties. This chapter describes mandated disclosure. The problem mandated disclosure addresses is both intensive and extensive. It is intensive because decisions are so truly unfamiliar and so greatly complex that considerable learning is needed to understand them. The problem is extensive because these decisions arise so profligately.

AN INTENSIVE PROBLEM

The decisions mandates commonly address are intensive; they turn on many factors that themselves are often intricate. To show what that means, we examine two kinds of decisions disclosure has classically tried to inform and improve—borrowing money to buy a home and choosing a medical treatment.

Borrowing Money

Few pecuniary decisions matter more than financing a home. No purchase costs more. Your choice sets your housing costs for years. Your house is probably your biggest investment, and one you can't really diversify. Your mortgage is your largest liability, and the monthly payments are the biggest chunk of your salary. Many houses in many neighborhoods are available, and they differ in ways that make comparing apples with oranges easy. You are picking neighbors and a school for your children. And houses can go expensively wrong, from leaky roof to flooded basement. You have *lots* of chances to make big mistakes.

So, how much house can you afford? You want a nice house in a nice neighborhood, and you don't want to be penny-wise and pound-foolish. But spending too much means disaster. The higher your payments, the less you have for everything else—college tuition, retirement savings, vacations, clothes, restaurants. If your income declines or your expenses increase (children could precipitate both misfortunes at once), you might have to borrow even more expensively or sell the house. If you stretch to increase your down payment, you cut into your investments and your cushion for emergencies. If you must sell in a bad market, you could lose your down payment *and* owe more on the mortgage than you get for the house.

You easily find general advice on how much house you can afford. A Web site says your housing expenses (mortgage principal, interest, taxes, and insurance) should not exceed 25–28 percent of your gross income and that your total debt should not exceed 33–36 percent. The amount you borrow depends on how much you put down. The Web site says lenders may want a down payment of up to 20 percent and that closing costs will be 3–6 percent. A Ginnie Mae calculator says you can get away with a down payment under 15 percent (much less if you get expensive private mortgage insurance). But as the 2008 mortgage crisis showed, the housing market is crucial. As prices fell even people with reasonable mortgages owed more than their homes were worth. For people with balloon payments, their down payment evaporated, refinancing was hard, and ruin loomed.

The people you deal with in buying and financing costly durable assets know a lot more than you do. The sellers know all about their house. It's as central to their finances as it will be to yours, so they've made it bright and shiny. True, you're working with a pretty swell broker (who gets paid sooner if you buy a house quickly and gets paid more if you pay more). You will encounter (and pay unexpected fees to) a closing agency. And you'll deal with governments waiting to tax you and with insurers glad to protect you against risks you hadn't considered at prices you didn't anticipate.

Then there's the mortgage. Lenders calculate risks and returns using long experience and information about your history and preferences. Competition often makes markets safer for consumers, but many of a loan's costs and consequences are either obscure to borrowers or can be obscured by lenders.[1] Furthermore, loans are individually packaged and priced, and market conditions change frequently, making it hard to rely on other people's experience. So you resolve to shop thoroughly and thoughtfully. You know little about this market, but Googling finds many apparently eager lenders, including mortgage brokers, local banks, credit unions, and national banks. Their loans are protean, with different costs, advantages, and commitments. In the welter of information sits a central datum—the annual percentage rate, which is intended to summarize a loan's costs.

But while this APR lets you compare, say, several thirty-year fixed-rate loans, it does not help with some crucial dilemmas. A few examples: long-term loans have higher interest rates but lower monthly payments than shorter loans. So, do you care more about a low APR (paying less interest) or a low monthly payment? If interest rates fall and you refinance, you may owe a prepayment penalty. Do you want a cheaper loan with that penalty or a costlier loan without it? How much costlier? You can lower your monthly payments by buying points (a kind of prepaid interest). Their value turns on your likelihood of paying off the loan early or refinancing, which turns on things like interest rates and your income. The adjustable-rate mortgage presents similar problems. Its interest rate fluctuates, so you cannot anticipate your payments. Moreover, ARMs sometimes offer tasty teaser rates and negative amortization, which make a house more affordable now but can increase the total you pay.

Then there are peripheral but substantial considerations. You soon discover that your closing costs will include some assortment of an application fee, appraisal fee, assumption fee, credit-report fee, mortgage-insurance application fee, lender's inspection fee, lender's attorney fee, loan-origination fee, points, mortgage-broker fee, mortgage-insurance premium, process fee, reserve-account funds, tax-related service fee, underwriting fee, wire-transfer fee, annual assessments, flood-insurance premium, homeowners-insurance premium, property taxes, attorney fees, notary fees, title-insurance fees, title-search fees, various inspection fees, recording fee, survey fee, and transfer taxes. Many of these cost little, many you can't affect, but some are larger, like the three kinds of insurance a creditor wants you to buy: title insurance (in case there's a legal problem with your ownership of the house); credit insurance (in case something happens to you or your income); and homeowners insurance (in case something happens to the house that is the collateral for the mortgage). To protect its collateral further, the lender must be sure you pay your property taxes and insurance premiums and so wants you to fund an escrow account for paying them. If you want to make these payments yourself when they are due instead of in monthly installments, you may need to pay a fee for an escrow waiver, and you had better know the financial and legal consequences of not making payments.

In this tangle of data and trade-offs, some things matter more than others. The question of how much to borrow at what interest rate dwarfs many of the junk fees that pop up, even if those are inflated. But all this is new to you, so you don't know what really counts and what can be ignored. You hear that borrowers often pay unexpected costs, so must you investigate things thoroughly? How do you allocate your attention? The Fed tells you not to "check your common sense at the door,"[2] but your common sense isn't answering all these questions.

In short, even a simple mortgage requires many decisions from a long menu of choices and options that cannot be revised, that have serious financial implications, and that depend on assumptions and factors even experts dread and miscalculate.

Choosing a Treatment for Prostate Cancer

To be diagnosed with prostate cancer, you will already have made decisions, since the diagnosis is made through a transrectal biopsy (often prompted by a high PSA) that few men think pleasant and so have reason to consider judiciously. Your biopsy shows cancer. As you regather your nerve and your wits, you find that treatments may include radical prostatectomy (nerve-sparing and non-nerve sparing), external-beam radiation, brachytherapy, combination external beam and brachytherapy, hormone therapy, cryotherapy, active surveillance, watchful waiting, and nothing. You may not be offered all of these; some may be inappropriate or unavailable. But not being offered a treatment may also mean you've been caught in the long battle between the two relevant specialties (urology and radiation oncology) that offer different treatments and disagree implacably.

Just learning what the treatments are is no small thing. What do the words mean? What do the treatments involve? How do they work? And there are three basic questions about each treatment: their necessity, efficacy, and collateral consequences.

One treatment is no treatment. Really. Much prostate cancer moves so slowly that you die of something else before the cancer gets you. But not all prostate cancers move slowly, so rejecting treatment may look scary. If so, you could try active surveillance. You would hope that the cancer is the indolent kind and see what happens. With luck, you are spared treatment and its risks. If the cancer begins to seem threatening, you treat it. Meanwhile, your PSA is monitored and you have more biopsies.

It would be easier if you could distinguish fast from slow cancers, but the measure—the Gleason score—is not ideal. Yours is $3 + 4 = 7$. Were it $3 + 3 = 6$, alert surveillance might make sense. Your urologist will do it even with your 7 but advises against it. Now your urologist points out that your transrectal biopsy sampled only twelve cores and suggests a transperineal saturation biopsy, which could take as many as eighty cores (your prostate is a bit bigger than a walnut). You agree, but the second biopsy stubbornly produces the same Gleason score. You're stuck.

You're offered two basic choices—radiation and surgery. The standard advice is that they treat the disease equally well. On inquiry, though, you find that the standard advice simplifies grossly. Success can only be assessed over long periods, so today's data evaluate treatments that are years old. Today's treatments are presumably better, but you can't be sure or know how much better.

If radiation and surgery cure equally well, the tie breaker may be the third issue—side effects, late effects, and complications, like impotence, incontinence, and difficulty urinating. Your urologist's chart says that several years out, surgery and radiation patients do equally well. So, which do you most want to avoid—impotence or incontinence? As you try to figure that one out, you realize that each term covers a range from mild problems to calamity. So, are the odds about the entire continuum or a particular degree of severity?

Then you realize that even a serious side effect might not matter if it can be treated. Your urologist says that both incontinence and impotence *can* be treated. You are relieved until you investigate the treatments, which raise completely new questions about efficacy and side effects. Will it be enough to take Viagra? (How effective is Viagra? And can it really make you blind?) If Viagra fails, how about more recherché alternatives? A vacuum pump? Penile injections? (Not to worry—the needle is thin.) A penile implant?

Then you learn that the likelihood and severity of side effects depend on your baseline, on how you're doing now. You re-examine your urologist's chart and find that surgery patients were younger and healthier than radiation patients, yet the two groups wound up about the same a few years out. Hmmm. More questions reveal that your chances of side effects are influenced by more than your baseline. If you *really* want individualized odds, you factor in your PSA, your Gleason score, the disease stage, your prostate's size and location, and more. Then you discover rare but horrible possibilities, like a recto-urethral fistula (a hole between the urethra and the rectum), that are hard to treat. The fistula is a risk of radiation but not surgery. And since surgery removes your prostate, you might find urinating easier, which would be nice.

Even if you could exactly predict your chance of each side effect, late effect, and complication and their severity and treatability, what would it all mean? How much would incontinence change your life? Impotence?

Your urologist says many patients would rather be impotent than incontinent. How can you evaluate this (to you counterintuitive) evidence?

You then ask about what happens during and immediately after treatment. What do you do to prepare for the surgery? (Briefly, things you would rather not do.) How debilitating is the surgery? What is wearing a Foley catheter (which runs to the bladder) for ten days like? Can you take the time for radiation treatments five days a week for eight weeks? How severely and how long will the radiation fatigue you? (Your doctor says it's like a long day at the office; your experienced friend was wiped out for weeks.)

You are not just choosing a treatment; you are choosing a doctor. Standard advice is to ask doctors about their success rates, but you hate to ask so rudely skeptical a question, and how will you understand the answer? How many different surgeons or radiation oncologists do you investigate? How do you compare a surgeon's success rate with an oncologist's? How do you account for the fact that the best surgeons take the hardest cases (lowering their success rates)? Assuming doctors are equally skilled, which one would you rather have caring for you?

Your urologist does not perform this surgery and sends you to a urologist who does and to a radiation oncologist. Having spoken with your urologist and having met the oncologist, you opt for surgery. You meet a surgeon of undoubted technical skill who sees you reluctantly, thinks you have studied your choices too carefully, says frostily that the side-effects data you studied do not apply to *his* patients, and tells you that surgery is the only proved way to survive. You begin to dislike him. You recall how much you liked the oncologist, who was a fine teacher, kindly, and gently persuasive.

Then your internist reminds you that you may not benefit from treatment, that your disease might progress so slowly that something else would carry you off first. Is it worth enduring treatment and its risks for an unclear chance of preventing something so uncertain?

INTENSIVE DISCLOSURES

These two examples suggest how intensive—how truly unfamiliar and complex—are the decisions that disclosure mandates ordinarily address. If so, the disclosurite ideal of informed decisions, of people empowered

to make autonomous choices, is demanding: Intensively complex problems demand intensive disclosures, a great deal of information for people
starting with little. Take our example of buying a house. Sellers' disclosure
baseline is the common law obligation to tell buyers all material facts
about defects in the house and to answer buyers' queries truthfully. But
numerous regulations (federal, state, and municipal) require specific disclosures in specific formats of dozens of items, including the property's
history, all known defects and hazards, zoning restrictions, conflicting
rights and disputes, and association fees. In California, for example,
sellers must disclose, among much more (the instruction booklet for disclosures is seventy-nine pages long), the location of registered sex offenders, a death on the property within the last three years, and neighborhood
nuisances like a dog that barks at night.

In shopping for a mortgage, the baseline is an APR index that summarizes a loan's interest rate and other costs. Then comes the intensive
disclosure. Instead of the one-page truth-in-lending disclosure with a
Fed box that highlights the APR and the total finance charges, borrowers
get a library of disclosures. The simplest mortgage can easily need fifty
(truly) documents and disclosures mandated by different agencies and
laws. There is the HUD-1 form—several pages—and a form comparing
the TILA and HUD-1 disclosures (which, because they are divulged on
different days, may differ), and an addendum (sometimes, addenda) to
HUD-1. There are disclosures related to the property insurance that borrowers must buy, and to the property appraisal, and to credit reporting
by the lender, and to compliance with federal nondiscrimination statutes,
and to privacy and data collection, and to the right to cancel, and to payment options, and to escrow, and many, many more. There are overlapping disclosures because many are mandated separately by federal and
state laws. There is even the Paperwork Reduction Act disclosure (from
a witty lawmaker).

Much can be bundled in the APR, but some factors cannot be, and
they are disclosed separately. A crucial one is the option to prepay. A disclosure must try to equip the borrower to compare a cheaper loan with a
prepayment penalty against a costlier loan without one. The adjustable-
rate mortgage presents similar problems. The monthly payments vary

with current interest rates. So you get a separate disclosure of synthetic examples, like simplified scenarios involving a $10,000 loan and how it would evolve in a representative history and in a worst-case scenario. These disclosures use terms like "index," "margins," and "adjustment caps."

Did we pick the knottiest decisions—loans and cancer? Alas, no. Intensively complex problems proliferate, requiring intensive disclosures. How intensive? The best answer would be to reprint the disclosures. But this would mean 10,000 words of contractual boilerplate or 2,500 words of privacy policy. Our publisher limits us to 80,000 words for the book, and besides we must avoid the error we criticize—overloading readers with more than they can (or care to) take in. So we'll illustrate intensity more compactly.

When disclosurites talk about mortgage disclosure, they think about the APR—the single score that summarizes the loan's cost. Low interest rates recently induced one of us to refinance his mortgage. His loan closing contained the APR disclosure *and* forty-eight others strewn over 101 pages, all looking ominous and demanding separate signatures:

Federal truth-in-lending disclosure statement (APR);
Borrower's promise to pay note;
Settlement statement (HUD-1);
Uniform residential loan application;
Addendum to HUD-1 settlement statement;
Addendum to HUD-1;
General closing instructions;
Specific closing instructions;
Addendum to closing instructions;
Itemization of amount financed;
Payoff schedule;
Credit-score disclosure;
Hazard insurance authorization requirements;
Request for transcript of tax return;
Request for taxpayer identification number and certification;
Certification addendum to HUD-1 settlement statement;
Borrower's certificate of net tangible benefit;
Acknowledgment of receipt of appraisal report;
Appraisal disclosure;
Certificate of loans to one borrower;

Owner's affidavit and indemnification agreement;
Borrower's compliance agreement;
Legal description;
Distribution form;
USA Patriot Act customer identification verification;
Federal Equal Credit Opportunity Act notice;
Notice concerning the furnishing of negative information to consumer-
    reporting agency (Fair Credit Reporting Act disclosure);
Occupancy- and financial-status affidavit;
Payment letter to borrower;
Privacy disclosure statement;
Quality control release and authorization to re-verify;
Servicing disclosure statement;
Signature affidavit and AKA statement;
Tax designation forms;
Inter vivos revocable trust as borrower acknowledgment;
Addendum to notice of inter vivos revocable trust;
Inter vivos revocable trust rider;
Illinois borrower information document;
Notice of right to cancel;
Mortgage;
Fixed interest rate rider;
Illinois civil union addendum to uniform residential loan application;
Evidence of joint application;
Collateral protection insurance notice;
Illinois notice of choice of agent insurer;
Payment instructions;
Illinois mortgage-escrow account;
Escrow waiver;
Illinois escrow disclosure statement;
Failure to close within specified commitment disclosure.

The disclosurite wisdom is that the financial crisis of 2008 was pre-
cipitated partly by mortgagors who made mistakes for want of information. President Obama has made targeted, simplified disclosures central
to his response to the crisis. Two documents in this list—the TILA disclosure and the settlement statement (HUD-1)—are revised products of this
simplification. But even if the two documents are simpler, they are buried
in the avalanche of forty-seven other forms, including new disclosures
required by the Dodd-Frank Act's response to the crisis.

Here, the disclosure's intensity came not just from individual disclosures but from multiple mandates for one transaction, but even a single document can be spectacularly intensive. Take a modest example. Contracts generally bind people only to terms they receive in advance. Reformers want to give people a "robust" opportunity to read contractual terms, which is why you're plagued by Internet pop-ups demanding your assent to terms. Terms can change rapidly, so you may be asked recurrently. Recently, iTunes told one of us to accept new terms of service (after he had agreed to many versions in the months before and anticipated more in the months to follow). He scrolled down the iPhone screen and found that he was reading the first of fifty-five pages but could accept the unread terms and e-mail them to himself. He did and printed thirty-two pages of minuscule font (8 point), pasted them into a scroll, and unrolled it in the University of Chicago Law School lobby (see plate 1).

Res ipsa loquitur—the thing speaks for itself. We could tell you how many words this (pretty typical) monster contains, or how often a new version emerges, or how each version lengthens its predecessor, or how hard comparing versions is. We could show you typos suggesting that even disclosers don't read the stuff very well. We could reproduce its language—say, the ALLCAP portions that must be more "conspicuous"— and tell you how baroque its prose and provisions are. But what is perhaps most droll is that all this is for a purchase of . . . 99¢.

Another illustration of an intensive disclosure is the California Retail Installment Sale agreement. This standard form integrates all the disclosures given someone buying a new car on credit. Attorneys call it a bed sheet. It's one piece of paper, but it's twenty-six inches long, and each side is crammed with print (see plate 2).

In 1961 this form was an unexceptional eight-by-eleven-inch page with four disclosures and two signature lines. In fifty years of consumer protection, it has acquired sixteen disclosure boxes on the front and a dense back. It is a patchwork of disclosures mandated by different lawmakers at different times addressing different concerns. Lawmakers enact mandates single spies; they rarely see the battalions that result.

The bed sheet is a quilt of the graphic designer's arts. Each box fights for the eye, and lawmakers have used every device short of three dimensionality, creating a merry motley of sizes, colors, spacings, fonts, distinctive shapes, and frames of varying thickness, area, and shade. The original document got by with four fonts; the 2010 form needs twenty-two typefaces and eight fonts. Some are **bold**, others *italicized*, some ***both***. Some items are in ALL CAPS, others in **BOLD CAPS**, others in RED (this is actually black, because our book is printed in black-and-white). While major topics must be in a font of no fewer than 6 points, the *really* major ones must be in **eight point boldface**, and the *really **really*** major ones in 10-point font or even a 12-POINT HEADING.

Because the bed sheet is standardized, terms must be filled in. The sheet is spotted like Mad Libs with lines for sellers and buyers to complete. The 2010 disclosure form had 199 blank lines, including sixty for prices. The 2010 version provides for eight signatures (up from two). Finally, the front of the 1961 sheet contained 743 words. The 2010 form—after fifty years of improved disclosure, during which TILA was enacted and the APR was invented—is 2051 words. With the boilerplate on the back, there are over 5,400 words (this chapter has about 6,400).

Intensive financial disclosures are common. Checking account overdrafts can provoke such high fees that in 2011 customers paid $38 billion.[3] To describe the many fees, the average disclosure is twice as long (and quite as dismaying) as *Romeo and Juliet* (111 pages). Fannie Mae's mandated mortgage-note disclosure has more than 10,000 words in nine pages of 7.5-point font. Simplified disclosures are often advocated but rarely achieved and, as chapter 8 will show, are afflicted with problems in pruning or compressing complexity. The cluttered bed sheet, one hundred pages of closing documents, and onion layers of medical perplexities abide.

In short, intensive problems—complex decisions exacerbated by unfamiliarity—evoke intensive disclosures. The intensity problem's magnitude may be surprising, but its seriousness is increasingly acknowledged (even if solutions are elusive). Yet, there is another way people may be overwhelmed by disclosures: unfamiliar and complex decisions are extensively pressed upon us. Even if you could master one, you could hardly master all (or most, or even many) of them. To this ubiquity issue we now turn.

EXTENSIVE PROBLEMS, EXTENSIVE SOLUTIONS

We now want to show how common unfamiliar and complex decisions are and how extensively disclosures are mandated. The obvious way is to list all the mandates, displaying the disclosure empire in all its exhausting detail. We did just that to write this book. But if disclosures fail partly because their number, length, and density repel recipients, how can we similarly repel you? You would skip the list as you skipped Homer's catalog of ships or the Bible's begats; if you didn't, you would drown in detail.

Just imagine. We might begin by surveying financial disclosures, since the truth-in-lending laws of the '60s are the crown jewel of consumer-finance protection. When people borrow, save, or invest; get a bank account or credit card; lease a car; or buy on credit, they get disclosures. From the familiar Schumer Box (of credit-card terms) to the legions of disclosures accompanying retirement investments, numerous devices are supposed to make consumer finance transparent. Then we might catalog mailings from financial institutions amending, augmenting, and renewing disclosures.

Next we might review health-related disclosures. Their centerpiece is the informed-consent doctrine, which obliges doctors to tell patients about their illnesses and treatments. But health law requires many more disclosures: warnings on drug packages, privacy notices, advisories on advance directives, conflict-of-interest notices, hospital report cards, and information about health-care plans.

Next, insurance. Insurers must explain their products, fees charged, coverage provided, what is not covered, how to withdraw from or revise coverage, how to avoid unnecessary coverage. Many states issue or require insurers to distribute "What You Need to Know" guides meant to be both educational (flash tutorials on insurance basics) and to provide information about policies. For example, Minnesota publishes a twenty-page booklet for consumers on auto insurance, how to shop for it, what it covers, how to file claims, and much more.[4] California requires disclosures to homeowners of types of property insurance. And who has not initialed a mosaic of insurance disclosures and disclaimers when renting a car?

Privacy and data collection are prolific topics for mandates. HIPAA is a federal statute purporting to protect confidentiality by (partly) making health providers, pharmacies, and health plans disclose how they handle records. A single HIPAA disclosure is an intensive document listing the many uses of different classes of information. But it is also part of a battery of privacy disclosures. Institutions must disclose what personal financial information they gather, how they protect it, and with whom they share it. Then there is the surge of privacy notices from the likes of Google, Apple, Facebook, and the telecom, retail, and other corporations that collect information about us. These notices average 2500 words. And, of course, the Paperwork Reduction Act disclosure adorns government and business forms (the version in the 1040 instruction booklet surpasses 600 words) to tell us that we need not "provide the information requested on a form that is subject to the Paperwork Reduction Act unless the form displays a valid OMB control number." Reading all the privacy disclosures we received in 2008 would take each of us seventy-six work days, for a national total of over fifty billion hours—an opportunity cost greater than the GDP of Florida.[5]

There are more, vastly more, disclosure laws we would shepherd you through. The *Miranda* warning discloses constitutional rights. Campaign-finance law discloses who contributed how much to whom. Every contract you accept (with mouse or pen) responds to a disclosure command. California's Proposition 65 famously requires warnings about products and facilities exposing people to toxic substances. And there are food labels, advertising disclaimers, product warning notices, store return policy and right-to-withdraw disclosures, campus crime reports, and restaurant hygiene grades.

Then there are product- and sector-specific mandates. Like the disclosure accompanying purchases of cemetery plots and caskets (e.g., "THERE IS NO SCIENTIFIC OR OTHER EVIDENCE THAT ANY CASKET WITH A SEALING DEVICE WILL PRESERVE HUMAN RE-MAINS"). Like the disclosure before they tow your car. Like the regiment of disclosures for real estate transactions and home improvement services. Or the battalions of mandates about specific foods; sales of pets, art, cars, or appliances; enrollment in schools, colleges, campgrounds, or timeshares; provision of services by brokers, restaurants, car repair shops; and installing home alarms. Or the oral disclosures consumers enjoy, like flight safety announcements, sales operators' telephone recitals, and the disclosures reminding people that comprehensive disclosures are available in writing.

So, we might march through the areas in which disclosures are mandated. Or we might trek through the categories of mandates. Disclosures are often long but may be short: the credit-card privacy disclosure or the Schumer box, the drug-warning insert or the drug "black box," the retirement fund's disclosure or the TILA Fed box. They are often written but may be oral: drug warning or *Miranda* warning, campus-safety report or flight-safety instruction, sales solicitation disclaimers by mail or by telephone. Disclosures may be standard but can be tailored: informed consent, truth-in-lending statements, and health-plan information can have both generic and personalized parts.

Sometimes a statute dictates a disclosure's words; sometimes disclosers choose their own. Drug warnings, for example, come in all styles. Some are specified by regulations; others emerge from principles of tort law. Consumer-credit laws state the *ipsissima verba*; informed-consent law threatens doctors with liability if they don't design defensible disclosures.

Some disclosure laws apply universally, some narrowly. For example, contract law requires parties to disclose terms before contracting. Because contracts govern so many transactions, that requirement lurks almost everywhere. The FTC calls failure to disclose fully "all material restrictions, limitations, or conditions to purchase" a deceptive act. Other rules apply to particular products, like halal meat or early-termination fees in cell phone plans.

Disclosures' content and purposes vary. Some tell people about rights or costs. Some warn people about dangerous products, unreliable individuals, and even themselves and their own imprudence. Disclosures seek to facilitate, to persuade, and to educate. Consider some species of the genus disclosure. Many disclosures tell people about their rights. Some describe rights against businesses: rights to return purchased goods, withdraw from a deal, refuse a proffered transaction, get a credit report, or have priority over someone else's claims. Travel services and agents must specify orally and in writing travelers' rights to some claims and refunds. Credit-repair services must tell clients of their right to a grace period for cancelling the service, to have accurate records kept, and to sue for violation of their rights.

A popular disclosure-of-rights species is the bill of rights—a summary of rights to be disclosed. There are bills of rights for patients, voters, credit-card holders, landowners' tenants, homeowners-insurance policy-holders, car buyers, depositors, local taxpayers, union members, energy consumers, and even taxicab riders. (How did the bill-of-rights locution descend from the Constitution to cab rides? And where are the Ten Commandments of extended warranties and the Magna Carta of car repair?)

Another species of mandated disclosure involves costs and fees. Some disclosures expose obscure costs, others highlight obvious ones. Thus financial regulations often require disclosures of APRs, finance charges, and creditors' fees—late fees, overdraft fees, usage fees, non-usage fees, and other arcana. Rent-to-own stores must disclose a potpourri of costs, in some states close to twenty items. Many products and services involve prices and charges that consumers cannot easily assess and compare: car-repair charges, insurance premiums, fees for medical treatments, and service or installation charges. More accessible information must also be disclosed: odometer readings for used cars or the news that signing a loan agreement creates a binding obligation.

Disclosures sometimes describe other perils. They warn that a choice may be unwise, unnecessary, or unproved. Brokers must say that the government does not advise using them. People seeking a viatical settlement of a life-insurance policy—exchanging the policy for cash, often to pay medical bills—must hear about other ways to get funds and why a viatical settlement may affect their taxes, their creditors' rights, and Medicaid and other benefits. Privacy statements warn of losing control over personal information and getting spam and solicitations. Further disclosures identify products that may harm the environment.

Disclosures can also warn of physical risks. Informed consent in health law is largely about medical risks. Drug warnings usually list side effects. Warnings are plastered on toaster plugs and lawnmowers because failure to list them increases the risk of liability for a harm. Risk disclosures range from the obscure to the obvious. Perhaps a hairdryer needs a sticker saying "Do Not Use in the Shower," but does a butane lighter need to say "Warning: Flame May Cause Fire"? You must be told that "you could lose your home, and any money you have put in to it, if you do not meet your [mortgage] obligations." And be warned not to use ATMs at night, alone, or in menacing circumstances. Traffic-violator schools must astonish applicants: "Students in the classroom include traffic offenders." Many service providers must disclose conflicts of interest—doctors, insurance agents, investment brokers, real estate agents, researchers. Financial brokers and residential landlords must disclose a catalog of past misdeeds.

Many mandates supply data to inform decisions. The Clery Act obliges colleges to disclose crime information to applicants. Barber schools must provide graduation and placement statistics. Restaurants must disclose calorie counts, SUV makers rollover ratings, distributors of some foods their country of origin, electric utilities rates and usage data, and hospitals report cards. Consumer-directed health-care is an elaborate disclosure campaign for equipping consumers to choose health plans and medical treatments. It envisions, as one HHS secretary put it, "a time, not far from now, when patients will be able to define and compare the cost of health care to create an informed value-based system."[6]

Contract law requires that consumers get the fine print before making a purchase so that they can shop more shrewdly. Some terms must be disclosed conspicuously, with large fonts, bold typefaces, and obtrusive hyperlinks, so that you "cannot help but see the notice."[7] The most ambitious presentations are intended to be educational, not just informational. Financial literacy, for example, has been a prominent goal for decades. Some disclosures are supposed to educate readers about privacy, nutrition, health, environment, safety, crime, insurance, condom use, and voting. The European Union's commission proposed a new consumer-sales law to tell consumers, before every sale, that they can contract under the old national law or the new European law, a choice summarized in a two-page "Standard Information Notice."

Some disclosures seek more to persuade than inform. The Patient Self-Determination Act, for example, requires telling patients about advance directives to encourage their use. Ulterior motives underlie many risk disclosures, like cigarette warnings or calorie labeling in fast-food chains. A campaign for GMO labeling not only wants to inform people but also to affect their choices and so change agriculture. California's Proposition 65 disclosures warn of toxic substances in products to deter producers from using them. In the subprime consumer markets, disclosures often insinuate that the transaction is dubious. ("You have the right to cancel your contract with any credit repair organization for any reason within 3 business days from the date you signed it.")

Disclosures target various audiences. Some are directed to the poor. Payday lenders, pawnshops, rent-to-own businesses, and doorstep sellers must proffer many disclosures to their rarely rich clients. Some disclosures are directed to the middle class, to inform salaried workers, homebuyers, checking account holders, and Internet shoppers. Mandates protect the wealthy when, for example, they buy fine arts, travel by air, invest in securities, or retire in a golf resort. ("Your home is subject to an easement for errant golf balls. This means that golf balls hit from the golf course may cross and land on your property causing substantial property damage or personal injury.")

CONCLUSION

We have wanted to describe disclosures but escape the full-disclosure syndrome, to show the ubiquity of this regulatory method without drowning you in its detail. Our exercise in *praeteritio*, in surveying a landscape of what we won't survey, may have brought us near the tedium of many disclosures. But it should now be clear how intensive and extensive the problem of unfamiliar and complex decisions is and how intensive and extensive disclosure mandates are.

Our exercise principally sketched the nature and scope of mandated disclosure, but it had other benefits. First, it revealed something inadequately recognized—that the same regulatory method is used in innumerable areas. Unfortunately, analyses of disclosures tend to be confined to a single area, allowing analysts to propose reforms that have failed elsewhere and to hope for a success that their method rarely achieves. Part of this book's purpose is to evaluate this regulatory method by looking at it in the whole range of circumstances in which it is used.

Second, when we lay out in such detail what mandated disclosure is asked to do, when we see the dimensions of its hopes and efforts, we can begin to ask our core question—can it work? Seen as a whole, mandated disclosure has loosed a tsunami of elaborate and technical information. Can people really find what they need in the flood and use it to make better decisions? To that question we devote chapter 3 and part II.

CHAPTER 3

THE FAILURE OF MANDATED DISCLOSURE

For more than forty years, I've studied the documents that public companies file. Too often, I've been unable to decipher just what is being said or, worse yet, had to conclude that nothing was being said.

—Warren Buffett

Chapter 2 revealed mandated disclosure's magnificent ambition. Thousands of disclosures provide billions of words to help us with millions of decisions, typically unfamiliar and complex, often consequential. If mandated disclosure works, it is truly the wonder its enthusiasts rejoice in. But if decisions are as complex and numerous as chapter 2 suggested, can it work? This chapter begins to answer that question.

Our evaluation comes in several forms and several stages. This chapter traverses a few. First, we ask a rarely posed question: by what standard should we assess mandated disclosure? We principally use the standard lawmakers and disclosurites set for it. We then apply that standard by recruiting several kinds of evidence. First, we survey the empirical studies of disclosure's success. We then look at laboratory evidence—at attempts to make disclosure work with research subjects. Finally, we describe signs of crumbling faith in disclosure among some sophisticated lawmakers and commentators.

These kinds of evidence make a strong prima facie case that disclosure mandates repeatedly fail to accomplish their goals. But this evidence does not explain *why* mandates fail and thus cannot show that the regulatory technique is fundamentally misconceived. That showing, however, can be made. Mandated disclosure, we said, depends on a long chain of fragile links. Lawmakers must impose the right mandates. Disclosers must obey the mandates. And disclosees must believe the disclosed information can help them, look for it, find it, read it, understand it, use it, and use it appropriately. If disclosures fail at any of these stages, they cannot reach their goal. Much of the evidence we have assembled describes breaks in this chain. That evidence is so extensive and persuasive that we examine it in detail in part II.

WHAT ARE MANDATED DISCLOSURE'S GOALS ?

Whether mandated disclosure works depends on its goals. Chapter 1 said that it principally seeks to help people confronting unfamiliar and complex decisions in transactions with knowledgeable people with interests of their own. Chapter 2 said that that problem is both extensive and intensive—that such decisions are common and that their unfamiliarity and complexity can be great. This suggests a standard of success—providing information that equips disclosees to understand their choice well enough that they analyze it and make a well-informed, well-considered decision.

This is in fact the conventional disclosurite understanding. Truth-in-lending laws are supposed "to assure a meaningful disclosure of credit terms so that the consumer will be able to compare more readily the various credit terms available to him and avoid the uninformed use of credit."[1] The Federal Reserve (chapter 1 reported) thinks that people choosing an adjustable rate mortgage should understand "indexes, margins, discounts, caps on rates and payments, negative amortization, payment options, and . . . most importantly, . . . what might happen to your monthly mortgage payment in relation to your future ability to afford higher payment."[2] Informed consent promotes "'patient sovereignty,' conceived as patient *choice* and *control* over medical decisions."[3] So patients must be told enough "to understand and make a rational choice." The informed-consent model assumes that from a "proper disclosure, and consequently understanding, will follow a rational and autonomous decision."[4]

This goal—which, needing a workable term for a complex idea, we will call "full disclosure"—sounds desirable but aspires mightily. Can disclosurites mean it? As we intimated earlier and will explain later, some lawmakers and commentators have tempered their hopes. But they are a minority and primarily address a minority of mandates. The conventional wisdom still embraces some version of full disclosure, as we see when we examine several kinds of evidence: First, the purpose of mandated disclosure. Second, the patterns of mandates. Third, the arguments disclosurites advance for mandated disclosure.

The Logic of Mandated Disclosure

The first reason to think that disclosurite expectations can generally be met only by full disclosure lies in disclosure's purpose—equipping people to make unfamiliar and complex decisions in transactions with more knowledgeable and not always friendly parties. These choices, like mortgage borrowing or retirement savings, health care or insurance, and the purchase of sophisticated products, are—as chapter 2 showed—so complex that many factors matter. So the Fed is right to say that the success of an adjustable-rate mortgage depends on many things and that overlooking even one may be disastrous. Since disclosures are ordinarily aimed at all the people facing a decision, and since there are few factors that everybody understands, disclosures must be thorough indeed.

Thus, after surveying evidence that people managing retirement accounts sail on seas of ignorance and lakes of misinformation, ignore navigational charts, yet intend to stay the course, one commentator concerned just with asset classes wants "communications" that, among many things, "include basic investment education about reasonable return and risk expectations for all pertinent asset classes."[5] Such communications should be so detailed that people understand why diversifying among asset classes is desirable and how to do it.

Similarly, the FTC requires that telemarketers must in a "clear and conspicuous manner" disclose "[a]ll material restrictions, limitations, or conditions to purchase, receive, or use the goods or services."[6] The White House says that "consumers have a right to easily understandable and accessible information about privacy and security practices." That right is so capacious that companies must disclose what data they collect, why they need it, how they will use it, when they will delete or "de-identify" it, whether and how they share it with third parties, and what the third parties do with it.[7] The Department of Education takes nearly 300 pages to tell colleges how to provide campus safety reports and admonishes them that the goal is to provide "accurate, complete and timely information about safety on campus" so disclosees "can make informed decisions."[8] Likewise, in discussing prepaid debit cards—which are sold primarily to the poor and often carry obscure but hefty fees—disclosurites envision "ensuring" that card users "understand how they work, . . . understand the terms and conditions that apply," and have the information available when they need it. Issuers must thus provide "clear, conspicuous, and full disclosures of fees."[9]

Full disclosure is crucial to the autonomy rationale for mandated disclosure, which expects people to make their own decisions, applying their own values, tastes, and analyses. This ideology holds that these values, tastes, and situations can only be understood by the person making the decision. And so a failure of full disclosure is an "affront to dignity."[10] Radin argues that contracts are only legitimate if people make them voluntarily and that assent isn't voluntary if people don't know a contract's terms. Firms' failure to explain those terms or, worse, tucking boilerplate inside a product's box, she calls "normative degradation."[11] Some disclosurites believe that giving people disclosures honors disclosees' autonomy whatever its effect on their decisions. As two law reformers write, giving consumers "an opportunity to read supports Llewellyn's idea of individual assent and autonomy, even if most consumers don't read."[12]

Full disclosure is consistent with another rationale for mandated disclosure—informing sophisticated intermediaries who transmit information to consumers. Thus one advocate of full disclosure of insurance policies (typically triumphs of obscurity) argues that "the intended audience of full disclosure includes consumer-oriented magazines and journalists, consumer advocates, academics, sophisticated consumers, and government actors" who "scrutinize the relevant data" and "inform the public of their findings."[13]

Finally, the need for full disclosure is apparent in the close relationship between mandated disclosure and education in the areas to which mandates are commonly directed. Many disclosurites realize that disclosures can be incomprehensible without the background and skills needed to interpret and use them. So education is often a significant part of the disclosurite agenda, and campaigns for financial literacy or health literacy (for instance) often accompany mandates. And disclosurites hope that disclosures themselves will gradually create a population informed enough to benefit from mandated disclosure.

The Pattern of Mandates

Chapter 2 was bedecked with mandates so intensive they could only be necessary if lawmakers wanted full disclosure. For example, it listed roughly fifty documents that mortgagors receive. It outlined a process of choosing a treatment for prostate-cancer that was like a matryoshka doll: open one and there's always another inside. It described the bed sheet that installment plan buyers encounter (and it is a napkin compared to the linen closet of information that investors or checking account holders receive). It displayed an iTunes scroll that is a masterpiece of full disclosure that is needed because you are not bound by a contract unless you can learn its terms. To be sure, mandates can always be broadened. But "full disclosure" usefully describes these mandates because they require far more information than disclosees will and can read.

The regulatory landscape is littered with full disclosures. HIPAA privacy forms list all the things doctors and hospitals might do with medical information, specify which of these can be objected to, describe how to object, and enjoin people to "review carefully" the resulting flow of fine print. The Privacy Act and the Paperwork Reduction Act require that "when we ask you for information we must first tell you our legal right to ask for the information, why we are asking for it, and how it will be used. We must also tell you what could happen if we do not provide it and whether or not you must respond under the law."[14]

Similarly, courts frequently sanction parties who failed to disclose a fact that, in hindsight, seems to matter. Product warnings abound because failing to list every hazard may expose the discloser to tort liability when an injury occurs. Even when an overload problem is recognized, full disclosure remains the mantra of the liability system because an injury's occurrence looks like proof that disclosure was necessary.[15]

We will later describe a ratchet effect—mandates tend to expand, rarely to shrink. As disclosures fail to solve the problems they address and as new problems are perceived, lawmakers expand old mandates and write new ones. A napkin grew into a bed sheet because lawmakers kept realizing that a really and truly informed decision required yet another fact. The Apple iTunes boilerplate, now thirty-two pages, was once seven. Thus do mandates press ever onward to full disclosure.

A telling measure of lawmakers' determination that disclosees learn everything needed to make good decisions comes from the IRB committees in universities and hospitals that approve every informed consent form that researchers give people participating in both social-science and biomedical research. As we will see in chapter 9, the regulating committees have steadily required longer and longer forms. In one study of eight IRBs, for example, the length of the forms for the same study doubled over seven years. Forms are longer because they contain more information, because, as a former secretary of Health and Human Services wrote, researchers must "ensure that subjects fully understand all the potential risks and benefits of a clinical trial. Full disclosure is a necessary precondition to free choice."[16]

Disclosurites have often advocated simplified disclosures, and sophisticated regulators and commentators now commend disclosures that rest on empirical evidence and that are something like a rating, score, or grade—"concrete, straightforward, simple, meaningful, timely, and salient."[17] But simplified disclosure is easy to require and hard to accomplish, as our discussion of simplification in chapter 8 explains. Most disclosures cannot well be reduced to a score, and reformers must often settle for making forms look less cluttered, more orderly, and more pleasing. When, occasionally, scores replace full disclosure, so much information must be squeezed into the score that distortions and obscurities are inevitable. Then pressure for more complete disclosure again mounts.

Preachments of Disclosurites

Disclosurites *must* think disclosees need full disclosure because they so often demand such detailed disclosures. Many disclosurites speak of "complete" information. Thus, "ultimately," we are told, "concern over incomplete information appears to underlie much or all of the demand for protecting consumers." Truth-in-lending laws "insist on 'full disclosure'" and require providing "any information that potentially might be useful to someone, sometime." This produces "a lengthy list of required disclosures," and "as new possibilities for disclosures arise or new problems surface in credit markets, new disclosures have been almost certain to be among the recommended solutions."[18] Graham believes that "the new disclosure systems are aimed at ordinary consumers and intended to inform comprehensively to change behavior." They "provide detailed information about specific companies and products" to "allow people with varied needs and values to make choices."[19] Thus nutritional labeling uses disclosure to reduce "deaths from heart disease, cancer, and other chronic diseases by designing a standardized system of disclosure for key nutrients that would let shoppers compare tens of thousands of products" and become alert "to the relationship between specific amounts of nutrients and risks of a variety of diseases."[20]

Calls for full disclosure permeate the informed-consent literature. The Institute of Medicine serenely asks for "clear, simple, unclouded, unhurried, and sensitive disclosure that gives the potential [research] participant all the information a reasonable person would need to make a well-informed decision."[21] This requires "that research participants fully understand the nature of scientific rationale and procedure; have insight into a set of risks of various types that might be identified on their behalf by ethicists or regulators; and have motives for participation that are not 'false.'"[22] One commentator wants "long discussions and detailed presentations of options and statistics" to "help patients to understand options, to consider the probability of benefits and harms and the supporting evidence, to explore beliefs and fears, to determine the desired level of control in making decisions, and to find motivation to engage with the primary clinician." This commentator "envision[s] offices of decision counselors" where patients "use high-speed Internet workstations, a complete library of decision aids, and other patient education materials."[23] As one scholar writes, from the "prevailing ethical and legal viewpoint, patients are capable of understanding the often complex and voluminous medical information communicated to them by physicians and placing that information into accurate, clinically usable perspective."[24]

Finding patients and research subjects still ill informed after decades of adjurations and effort, disclosurites urge expanding disclosure almost past the "full" standard by asking providers to (1) explore patients' "affective and cognitive processes" in depth; (2) "explore uncertainties and limitations" in the provider's knowledge and in science; (3) "understand and disclose their own motivations, beliefs, and values"; (4) explore patient's expectations about decision-making; and (5) offer individualized informed consent "in the context of an ongoing relationship with a trusted health-care provider."[25] At such moments, the goal soars past full disclosure to full understanding.

Distrust of Disclosers

The full-disclosure goal can also be inferred from the common fear that disclosers will abuse the power their expertise gives them. In this world of distrust, disclosees must make decisions personally—or at least understand them well enough to detect disclosers' deceptions, biases, and self-interest. This requires considerable knowledge.

Distrust of disclosers has grown markedly. Under the doctrine of caveat emptor, sellers did not have to volunteer information to buyers, even if, say, a seller knew that the house had termites and the buyer thought it did not. (Sellers could not defraud buyers, that is, lie to deceive them about material facts.) Courts have been replacing caveat emptor with disclosure. They began requiring sellers, for example, to tell buyers about the termites. At first, this did not mean full disclosure, just revealing a few things buyers really cared about. If willingness to buy depended on an understanding sellers knew to be false, they had to correct the mistakes. Courts have also allowed buyers to sue manufacturers (not just sellers) for nondisclosure. Traditionally patients who wanted information that doctors hadn't volunteered had to ask; doctors needed consent, but not informed consent. Courts now require doctors to tell patients about a proposed treatment's benefits, risks, alternatives, and increasingly more.

Legislatures soon followed and even surpassed courts. Home sellers in most states must give buyers a four-to-six page disclosure of dozens of problems. In interstate sales, subdivision developers must give buyers a "property report" that can reach thirty pages. Deep distrust of subprime businesses like rent-to-own stores prompted legislatures to mandate disclosing full lists of fees and rights. Legislatures began to require informed consent statutorily and to elaborate on it (e.g., requiring doctors to disclose specified choices, like lumpectomy as well as mastectomy).

Yet further evidence of the way distrust leads to broad disclosure mandates is the proliferating requirement not only to describe products and transactions but also to tell disclosees about their rights against the discloser. For example, FERPA (an education privacy law) obliges schools to tell students their rights and how to complain about violations. Disclosures about sellers, creditors, debt collectors, data collectors, credit-repair organizations, rent-to-own operators, direct marketers, and remote-sales operators must now describe rights against disclosers and how to enforce them. Thus, credit bureaus must give consumers two pages summarizing their rights under the Fair Credit Reporting Act. Credit-repair organizations must distribute a summary of rights under the Credit Repair Organizations Act (like the right to cancel the credit-repair contract within three days). Lenders denying credit must list consumers' rights under the Equal Credit Opportunity Act; debt collectors must tell debtors about their rights under the Fair Debt Collection Practices Act; door-to-door sellers must tell people in writing that they have three days to abjure a transaction.

Distrust of disclosers inspires many conflict-of-interest warnings. Disclosers must say something like, "Believe me, you can't believe me." The number of people who must reveal such conflicts and the detail of self-denunciation demanded has increased considerably.[26] For example, the problem so agitates the world of research regulation that a conflict-of-interest committee chair can think that "[t]he future of academic health centers depends on [conflicts oversight] being done right."[27]

EVIDENCE OF THE FAILURE
OF MANDATED DISCLOSURE

We have described the problem mandated disclosure addresses, how it seeks to solve it, and the standard of success inferable from mandates and from disclosurites. We can now begin to assess that success. We first survey research indicating that actual disclosees do not make better decisions because of mandated disclosures. We next examine laboratory evidence (of experiments with research subjects). We then investigate an indirect but telling kind of evidence—the doubts lawmakers and commentators display about disclosures.

These kinds of evidence, however, only introduce our argument that mandated disclosure is a fundamentally defective regulatory method. We also argue that because disclosees so often do not notice, read, understand, or use disclosures, mandates cannot achieve the goal disclosurites set for them. The evidence of this failure is so voluminous but so dispersed that we devote all of part II to distilling it. Part II shows that in area after area, each link in this chain is fragile. People do not aspire to make decisions in the way that disclosurite ideology assumes and often could not do so even if they wished to.

Studies of Mandated Disclosure in Action

The usual understanding is that a regulation's proponents have the burden of showing that it does more good than harm. Mandated disclosure, however, has escaped this regulatory discipline and has borne little more than a rhetorical burden. The few disclosurite books confine themselves to a handful of examples, and even these are not reliably convincing. For example, in *Full Disclosure*, which advocates a version of mandated disclosure they call targeted transparency, Fung, Graham, and Weil proffer eight examples. The one they think most successful is the ordinance requiring that restaurants post a hygiene grade in their window.[28] An early study showed that such ordinances caused a remarkable 20 percent decline in food-borne illnesses, but a newer and more comprehensive study concluded that grades (however plausible) "do not convey meaningful information that would enable consumers to choose between riskier and less risky establishments." Worse, grading shifts agencies' resources from inspections in restaurants with bad scores to reinspections at restaurants with better scores.[29] Similarly, while Mary Graham (in *Democracy by Disclosure*) calls food-labeling mandates "the most important change in national food policy in fifty years,"[30] she concedes that "[o]n the important question of the degree to which new food labels influenced consumers' product choices, most surveys did not find significant effects." And she concludes that "[n]o sudden changes in the mid-1990s suggested a notable impact of nutritional information on labels."[31]

Studies of many kinds in many areas find disclosures failing to achieve their goal. Surveys of such studies in some of the fields in which mandates matter most reach just such melancholy conclusions. As chapter 1 reported, Willis concluded that federal home-loan disclosures did not produce "good deliberate decision-making about risk."[32] Rubin found that consumer-credit disclosure has not achieved its goals.[33] The Treasury Department, in a comprehensive study, averred that even improved disclosures will not "curb abusive and predatory lending. Disclosure of costs does not, by itself, prevent unfair terms and other abuses [and] can have the unintended effect of insulating predatory lenders where fraud or deception may have occurred."[34] Research now justifies the jests about consumers blindly clicking online disclosures, since readership rates of privacy statements and end-user license agreements are virtually zero.[35]

Likewise, reviews of the informed-consent literature repeatedly find that it falls short of its goals. A 1980 survey concluded that "while consent has remained a focus of intense interest" since Nuremberg, it "often fails to accomplish its intended objective." The studies surveyed showed that "patients remain inadequately informed, even when extraordinary efforts are made to provide complete information and to ensure their understanding. This appears to be true regardless of the amount of information delivered, the manner in which it is presented, or the type of medical procedure involved."[36] A 1999 annotated bibliography of empirical research on informed consent called its picture "not pretty."[37] In 2003 the National Research Council acknowledged that despite decades of effort "there appears to have been little progress in devising more effective forms and procedures."[38] In 2011 Lidz asked whether informed consent has "produced the rational autonomous decisions that the legal and ethical theorists envisioned" and found the answer "pretty simple. There is very substantial empirical evidence that the large majority of both research subjects and patients do not carefully weigh the risks and benefits." In short, while some studies show that some methods can produce some improvement in some people's understanding, the disclosurite goal remains distant.

But what does it mean to say that "patients remain inadequately informed, even when extraordinary efforts are made to provide complete information and to ensure their understanding"? That even when *expert* disclosers lavish information on patients, many neither understand nor remember it well enough to make decisions. That despite extravagant educational efforts, patients cannot recall and presumably have not really understood the risks of treatment. While memory of risk disclosures is most often studied, there is also persuasive evidence that patients do not properly understand proposed treatments' benefits. In one study, for example, "patients' expectations of improvements in their functional status after infrainguinal bypass operation were greater than those suggested by previous research."[39]

Even where good decisions might seem most necessary, informed consent disappoints. Despite decades of legal and medical efforts, patients making life-and-death choices are regularly ill-informed and even mistaken. In one large study, for example, fewer than half the breast cancer patients understood survival rates and fewer than a fifth understood recurrence rates, even though the patients thought those factors important and had consulted "a relatively large variety of information sources."[40]

Couldn't doctors try harder? One study *truly* strove to enlighten patients about conflicts of interest created by the ways HMOs paid doctors. It "went to unusual lengths to ensure that the essential information was conveyed." Disclosures by mail were "followed by phone calls in

which subjects' understanding was tested and reinforced through repetition and simple quiz questions." While knowledge of incentives was
considerably increased, a majority still could not correctly answer more
than half the questions. "[E]ven the extensive and [desperately] impractical methods used here to attempt to convey only limited knowledge of
incentives fell well short of complete success."[41]

Even in ideal circumstances informed-consent disclosures fail. For
example, in one study patients facing routine neurosurgical procedures
were taught in three stages. First, the neurologist explained spinal anat-
omy and physiology, the procedure, the reasons for considering surgery,
the surgical techniques, the nonsurgical alternatives, the operation's
goals, and aspects of postoperative care. The surgeon used printed materials and anatomical models to make points clearer, invited questions,
and asked patients to say in their own words what they had learned. Second, patients, families, and friends attended an education conference
conducted by a master's-level nurse educator covering the same topics.
The nurse too used visual aids, solicited questions, and tested patients.
Third, patients revisited the surgeon to ask questions and receive information. *Immediately* after these sessions, patients answered only 53
percent of the multiple-choice and 34 percent of the open-ended questions correctly. Better-educated patients did better, but even patients with
graduate education scored only 64.8 percent (multiple-choice) and 36.5
percent (open-ended).[42]

Even when legislatures have made special efforts to use informed
consent in focused ways, the results have been discouraging. Statutes have
used expert boards to formulate special disclosures about mastectomies
and have even threatened physician disciplinary procedures.[43] But while
these statutes were "associated with slight increases (6 to 13 percent)" in
the use of lumpectomies, the "increases were transient" and lasted from
three to twelve months.[44]

If informed consent should work anywhere, it is in consent to participate in research. There each disclosure's exact words and procedures
must be approved in advance by a board called an IRB that is institution-
ally and ideologically determined to make researchers inform prospective subjects *really* thoroughly. But again the evidence is disappointing.

For example, trials of cancer treatments are riskier than most research, so disclosures about them are attentively designed by researchers and much scrutinized by regulators. Disclosees—research subjects—presumably have urgent reasons to understand their choices. In an especially careful but otherwise typical study, impractical amounts of time were spent educating the subjects, who lengthily assessed their choices and consulted "additional sources of information and had support from family or friends." But "knowledge varied widely and there were important misunderstandings." Many "did not realize that the treatment being researched was not proven to be the best for their cancer, that the study used nonstandard treatments or procedures, that participation might carry incremental risk, or that they might not receive direct medical benefit from participation."[45]

Similarly discouraging results are reported in yet other areas. The Federal Trade Commission recently studied privacy protection in the digital era. It reported a "consensus among roundtable participants that most privacy policies are generally ineffective for informing consumers about a company's data practices because they are too long, are difficult to comprehend, and lack uniformity." It noted "the lack of transparency about the practices of information brokers, who often buy, compile, and sell a wealth of highly personal information about consumers," who often don't know about the brokers and what they do. The report's response to ignorance in the face of strong mandates to disclose data collection was typical: "privacy notices should be clearer, shorter, and more standardized to enable better comprehension and comparison of privacy practices." Loyal to the disclosurite faith, the report preaches that "all stakeholders should expand their efforts to educate consumers about commercial data privacy practices."[46]

The list of surveys concluding that disclosures have failed continues. An FTC report's title speaks for itself: "Mobile Apps for Kids: Current Privacy Disclosures are Dis-*app*-ointing." One survey of the literature found "no evidence that consumers benefit from government-mandated disclaimers in advertising" and said that consumers "may fail to respond to government-mandated messages and disclaimers in the ways that the regulators intend them to."[47] A survey of evidence on *Miranda* concluded that researchers generally thought it had not changed the rate of confessions meaningfully, that police have adapted by inducing waivers or questioning "outside Miranda," and that "next to the warning label on cigarette packs, *Miranda* is the most widely ignored piece of official advice in our society."[48] Stuntz wrote that "*Miranda* does nothing to protect suspects against abusive police tactics" because letting suspects decide whether police are behaving coercively "has failed."[49]

In sum, in field after field there is good evidence that mandated disclosure does not achieve disclosurites' goals. The evidence comes from numerous studies, many conducted by researchers truly committed to making disclosure work, many pouring impractically generous resources into disclosure. The evidence does *not* say that no disclosure ever improves any disclosees' understanding. *Many* studies show some improvements. But repeatedly even strenuous efforts to educate disclosees do not bring them near the level of understanding needed to make good decisions. If you take a multiple-choice test covering basic information about a choice and can answer only half the questions, you don't know or are wrong about too many things to evaluate your choices the way disclosurites want.

The Laboratory Evidence

As the FTC privacy report suggests, many disclosurites believe that "clearer, shorter, and more standardized" disclosures can "enable better comprehension." But designing good disclosures has proved an agony. Many studies have tried to analyze disclosures more accurately by studying how research subjects respond to them in laboratory settings. These studies reveal fundamental problems with disclosures.

One advantage of such studies is that they can be conducted in something like ideal circumstances. If a disclosure fails in the laboratory, it cannot withstand the tumult of real life. For example, many disclosures fail because disclosees lack the literacy, intelligence, and sophistication to understand them. Choi, Laibson, and Madrian eliminated this problem by assembling 730 white-collar Harvard staff members of above-average education (88 percent with a college degree, 60 percent with graduate education), MBA students from Wharton (average SAT scores in the ninety-eighth percentile), and Harvard College students (ninety-ninth percentile SATs).[50] Their financial literacy was much higher than the typical retail investor's.

The Choi group knew that disclosures fail because they present too many choices. So the group assigned subjects a single, relatively simple task: allocating $10,000 among four real S&P 500 index funds whose prospectuses they were given. Generally, "funds tracking a given index offer virtually identical portfolio returns before fees," so what mattered was fees (which differed). Yet, almost none of the subjects minimized fees. Staff, MBA students, and college students averaged (respectively) 201, 112, and 122 basis points more in fees than necessary. Staff and college students acknowledged that "fees played relatively little role" in their choice; "MBAs claimed that fees were the most important decision factor for them, but their portfolio's fees were not statistically lower than college students' fees." All groups "reported placing high weight on past returns." This was a mistake, if only because the funds had operated during different periods (so their returns weren't comparable). In short, "chasing the past returns reported in the prospectuses lowered future expected returns" even with these exceptional disclosees. Furthermore, "[e]ven subjects who claimed to prioritize fees in their portfolio decision showed minimal sensitivity to the fee information in the prospectus."[51]

Laboratory experiments can also eliminate the noise that disrupts people's choices and focus the disclosees' attention on their task. This should help conflict-of-interest disclosures, since in real life they are often mixed with other information and distributed at stressful moments. Experiments by Cain, Loewenstein, and Moore raise fascinating questions about the fundamental assumptions of these mandates. In the basic experiment[52] subjects had to estimate the money in a coin jar and were paid according to the estimate's accuracy. The subjects were advised by other participants who had more time to examine the jars and make better estimates. These advisors had a conflict of interest: their payments depended on how high advisees' estimates were, not how accurate. In the treatment group the advisors had to disclose this conflict; in the control group, they did not. Conflicts disclosures are supposed to permit disclosees to eval-uate disclosers' advice and to dampen disclosers' tendency to promote their own ends. But no. Subjects told about the conflict of interest made *worse* guesses and earned less money than those who were not. And ad-visors who had to disclose their conflict exaggerated more and gave more inflated advice than advisors who did not have to disclose. At least in this experimental setting, disclosure "benefited the providers of information but not its recipients." The Cain group did not think this would always be so but thought the experiment challenged "the belief that disclosure is a reliable and effective remedy" for conflicts.[53]

How can this be true? Partly, disclosees need to know not just that disclosers have a conflict; they need to know how it affects what they say, something disclosures cannot reveal. In addition, other experiments found that people who received disclosures relied on the discloser *more*, not less. This is not so strange. Patients told that their doctor's research is funded by a drug's manufacturer might conclude that the doctor is open, honest, and "'deeply involved' and thus knowledgeable."[54] In addition, disclosing conflicts may create "insinuation anxiety," disclosees' fear that rejecting proffered advice implies that they think the discloser morally corrupted by the conflict.

And how might the disclosure affect the discloser? Does it diminish disclosers' concern about giving biased and misleading advice? Does it grant a kind of moral license to be biased? Is there a "yelling louder" effect? Do advisors say, "I know that I try to give accurate advice, but now the disclosee thinks the advice is biased, so I'd better exaggerate my advice to offset the disclosee's error"?

Not all laboratory disclosures fail so badly. Many show a small im-provement. Isolated from other concerns, focused on a particular task, and led by researchers anxious to make disclosure work, some studies show some benefits some of the time. Such success is reported, for exam-ple, in the FTC's test of new mortgage disclosure forms (under a highly motivated regulatory agenda of "Know before You Owe") and in attempts to summarize health-insurance benefits better. Part III discusses this work as part of our examination of simplifying disclosure. But measured against disclosurite goals, these improvements fail.

Lawmakers' Discontent with Disclosure

Lawmakers seem chronically dissatisfied with disclosures because their mandates are often followed by revised mandates implicitly (sometimes explicitly) admitting their predecessor's failure. Many mandates in many areas are reconsidered and reformed. Sometimes these reforms build on what looks like success. For example, hopes for new food-labeling mandates build on studies finding merit in nutrition labeling. But in major areas mandates have been reformed because they seem to have failed.

TILA's history, for example, reflects a cascade of disappointments. The statute was enacted in 1968 and implemented by the Federal Reserve's famously baroque "Regulation Z." A few years later, Congress found that "significant reforms" were needed if borrowers were to have "greater and more timely information" and be "protected from unnecessarily high settlement charges." Congress enacted a detailed mortgage-disclosure statute, the Real Estate Settlement Procedures Act of 1974 (RESPA).[55] To the already considerable disclosures that mortgagors received courtesy of TILA, RESPA added a multipage form called HUD-1.

The 1968 and 1974 mandates were so complicated and cluttered that in 1980 Congress passed the Truth-in-Lending Simplification and Reform Act.[56] The Senate wanted legislation because typical disclosures were ineffective, long, and legalistic, and critical terms were mingled with mundane ones. The result was a piece of paper that looked like "'just another legal document' instead of the simple, concise disclosure form Congress intended."[57]

But the 1980 reform, in its retracing search after its missing success, only found another failure. The "good faith estimate"—a disclosure made early in the loan application process—was three pages long with more than a hundred items. During the 1990s the government adjusted the mandate with restraint, but the 2000s brought another round of reform. For example, RESPA disclosures were significantly changed to stop disclosers from itemizing some costs and instead to require disclosing aggregate settlement costs.[58] By 2008 a regulation titled "Simplifying and Improving the Process of Obtaining Mortgages to Reduce Settlement Costs to Consumers" sought "to ensure that consumers are provided with meaningful and timely information" and to create a form simplifying and standardizing "estimated settlement cost disclosures to make such estimates more reliable."[59]

After the 2008 mortgage crisis all this reengineering seemed to have failed and was re-reengineered. Because disclosures did not explain mortgage terms well enough, the Dodd-Frank Act of 2010 required new forms that would "improve consumer understanding of mortgage transactions." The Consumer Financial Protection Bureau (CFPB)—the agency now in charge of consumer-credit disclosures—said that disclosures had overlapping information and inconsistent language, that people often thought the forms confusing, and that "lenders and settlement agents find the forms burdensome to provide and explain."[60] In 2012 the CFPB introduced new formats improving much that had earlier been improved, even the 2008 reform. The new templates are based on laboratory experiments and intended to account for consumers' behavioral and psychological tendencies. (The sense that past failures require a behavioral toolkit is another recurring sentiment. For example, the 1980 TILA round, like the Dodd-Frank round, was informed by "testimony from a leading psychologist who has studied the problem of 'informational overload.'")[61]

In sum, the pattern of rejected reforms shows lawmakers repeatedly recognizing that laboriously built mandates had failed. And other mandates in other areas replicate this history.

The Sea of Faith

The Sea of Faith in mandated disclosure was once at the full. Lawmakers confidently mandated disclosures; commentators confidently applauded. But now we begin to hear faith's melancholy, long, withdrawing roar. Disclosurites speak more cautiously. Veteran Federal Reserve economists Durkin and Elliehausen "strongly believe that the disclosure of information to consumers in the financial area—truth in finance—provides clear benefits." But the regime suffers from defects like loading disclosees with so much information that they can actually make worse choices. "And the fact that its problematic condition stems from a long history of efforts to improve it suggests that further attempts at reform can easily add to rather than reduce the problem."[62]

Commentators who never took the disclosurite pledge have become more prominent. Issacharoff sees every reason to expect the success rates of most kinds of disclosure to be low. He explains the decline of faith among sophisticated lawmakers and commentators by the emergence of "an important second generation of literature on the behavioral dimensions of consumer protection, showing that disclosure by itself is not enough. Product attribute disclosure alone is ineffective, given the innumerable errors that consumers are prone to make."[63] Likewise, Sovern thinks mortgage disclosures "have gone about as far as written disclosures of such information can go" and that "writing alone is not always enough." Rather, "the future of our economy" depends on mandatory counseling.[64] And Barr et al. conclude that "disclosure alone is unlikely to help," for "how many homeowners really understand how the teaser rate, introductory rate and reset rate relate to the London interbank offered rate plus some specified margin, or can judge whether the prepayment penalty will offset the gains from the teaser rate?"[65]

Much of this doubt has emerged from long struggles in core areas to make disclosure work and from a growing literature describing disclosure's shortcomings in many areas and aspects. Studies of disclosure in various sectors detail those shortcomings and express discouragement with disclosure. For example, hospitals' report cards include various kinds of scores assessing virtually every aspect of the care they offer "to help you to become a more informed consumer and to make better health care choices."[66] However, finding that report cards meant more resources were spent while outcomes (especially for sicker patients) worsened, Dranove et al. concluded that report cards "decreased patient and social welfare."[67] Dafny and Dranove found that disclosing quality measures did not affect decisions to enroll in health plans (and that the only disclosure that affected disclosees was consumer satisfaction).[68] While there is evidence of some success in using disclosures to help people identify superior hospital care, "there is also considerable evidence from healthcare and education that sellers have attempted to game the system at the expense of consumers, especially if the measured quality does not cover all dimensions of quality or does not adjust for characteristics of consumers that can affect the rankings. There is no consensus as to whether the benefits outweigh the costs."[69]

In the preceding section we said that some lawmakers showed their doubts about mandates by reforming them so often and so much. Some sophisticated regulators are expressly critical. In 2005 the acting Comptroller of the Currency said that despite "enormous resources expended," disclosure "is not working as well as it should," a problem so severe that "just about every major participant in the process of developing, designing, implementing, overseeing, and evaluating consumer disclosures for financial products and services needs to rethink the approach to those tasks."[70] Even Cass Sunstein, then head of the White House Office of Information and Regulatory Affairs, while avowing great hope for empirically tested disclosures, warned of the many pitfalls of mandated disclosure.

Declining faith is more marked among commentators. As Hillman wrote, many of them "seem to have lost faith in disclosure as a remedy for market failures in standard-form contracting." Commentators have seen "the relative failure of laws such as Truth-in-Lending." They have read the literature explaining why people don't use disclosures. And they have faced the considerable evidence of the failure of Web site disclosures. The literature on informed consent in clinical medicine also reflects doubts, as the rise of "shared decision-making" suggests. It offers a "middle choice" between paternalism and "the informed decision-making model." In that middle choice patients get "some say without total responsibility," and doctors not only give patients information but may participate in, while not dominating decisions.[71]

The sea of faith may be ebbing, but it is still a sea. Lawmakers mandate disclosures prolifically. Agencies that recognize failures commonly persist in seeking a better mandate. Evidence of a mandate's failure ordinarily inspires commentators to propose ways to improve the disclosure. Even those who acknowledge the evidence about disclosure's failures as a regulatory tool cling to hopes for improved transparency.[72] There are even commentators who once criticized disclosures to protect consumers who now make it the star of their reforms.[73] Rarely does someone assemble the data, notice their pattern, and ask basic questions about mandated disclosure's regulatory usefulness.

CONCLUSION

In this chapter we have begun to assemble the evidence that mandated disclosure is a regulatory device whose ambitions outstrip its abilities. Disclosurites aspire to mandate disclosures that improve the decisions people make about unfamiliar and complex problems. We have assembled several kinds of evidence of the unreliability of that regulatory device. Studies repeatedly show disclosees falling far short of the level of understanding needed to make decisions in the way disclosurites intend. Studies repeatedly show disclosees lacking information and misunderstanding their situation. Laboratory experiments in circumstances greatly favorable to mandated disclosure confirm these discouraging results. And the repeated acknowledgments, explicit and implicit, of lawmakers and some commentators that some version of mandated disclosure has failed are yet further evidence.

But why does mandated disclosure fail so often to achieve the goals disclosurites set for it? Particularly, does it fail in ways that can be fixed? Part II will address these questions and find that much of the explanation lies in disclosees' attitudes and abilities. Our inquiry will identify numerous breaks in the chain of events on which success depends. And we will conclude that the reasons for mandated disclosure's failure run so deep that—whatever its occasional usefulness—lawmakers should regard it as presumptively unsuccessful and should use it only when they have strong evidence that it really will work.

WHY DISCLOSURES FAIL

Part I concluded by introducing evidence that mandated disclosure does not achieve the results set for it. Part II has three primary tasks: First, to explain *why*. Second, to present evidence confirming our argument that mandated disclosure doesn't work. Third, to begin to argue that the reasons it fails are so basic and so many that it is irreparable.

At the heart of disclosure's failure is that people want and use it too little. Studies numerously testify that people don't notice disclosures, don't read them if they see them, can't understand them if they try to read them, and can't use them if they read them. If mandated disclosure mismatches people's lives, if they reject the project of mastering information in order to make their own personal decisions, if they think disclosures unhelpful or even noxious, then mandated disclosure is fundamentally misconceived. It asks people to do something they don't want to do and cannot be made to do. It cannot be fixed.

Part I accepted the conventional formulation: mandates address problems arising from people's failure to understand choices. That formulation has shaped disclosurite writing. It is primarily about disclosures as decision aids, and when it recognizes the difficulty of disclosure in particular areas it asks how to revise the disclosure. This conventional formulation evokes the conventional explanation—mandated disclosure fails because it is done incorrectly. Disclosures come at the wrong time in the wrong form. But why have decades of effort in dozens of areas not produced effective disclosure regimes?

To answer that question, we shift our focus—from disclosure to disclosee. Instead of asking whether disclosures communicate data, we ask how disclosures fit the way people organize their lives, approach problems, and make choices. From this perspective—from the perspective of daily lives and common experience—things look different. When we take the disclosee's perspective, we find people crucially less enthusiastic about making decisions—and making them in the disclosurite way—than disclosurism assumes. In short, disclosures must at every stage overcome the resistance of their audience.

Part II essentially defends this recusant attitude. It is so much part of people's lives that it will not be changed by any means known to public policy. But more: ignorance is rational where the cost of collecting and analyzing information outweighs the benefit. Specifically, chapter 4 argues that people are decision averse in the sense that they make decisions less willingly and less thoroughly than disclosurites expect. A primary reason for this attitude is the burden disclosures impose on people, a burden that is intrinsically unpleasant and that distracts people from things they would rather do. Mandated disclosure is at core an enormous educational enterprise of a kind academics may enjoy but that most people do not. Most people have little reason to think that the yield from studying disclosure will repay the effort.

Chapter 5 argues that informed decisions are made more difficult and forbidding by literacy problems (broadly defined). People are hobbled and thwarted by various forms and degrees of illiteracy and innumeracy. Nor are most disclosees competent enough in the sectors in which disclosures are made to interpret them productively. These literacy problems can be so severe that many people find many disclosures simply useless.

Chapter 6 argues that disclosures are made yet more forbidding by what we call the quantity question. It has two aspects. First, the overload problem: Many disclosures are so intensive and taxing that disclosees cannot cope with the flow of data. Second, the accumulation problem: Disclosures have become so numerous that none of us can begin to read and assimilate all of the disclosures thrust upon us.

Chapter 7 argues that even if these (essentially) cognitive problems with information could be overcome—even if disclosees were offered, accepted, understood, and remembered disclosures—people might not make better decisions. First, much of the information disclosed is unneeded and cannot improve decisions. Rational people make many decisions without the guidance that disclosures offer. Deciding *not* to be informed and not to use disclosures is often patently rational. The second reason disclosures may not improve decisions is the opposite: the relevant facts are so many that even under the full disclosure model, and certainly under the summary disclosure model, crucial facts are missing. In addition, people may need kinds of information that disclosures rarely provide, like information about themselves. Finally, there is the problem explored by a literature in social psychology and behavioral economics— that the human mind distorts information and reasoning. Disclosurites believe this literature is the key to effective disclosures, but we doubt that it provides a firm foundation for adjusting disclosures to account for the great tangle of biases and heuristics that affect decisions.

CHAPTER 4

"WHATEVER": THE PSYCHOLOGY OF MANDATED DISCLOSURE

> *Freud was once asked what he thought a normal person should be able to do well. . . . [He] is reported to have said:* Lieben und arbeiten *(to love and to work).*
>
> —Erik H. Erikson, *Childhood and Society*

When one researcher gave her subjects the consent forms that the law mandated, they would say, "Whatever."[1] That whatever—that verbal rolling of the eyes—captures much in disclosees' response to disclosures. Why?

"Whatever" is the first of several obstacles in mandated disclosure's path, for the attitudes it reflects are inimical to disclosurite assumptions. We begin describing those obstacles with evidence that many disclosees resist making the decisions the disclosures address, make them with incomplete information, and thus skip or scant many disclosures. Such disclosees are unlikely to use disclosures in ways that would make mandates effective.

We open our "whatever" discussion with an "if you say so" story. Rhonda Castellana signed five documents when she bought a car on credit from Conyers Toyota. These were the Georgia equivalents of chapter 2's California bed sheet for installment sales. She later testified that for almost three hours she read them and thought she understood them. When Ms. Castellana's credit application was denied, Conyers repossessed the car. Ms. Castellana said that the salesman had falsely assured her that her application had been approved. The court replied rather crossly, "The only reasonable construction of these documents is that no approval of the purchaser's credit application had been made when she signed them, nor would this occur until [the credit issuer] processed and approved it, and that [the seller] was authorized to repossess the vehicle if her credit application was rejected or disapproved." And what about the salesman's oral assurances? The court reproved Ms. Castellana, because "absent fraud, parole evidence is without probative value to vary the terms of a written contract." Furthermore, she should have exercised "ordinary diligence in making an independent verification of contractual terms and representations."[2]

This story illustrates many of mandated disclosure's problems. Ms. Castellana did not say "whatever"; she did what she was supposed to. She tried to make a well-informed choice about an unfamiliar and complex decision while dealing with a knowledgeable party whose interests were not hers. Why does someone living the disclosurite life seem so strange?

DECISION AVERSION

Disclosurism misconceives human nature. It rests on a plausible assumption about human nature and plausible inferences from it. Both the assumption and the inferences are importantly correct, but they fail in ways that lead policy astray.

The plausible assumption is that people demand "control." The plausible inferences are that therefore people want to make all the decisions that could significantly affect their lives and to make them carefully and well. In other words, disclosurism implicitly imagines a world populated by what (in the tradition of *homo economicus* and *homo ludens*) we call *homo arbiter*. *Homo arbiter* cherishes decisions, embraces them, makes them meticulously. *Homo arbiter* represents not just an assumption but a moral view. Iyengar writes,

> "Modern individuals are not merely 'free to choose,' but *obliged* to be free,
> to understand and enact their lives in terms of choice. . . . Their choices
> are . . . seen as realizations of the attributes of the choosing person—

expressions of personality—and reflect back upon the person who has made them." So to be oneself is to make the choices that best reflect the self, and these choices—taken cumulatively—are the expression and enactment of that most treasured value: freedom.[3]

There is truth in the assumption, the inferences, and the view of human nature, but it is partial and omits much that is crucial. First, the assumption: Control matters, but plenary control is impossible, and seeking it means mastering balky subjects to reach hard conclusions. Control may be comforting, and impotence would be misery, yet who does not leap to decisions with modest information and little reflection?

Next, the inferences. The first is that if people want control, they must want to make decisions. But making decisions well enough to approach control is so time-trashing and soul-sucking that it interferes with working and loving. And who relishes decisions? The drudgery of learning, the boredom of reading, the miseries of indecision, the risk of responsibility, the dread of error are charms cheerfully foregone.[4] The second inference is that, given information, people will make decisions—and make them well. But that is horribly hard. The cognitive problems that unfamiliar and complex decisions pose are forbidding, and analyzing choices is a process less rational than the *homo arbiter* model implies.

In the disclosurite world nobody says "whatever," and everyone is Rhonda Castellana (only better). In that world people (1) recognize that unfamiliar and complex decisions matter and depend on their own interests and circumstances and (2) learn enough to make informed and considered decisions that promote their interests and preferences. In the real world, however, people in surprising numbers and circumstances (1) resist making even significant decisions and (2) make them with incomplete information and inconsiderable effort. People are, loosely and broadly, decision averse. They are therefore unlikely to seek out or study disclosures. So mandated disclosure is short-circuited before it begins. Because decision aversion so affronts disclosurite assumptions (and the academic mind), we devote this chapter to it. We first explain our description, then the aversion itself.

When we say people are decision averse—are less eager to make decisions and make them less carefully than disclosurism hopes—we are easily misunderstood, but two clarifications may help. First, while people may be decision averse, they do not avoid or scant all decisions. Many decisions can only be made personally (like choosing a school or a spouse). Some decisions some people enjoy (like buying shotguns or shoes). Sometimes learning can be fun (like reading box scores or gossip columns). But these are not the decisions and information at which mandated disclosure is usually aimed.

Second, we are not saying that people rarely make good decisions. People manage their lives just fine because most decisions are familiar. Making decisions repeatedly teaches you what your choices are, what works or fails, and how to choose. Experience *is* the best teacher. But these advantages evaporate when you tread unfamiliar ground, and mandated disclosures take you deep into that ground. Furthermore, ignoring disclosures in making unfamiliar and complex decisions often is good sense.

Avoiding Decisions

Decision aversion occupies a long continuum—from declining to decide, to delegating decisions, to keeping options open, to postponing decisions, to deliberating sketchily, to making decisions loathing every step. The degree of deliberateness in avoiding decisions also varies, from ignoring them, to intending to make them soon, to conscious avoidance. So what is the evidence of this decision aversion in the areas in which mandates bloom?

On disclosurite principles if people wanted to make *any* decisions, it should be decisions about their health (about treatments, health-care plans, physicians, and more). These can be literally life-and-death matters, and because preferences about them vary, personal decisions may look prudent. Patients' desire to make decisions about treatments has been much studied, so with it we begin.

Nobody doubts patients' authority to decide, and some espouse a duty to do so. Nevertheless, many patients reject the gift of decision, both in pronouncement and practice. Asked whether they wanted information, patients' mean score was 80 on a 0–100 scale; asked whether they wanted to make decisions, the mean was 33. Not only was patients' desire to make decisions generally "weak," but the sicker and older they were—and thus the more the decisions generally mattered—the more they resisted.[5] In another study nearly half the patients wanted their doctor to make decisions for them, a third wanted the doctor to make decisions but "strongly consider the patient's opinion," a fifth wanted to share the decision with the doctor equally, and 3 percent wanted to decide for themselves.[6]

Some patients actually are *homo arbiter*. William Martin, a Rice sociologist with prostate cancer, describes studying his treatment choices as though he were investigating a nifty problem in ethnography. He interviewed doctors. He read articles, popular and professional. He became "totally engrossed in trying to unravel the riddles of prostate cancer, sometimes almost to the point of forgetting just why I had developed such a keen interest in the subject."[7] But few patients' memoirs of illness even mention participating in their medical decisions.

Some health-care decisions almost invite evasion. Picking a health-care plan presses patients to choose and economize. Choosing is labor, and economizing means giving up things you want. Not only is examining health-care choices distasteful, it is delightfully easy to avoid. If you have a doctor, follow the doctor's advice. If you are choosing a health plan, focus on one or two plan attributes and rest your decision on them. Or follow your coworkers' lead. Check a box. File and forget. Since the decision is revisable annually, people might eventually switch plans and improve their choice—not because of careful reflection and study but largely because of bad or expensive experiences. In short, as Brown writes of consumer-directed health care, "The public is not running to government demanding longer lists of plans and therewith more chances to ask more probing questions, sift more information, and wage a more valiant inner struggle against their suspicions of purchasers, plans, and providers."[8]

On disclosurite principles people should also take command of retirement accounts. Large sums are at stake, people who plan for retirement do better than those who don't, the decisions recur, information (mandated and not) is copious, and many employers offer incentives to act. However, one representative study found considerable decision aversion. Typical employees take over a year to enroll in a retirement plan and then overwhelmingly accept the plan's default choices (often a poor long-term option). Decisions to consume or save are based on mechanical criteria.[9] In a study of people more than fifty years old (most already retired), only 31 percent had tried to make a retirement plan, and of them only 58 percent had done so.[10] (And lest academics feel smug, at one time Harvard contributed to assistant professors' retirement accounts, but no interest accrued until they filled out a form specifying how to invest the money. But "most assistant professors filled out their forms only five or six years later, when they were leaving Harvard."[11])

Scanting Data and Deliberation

Not only do people say and show that they are reluctant to make their own decisions with anything like the zeal that disclosurites assume, but they often make decisions with little information or deliberation. On the contrary, people often simplify choices by pruning factors, sometimes down to just one. So even if disclosees got a well-judged disclosure program, many would ignore data to make their task more manageable and would deliberate too shallowly to evaluate disclosures well.

For example, patients generally receive far less information than disclosurite standards call for, yet they seem content with what they receive, as suggested by studies and the paucity of informed-consent suits.[12] Patients often hear horrifying things in informed consent, but a number of studies "strongly suggest that refusals attributable to disclosures are rarely, if ever, seen."[13] Thus a study of why patients refuse treatment found an average of only 4.6 refusals per 100 patient days, and for reasons that did not suggest that patients had considered their choices fully and rejected some as inferior.

It is easy to imagine reasons that patients might defer to physicians (like being sick, tired, and scared). But this makes choosing health plans and physicians crucial, and that is a choice that people can often make at leisure and in health. Much effort—including an elaborate disclosure regime—tries to induce people to select health insurance learnedly. Nevertheless, people regularly use little of the information furnished. For example, only about half the people in consumerist plans that provided information about the quality of physicians or hospitals said they had tried to use it. Only a third had tried to use cost information about doctors or hospitals.[14] For another example, only 10 percent of Medicare beneficiaries who had had high-risk surgery seriously considered going elsewhere for the surgery. Few (11 percent) sought information to compare hospitals. And 94 percent thought their hospital and 88 percent thought their surgeon well reputed.[15]

Nor do individual investors devote the effort to their finances that disclosurite doctrine expects. For instance, a majority of the USC nonfaculty employees surveyed spent less than an hour planning a portfolio for their defined-contribution plan.[16] One study found investors preferring portfolios chosen by someone else to portfolios they chose.[17] Nor do insurance buyers spend much time or effort shopping.[18] We have already explored mortgages' complexities, yet one study found that 40 percent of mortgagors had done little or no searching, 32 percent searched a moderate amount, and 28 percent searched a lot or a great deal. Mortgagors considered a median of three loans and six terms or features.[19]

People's willingness to make little-considered choices is suggested by the way they can make crucial decisions too quickly to have time to consider many factors. Asked to donate a kidney for transplantation, people often decide instantly. Despite determined attempts to have donors give truly informed consent, no donor "weighed alternatives and rationally decided." Many said they had decided immediately when the subject was raised over the phone, "'in a split-second,' 'instantaneously,' and 'right away.'" In short, all the donors and potential donors described decisions that were "immediate and 'irrational'" and could not meet the AMA's standards for informed consent.[20] Tellingly, patients' memoirs rarely reflect on how authors made decisions, and those that do often describe aborted processes. One breast cancer patient "knew right away what my decision would be."[21] For another cancer patient "[n]ot even a split second was needed to opt for chemotherapy despite all I had heard about it."[22]

Not only do patients often make complex choices too quickly to gather and consider the relevant facts, but many patients rely on only a few factors, or even one. If informed consent works anywhere, it should work for choosing breast cancer treatments. The choices are (relatively) well defined, specialists are practiced in presenting them, and informed consent and decision aids for breast cancer have been long studied. Yet one investigation concluded that the leading influence on decisions was "perceived salience." That is, patients relied on a single aspect of the treatment. They reported no "conflict about what course to take or the need for further information or deliberation."[23] Even patients who gather more information often choose "with nothing like adequate understanding."[24] Similarly truncated decisions were observed in prospective dialysis patients. They often listened until they heard some arresting fact and then based their decision on it. "[A]s soon as some patients hear that hemodialysis requires someone to insert two large needles into their arm three times a week, they opt for whatever the alternative is. When some other patients hear peritoneal dialysis means having a tube protruding from their abdomen, they choose 'the other kind of dialysis.'"[25]

Not only do patients often make decisions quickly and consult few criteria, even patients well educated and reflective enough to write memoirs commonly describe no decisional process at all. Instead, they invoke intuition and impulse, despite having little experience or reason to fall back on instinct. An AIDS patient, for example, said that if he got "a 'ding' (a strong instinct) about a vitamin, herb, drug, or other treatment, I try it."[26] A multiple sclerosis patient "got a flash."[27] Anatole Broyard wryly defended this: "I think that if a man should ever give in to his prejudices, it's when he's ill." His prejudices reflected "the intelligence of my unconscious, and so I go with it."[28]

Even patients apparently committed to thoughtful, informed decisions can falter. Michael Korda (editor-in-chief at Simon & Schuster and author of books like *Power!*) believed in understanding his prostate cancer and making his own decisions. He consulted a prominent surgeon, asked questions, then found that his "mind had gone blank" and he was "feeling the inevitability of the thing."[29] Even that disclosurite model, the Rice sociologist William Martin, wrote, "Without knowing precisely why or being able to provide a clear rationale, I decided I would ask Peter Scardino to perform my surgery."[30]

If people revisited initial choices, all this could matter less. But, Francis Bacon warned, when the mind adopts an opinion it "draws all things else to support and agree with it. And though there be a greater number and weight of instances to be found on the other side, yet these it either neglects and despises, or else by some distinction sets aside and rejects."[31] With more evidence but less eloquence, Nisbett and Ross say that "once subjects have made a first pass at a problem, the initial judgment may prove remarkably resistant to further information, alternative modes of reasoning, and even logical or evidential challenges."[32]

People can ignore even dramatic lessons publicly taught. For example, a flurry of bankruptcies in which employees who had put much of their pension funds into company stock and lost both job and savings seemed to teach a stark lesson: diversify! But one study estimated that all the to-do about "the Enron, WorldCom, and Global Crossing bankruptcies reduced the fraction of aggregate 401(k) assets held in employer stock by at most 2 percentage points, from about 36 percent to about 34 percent." The study concluded that "educational interventions yield remarkably small changes in saving behavior."[33]

Skipping and Skimming Disclosures

We have suggested that many people tend to avoid making the unfamiliar and complex decisions that mandates generally address and make them with less data and deliberation than disclosurites expect. If so, a principal motive to read disclosures is gone. Much evidence suggests that people often overlook disclosures, ignore them when they notice them, treat them perfunctorily when they read them, forget and misinterpret much they have read, and incorporate little of their learning into decisions.

The Internet transactions of disclosees are easily tracked, so we *know* that nobody reads the terms (like the iTunes contract) they agree to. Many disclosurites passionately believe that such contracts ought not bind those who have not had a chance to read them. So contract law, bolstered by federal statutes and decades of court decisions (with occasional exceptions), mandates disclosure of their terms. For example, EULAs (end-user license agreements) are boilerplate contracts governing the use of most software. They are hyperlinked at the checkout page or pop up during installation to demand an "I agree" click. Similar disclosures include privacy and data-collection policies, Web sites' terms of service, and dispute resolution agreements. So what do disclosees do with this classic fine print?

Just what *you* do. Lord Denning once said of analogous disclosures that "[n]o customer in a thousand ever read those conditions." He may have meant this metaphorically, but a study tracking the visits of 45,091 households to the Web sites of sixty-six software companies found that "only about one or two in one thousand shoppers accesses a product's EULA for at least one second."[34]

Are the disclosures just too hard to find? No. Making them more obvious did not increase readership significantly. Even putting the "I agree" right next to the terms increased readership (at best) about 1 percent. Forced-to-click terms were read only 0.36 percent more than linked terms, which users need not even click. Overall, readership of the fine print of Web sites ranges from 0.1 percent to 1 percent, and this is marvelously conservative, since "readers" are shoppers who accessed the contract (mean, 2,300 words) for an average of less than thirty seconds.[35]

But even if consumers click blithely past Internet disclosures, don't people with more at stake—like investors—scrutinize disclosures? Securities laws require disclosing data about stocks, bonds, and mutual funds, but only 15 percent of shareholders report reading the whole prospectus (a report we doubt, because they are hideously hard). Even people who owned direct-marketed funds or who said they were self-reliant read little.[36]

Nor do other financial disclosures seem to fare better. For example, experts doubt that people read TILA disclosures, and they find some support in consumer surveys.[37] Asked whether most people read those disclosures carefully, 70 percent of the respondents in a Fed survey said no.[38] The subprime-mortgage meltdown showed not only that subprime borrowers didn't read mortgage documents, professional investors ignored the prospectuses for mortgage-based securities. Michael Lewis's *The Big Short* describes the triumph of a few investors who studied the fine print and noticed that the underlying assets were riskier than rating agencies supposed.[39] Kirsch writes that consumers pay little heed to disclosures like buyers' guides that insurers and producers must distribute and that people who know about them find them of little use.[40]

But even if people speed-click through Internet disclosures and skip over investment and insurance information, don't patients and potential research subjects read medical disclosures? They are typically presented just when the decision must be made, and they tell patients and sub-jects things they might well care about. Yet Baren, for example, used trained research assistants to get consent to an emergency-room sur-vey of intimate-partner violence. Potential subjects got a brief form (two pages, eleven paragraphs). Only 53 percent could read it at all. Of these, 20 percent spent less than ten seconds, 38 percent less than a minute, 30 percent between one and two minutes, and 13 percent more than two minutes. Only a fifth asked questions. They could not have understood the form in two minutes, nor can we know that they were actually read-ing it (instead of pretending to, to be polite or to show that they were not illiterate).

A principal hope for educating patients is the report card on hospi-tals and health plans. However, surveys of patients and clinicians suggest that report cards have little effect.[41] Patients rarely know about them and yet more rarely understand and use them.[42] Ninety percent of Medicare beneficiaries, for example, knew nothing or little about HMOs, and only 16 percent knew enough to choose between traditional Medicare and an HMO.[43] In another study two-thirds of the respondents lacked a good grasp of differences between traditional fee-for-service and HMO plans, and many did not know fundamental facts about HMO plans. Only about 20 percent of insurance purchasers reported using any systematic ap-proach for selecting good plans; most just looked to see whether the plan was accredited.[44] Even people given the best disclosures seem not to have used the information to decide whether to switch plans.[45]

Skimming and scanting information is not confined to mandated disclosures but seems to be part of people's attitude toward even signifi-cant choices. For example, patients looking for drug information on the Internet spend only four seconds per page, and most give up if informa-tion can't be found in twenty minutes.[46]

In sum, plentiful evidence shows people skipping, skimming, and scanting disclosures. "Whatever" is not the only reaction, but it begins to look like the modal one. Even Judge Richard Posner, faced with hundreds of pages of disclosures for a home-equity loan, is quoted as saying, "I didn't read, I just signed."[47]

MANDATED DISCLOSURE AND SOCIAL PRACTICE

We have been arguing that disclosurite psychology is wrong, that people live differently than disclosurites imagine and therefore make decisions in ways disclosurites must think feckless. This aversion to disclosures, deliberation, and decision may look like a fool's path to disaster. People's affairs surely can suffer because they avoid or defer decisions or trust poor data and paltry deliberation. As Gilovich observes, relying on incomplete or inaccurate information is a common reason people's beliefs are wrong.[48] Were individual investors better informed and more thoughtful, for example, they might be less prone to trade too much, diversify too little, hold losers too long, and buy their own employer's stock too much.[49]

Nevertheless, the benefits of decision aversion often outweigh its costs. Not least, people are confirmed in their apparent fecklessness by their personal experience with disclosures and the social experience with them, the experience of overlooking, ignoring, and skimming disclosures without apparent disaster. Social practice has a term—fine print—reflecting this judgment. Personal and social experience also gives people a repertoire of justifications (more or less explicit) for dismissing disclosures.

Let This Cup

Applying Ms. Castellana's method to every unfamiliar and complex decision would mean a life-time educational project like the worst of high school—boring subjects and nasty tests going on your permanent record. Most of us are glad to have graduated and loath to return. Give people a disclosure and tell them to make a choice familiar and comprehensible and hear, "This looks like work to me, hard work, work I'm not interested in, work I'm not good at, work I would rather avoid, and (hallelujah) work I *can* avoid. I shall." The drudgery of learning, the inevitability of incompetence, the certainty of uncertainty, the labor of weighing risks and wants, the pain of indecision, the burden of responsibility, and the dubious return for your misery hold charms for few.

For most people facing unfamiliar and complex decisions, the "more information is better" mantra is wrong. In these areas knowledge is not intrinsically valued. Many people want to know less, not more, and information brings anxiety, not confidence. They dislike reading contracts, manuals, warnings, notices, forms, charts, instructions, lists, scrolls, and bed sheets. In short, asking novices to master expert information is setting them a repellent task. Few people have the academic's zeal for study; fewer still share that zeal when the subject is wearisome; almost no one shares it when the study is arduous and unrewarding.

This book overflows with evidence about how onerous disclosees' work can be. Educating yourself about even one of these decisions can mean starting from a base of ignorance that can be diminished only by reading texts indecipherable to many and daunting to many more, especially since people lack the background to interpret even the sentences they can read. Even if you rightly interpret what you read, the labor of analyzing a complex choice (often pockmarked with uncertainties) can be bruising. There are so many decisions in so many fields. It's hard, unending, unpleasant. It's education. And who cares? Do you really want to know everything that can go wrong when you book a cruise vacation? Or what Web sites do with their data on your shopping? Or how many calories you spend on every bite of a decadent dessert? As Schwartz writes, "We can't make ourselves sufficiently well informed about everything so that the need for trust goes away." But wariness "makes each transaction a contest, a confrontation. It leaves us feeling all the time that we've probably been taken. It makes acquisition a full time job."[50]

Opportunity Costs

Not only can the disclosurite lifelong-learning program be repellent, it interferes with things people *like* doing; it distracts people from more agreeable and valued activities. When people think about their lives, they think about what they like to do, what they care about. They surf the Internet to find things that interest them and to play and work, not to read privacy policies and terms of use. They go on cruises and rent cars to enjoy the beach, not to read disclaimers or insurance terms. And they visit the doctor to get rid of headaches, not to get them from reading HIPAA disclosures.

The hours spent studying disclosures cannot be spent doing things you like. And all kinds of effort—"cognitive, emotional, or physical—draw at least partly on a shared pool of mental energy." The attention it takes to analyze disclosures requires exerting self-control, which is "depleting and unpleasant." After spending so much on an unfamiliar and complex decision, you begrudge the self-control another effort demands.[51]

Disclosurites forget another opportunity cost. Reading a disclosure means you cannot spend time reading other disclosures. If you want to read fine print, you soon find yourself thwarted by the enterprise itself. Reading some fine print precludes reading other fine print. And even the disclosure you read is soon revised and modified again and again. As disclosures proliferate, more of them must be ignored to free time for the really important ones.

For What?

Mastering disclosures, then, can mean sacrificing the pleasant for the un-pleasant. People need good reasons to do this. The reasons depend partly on how much education improves decisions. Disclosees gain little if there is little to gain, yet disclosures are often mandated even where disclosees can hardly improve a choice. Acres of disclosures are insignificant. Most click-through and shrinkwrap forms and many contractual disclosures explain contingencies so remote and recherché that you *should* ignore them. The boilerplate arbitration agreements whose disclosure so stirs consumers' champions excite few consumers. As James J. White put it, "For a nickel or a dime, almost all of us would give up our right to resell software, and would agree to arbitrate."[52]

Even when we care, disclosures may mean little. HIPAA and financial-privacy disclosures tell us about confidentiality practices. It can matter how private information is marshaled, sold, and used. But to understand how our bank, retailer, or Web service uses it, we must decipher cryptic legalisms that tells us that our information is shared "as permitted by law" (as if we knew the law) with "affiliates" and "service providers" (as if we knew who they were). And even if we understand, what do we do? If we don't want the bank sharing our financial DNA, do we to go to another bank (with heavy switching costs)? Is the other bank's policy better (improbably)? Call the 800 number and try to opt out? We are back to "whatever" land.

Furthermore, disclosures can change rapidly. As Google warns, it will "modify these terms or any additional terms that apply to a Service to, for example, reflect changes to the law or changes to our Services. You should look at the terms regularly." Google will helpfully "post notice of modifications to these terms on this page" and "notice of modified additional terms in the applicable Service."[53] Will you really monitor evolving terms in various places with no tracked-changes feature to learn things you probably don't care about and surely can't change?

But aren't undisclosed terms unfavorable terms? Radin laments that people "do not even know that they are receiving boilerplate purporting to impose obligations or to remove background rights." Terms are so bad that getting boilerplate is "like being hit by one of thousands of dumped projectiles."[54] But Marotta-Wurgler found that fine print wrapped in the box and available only after purchase is no worse than predisclosed fine print and even a bit better. She thinks sellers are not sneakily hiding one-sided contracts. Rather, sellers protect one-sided contracts by making them prominent enough that buyers cannot claim undue surprise.[55]

The return on disclosures is also slight where disclosees have good advice to rely on. Thus Hung's inexperienced investors relied on plan administrators.[56] Patients doubt they can make a better decision than their doctors and don't try. They may retain a veto ("You want to do *what* with that big needle?"), but they delegate much to their physician.

Finally, disclosees gain little from disclosures they don't understand. Thus in one study inexperienced investors "were unwilling to commit time to seeking out additional information that they felt they had little chance of understanding."[57] The chapters in this part will show how often that chance is small.

In sum, "whatever" often makes sense. The cost of reading disclosures is often high, the benefits often low. As Willis says of financial decisions, making people be "their own financial experts is inefficient. People are financially illiterate not because they are stupid, but because they have better things to do with their time. The hours of study they would need to invest to attempt to reach literacy are unlikely" to pay off.[58]

Our argument conflicts with one version of the autonomy principle—the version that sees autonomy as knowledgeably making decisions that affect you. As a seminal case put it, "True consent to what happens to one's self is the informed exercise of a choice."[59] This version of autonomy is right for everyone sometimes. But people often prefer a different version, one in which they decide when to make decisions personally and how well to inform themselves. They value autonomy not for itself, but instrumentally—as a way to get what they want. If they can get it without plowing through disclosures, great.

This view makes the informed choices that disclosurites advocate look more like threats to than shields for autonomy.[60] Studying disclosures can *detract* from your sense of control. Few things make you feel *less* autonomous than studying a choice that hourly becomes more convoluted and confusing. You feel even less autonomous on realizing that you may never understand. And less autonomous still when you realize that the choice is essentially illusory. The kind of control over life's choices that disclosurism seems to promise is an illusion.

Decision aversion neatly fits another ideological basis for disclosurism: it is standard economics that searching for and acquiring information are costs justified only by sufficient benefits. Since the cost of acquiring information can be high even when disclosures are near to hand, ignorance can be both rational individually and efficient socially.

Personal and Social Experience

We have been explaining why disclosurism so badly fits people's lives. We can get a richer sense of why by taking the disclosee's perspective, particularly by reviewing disclosees' repertoire of explanations for ignoring disclosures. The explanations are not always convincing, but they are at least plausible enough that people are unlikely to abandon them readily.

I already know it. People ignore disclosures because they think they know what they say. Sometimes rightly, sometimes wrongly. Many people think they know more than they do about loans, mortgages, flu shots, Viagra, warranties, mutual funds, living wills, car rentals, and freezers. When you don't know what you don't know or what questions to ask, it's easy to be ignorant but confident. For example, consumers greatly underestimate the differences in price and products and therefore may not see the need to shop.[61]

It's irrelevant. People ignore disclosures because they look irrelevant. We have argued that they are often right. Sometimes, to be sure, they are wrong, because when decisions are unfamiliar and complex, people often don't know enough to see the disclosure's relevance. And when people make decisions rapidly, they often fix on a criterion (or a few criteria) to rely on, ignoring relevant criteria. If you have decided to choose a loan by asking whether you can afford the monthly payment, the rest of the information in the pile looks superfluous.

Disclosures don't matter; people do. People ignore disclosures because they think that what they get and how they are treated depend more on the person or place they're dealing with than any disclosure. Patients take the statin because they think their doctor wouldn't prescribe it unless they needed it. People conclude (rightly) that whether a company backs its products depends more on its customer-service practices than what its lawyers stick in the warranty. People buy Apple computers and use iTunes despite thirty-two pages of terms and conditions.[62] People (and businesses) dealing with businesses expect relations to be governed by cooperation and accommodation and think the fine print—norms that require legal proceedings to enforce—mostly irrelevant and of risible use to consumers.[63]

It must be safe to ignore this disclosure. People can imagine that disclosures don't matter because they think transactions are safe: "They couldn't do this unless it were OK." In a regulation-rich society, people may assume that the government's rod and staff will protect them. People may also assume that the market punishes anyone proffering bad deals. And when you (and your friends) have entered into thousands of transactions and can't remember suffering from neglecting a disclosure, these assumptions look reasonable.

I've got to have this no matter what the disclosure says. Why read a disclosure if it just keeps you from getting what you have to have? If your doctor says, "It's the operation or death," what matters the consent form? One of us was once handed a document that covered *all* the unit's procedures, so he read about lots of dire things. When he asked why anyone signed this gruesome form, the technician replied frankly, "Because we won't treat you if you don't." When closing on our homes, both the property professor and the contracts professor stared at the pile of papers and never thought of rejecting one. We had already sold our old homes, hired the mover, ordered the new appliances, and had nowhere else to live. What choice did we have?

The disclosure doesn't help me; it protects them. Two scholars put well what most people think, that CYA "is a master principle that rivals Freud's pleasure principle or Bentham's felicific calculus."[64] Don't companies use fine print to protect themselves? Even the IRB system's foremost apologist says, "In the 'cover your ass' mentality that has developed over the last decade, . . . IRBs do really foolish, stupid things in the name of protecting human subjects but really to cover themselves."[65] In an English study almost half the patients thought the consent form's main purpose was to shield the hospital from suits.[66] In an Irish study 86 percent of the patients thought the form primarily protected the doctor and hospital.[67] Nor is this just cynicism. Warnings about products shelter manufacturers from tort liability. Warnings about consumer loans save lenders from fraud liability. Disclaimers protect sellers from much contract liability. And as chapter 11 will show, disclosures can badly undermine consumer protections and bolster businesses' immunity.

I couldn't understand it anyway. Part I described how complex, convoluted, and confusing disclosures can be. Disclosees soon learn (to paraphrase Thurber) that disclosure tells them more about penguins than they wanted to know, but incomprehensibly. Most (all?) disclosees have tried and failed to understand disclosures. So disclosees learn that reading disclosures may mean wasted time, and the disclosee who tries to read a complex disclosure soon relearns the lesson.

That's not what I wanted. Consumers often prefer plenary recommendations from people they know and trust to detailed disclosures. "Preference for nontechnical, informal sources of quality information is reflected in a number of focus group studies and surveys on the topic of consumers' use of health-care quality information. This preference appears to be driven by a perceived lack of understanding of process-based measures."[68] Failing such help, people may prefer to consult organizations they trust. Suppose you truly care about how a Web site collects and uses information about you. The "Important Notice Concerning Your Privacy" is obfuscatory and obscure. Better to consult an intermediary that studies and rates (with a seal or a grade) the site's behavior.

Oh, was I supposed to read that? Disclosees do not always recognize that they are being given information they are supposed to study and use. Relevant information may be so mixed with irrelevant information that disclosees think the whole document is meant for somebody or something else. Unfold a drug insert. Are you *really* supposed to read all that fine print? In fact, no. Most of it is for your doctor; your part is at the tag end. The beginning tells your doctor about the drug and when and how to prescribe it. And disclosures (like your bank's latest overdraft policy) may arrive in envelopes so resembling junk mail that you toss them out.

Boring! As literary works, disclosures fail. Graceless sentences, dubious grammar, and vulgar syntax rule. The story is plotless, lifeless, humorless, endless.

Weird! That person in front of you at the airport car rental counter who reads all the fine print, asks the clerk to explain it, demands full disclosure, and scribbles new clauses to replace the boilerplate is not normal. You don't want to be like that.

In sum, not only do people begrudge the labor of learning enough to make good decisions independently, not only do they have things they would rather do, but they have a repertoire of explanations for dismissing disclosures. And these explanations and that attitude are strengthened by the psychology and culture of "whatever" that surrounds disclosures.

Conclusion

Far from reaching out to make well-informed decisions in the way disclo-surites imagine, people chronically avoid decisions, postpone them, rush them, delegate them, and make them with little information. Insofar as they do, their incentive to scrutinize disclosures lessens. And for many disclosees a cost-benefit analysis further reduces that incentive. And this is not the end of the cost-benefit analysis. To its other elements we now turn.

CHAPTER 5

READING DISCLOSURES

All too often, visiting the doctor is like being a seventeen-year-old buying our first used car: we go into it in a thicket of hope, ignorance, and anxiety, hoping to get good, reliable information with which we can make a sensible decision; but once we're on the spot we are told things we barely hear, let alone understand, consider, or remember.

—Tim Brookes, *Catching My Breath*

Chapter 4 identified a principal reason mandated disclosure fails: it rests on false assumptions about how people think, act, and live. People tend to be averse to making many unfamiliar and complex decisions, so they are inclined to avoid making (or at least to postpone) choices about them and tend to make them with less information and care than disclosurites desire. This reduces people's incentives to read, study, and use disclosures. Those incentives are further diminished by the conclusion many disclosees reach—at varying degrees of awareness—that the costs of using disclosures often exceed the benefits. People are confirmed in this judgment by their own experience and social experience, which we saw reflected in the list of reasons people can readily adduce for ignoring disclosures.

This chapter examines one reason disclosees decide that disclosures aren't worth the trouble—they often can't read them. We use "read" broadly to mean "extract useful meaning from." Many people cannot read many disclosures because they are not literate or numerate enough to decipher them with reasonable effort. This is both because levels of literacy and numeracy are surprisingly low and because the reading levels of disclosures are surprisingly high. But disclosees cannot read many disclosures for yet other reasons. These reasons grow out of the very justification for disclosure mandates—that people must make decisions about unfamiliar and complex issues. Understanding disclosures about such issues takes more than understanding words, sentences, paragraphs, and figures; it often requires what we call sector literacy—understanding a decision's context and an industry's practices as only proficients do.

LITERACY

Chapter 2 showed how intensively unfamiliar and complex are the problems that mandates are intended to help people with and thus how intensively complex disclosures must be. Examples included a pile of fifty mortgage disclosures, the iTunes scroll, and the consumer-credit bed sheet. So, how hard are the sentences in these disclosures? Here are several examples. Words and passages like these are so common that anyone who can't manage them comfortably is unlikely to understand (or even trudge through) such disclosures.

A common and important provision from the bed sheet: "Any holder of this consumer credit contract is subject to all claims and defenses which the debtor could assert against the seller of goods or services obtained pursuant hereto or with the proceeds hereof. Recovery hereunder by the debtor shall not exceed amounts paid by the debtor hereunder."

A sentence from the iTunes contract: "By using any location-based services on your iPad, you agree and consent to Apple's and its partners' and licensees' transmission, collection, maintenance, processing and use of your location data and queries to provide and improve such location-based products and services."

A passage from the Fed's Consumer Handbook on Adjustable Rate Mortgages: "The interest rate on an ARM is made up of two parts: the index and the margin. The index is a measure of interest rates generally, and the margin is an extra amount that the lender adds. Your payments will be affected by any caps, or limits, on how high or low your rate can go."

A clause from Walmart.com's terms: "You agree to defend, indemnify and hold harmless Walmart.com and its affiliates from and against any and all claims, damages, costs and expenses, including attorneys' fees, arising from or related to your use of the Site or any breach by you of these Terms of Use."

And just for fun, a sentence from a pre-need contract for burial merchandise: "THIS CONTRACT AUTHORIZES THE DELIVERY OF MERCHANDISE TO A LICENSED AND BONDED WAREHOUSE FOR STORAGE OF THE MERCHANDISE UNTIL THE MERCHANDISE IS NEEDED BY THE BENEFICIARY. DELIVERY OF THE MERCHANDISE IN THIS MANNER MAY PRECLUDE REFUND OF SALE PROCEEDS THAT ARE ATTRIBUTABLE TO THE DELIVERED MERCHANDISE."

The reader who has plowed through this prose may well have understood some of it. (We ourselves aren't sure we understand all of it.) But how will typical disclosees fare?

Levels of Literacy

People learn little from disclosures they can't read. But our readers (and their friends and colleagues) are in the highest percentiles in literacy, and they may doubt that in a country with universal education and excellent universities so many people are so much less literate. Therefore, we briefly chart American literacy levels.

The 2003 National Assessment of Adult Literacy described four levels of literacy among English-speaking adults: (1) below basic (14 percent); (2) basic (29 percent); (3) intermediate (44 percent); and (4) proficient (13 percent). People in level 1 have only the simplest and most concrete reading skills. They "would likely [*sic*] be able to locate the words *child, children, pediatric* on a package of cold medicine" but not to tell how much to give a fifty-pound ten-year-old. People in level 2 "can locate information in moderately complicated text, make low-level inferences using print materials, and integrate easily identifiable pieces of information." But they have trouble reading a dosage chart and are not literate enough to participate fully in American life.[1] People in level 3 can manage moderately difficult literacy tasks; people at level 4 can "perform more complex and challenging literacy activities."[2] In short, much of the population has trouble reading even quite simple things.

A few specifics: A third of the English-speaking patients at two public hospitals could not read basic materials about health. Over two-fifths could not understand "directions for taking medication on an empty stomach," a quarter could not use an appointment slip, and three-fifths could not read standard consent forms. Because of patients' trouble reading "about disease management, prevention, and informed consent" doctors cannot give their patients essential information.[3]

Not only do many people read poorly; few read well. A 1993 Department of Education survey divided a 0–500 point scale into five levels. Level 5 comprised people with scores from 376 to 500 (average 423). A question worth 410 points gave people a question-and-answer pamphlet of 648 words written for prospective jurors. The pamphlet included this:

> When an attorney believes that there is a legal reason to excuse a juror,
> he or she will challenge the juror for cause. Unless both attorneys agree
> that the juror should be excused, the Judge must either sustain or override
> the challenge. After all challenges for cause have been ruled upon, the
> attorneys will select the trial jury from those who remain by exercising
> peremptory challenges. Unlike challenges for cause, no reason need be
> given for excusing a juror by peremptory challenge.

The question: "Identify and summarize the two kinds of challenges that attorneys use while selecting members of a jury." *Three* percent of the population reached level 5.[4]

Levels of Reading Difficulty in Disclosures

When almost nobody can answer the question we just described and only 13 percent are "proficient" in literacy, disclosures must be *very* accessible to be widely useful. Thus the conventional wisdom is that consent forms for research should be written at an eighth-grade level.[5] Minnesota law requires that consent forms "be written at a 7.5-grade reading level to ensure that patients understand the therapeutic options available."[6]

In many areas this standard is much flouted. Consent forms tend to be so long and dense that the average person finds them hard going.

Forms for oncology trials ranged from 955 to 6453 words and from four to twenty-six pages, and they required reading levels from 8.3 to 17.5 years.[7] Grossman studied consent forms that had been approved by an oncology center's clinical research committee, an IRB, and three national cooperative groups. Forms were too hard for most patients and families.[8] Even regulators' *model* consent forms usually exceed the regulators' reading-level standards.[9]

Privacy notices are now thick as leaves in Vallombrosa. But financial-privacy notices are written at a third- or fourth-year college reading level.[10] Two-thirds of the privacy forms that academic medical centers use require some college education, and 90 percent are "difficult." IRB privacy forms can add two pages to consent materials and use language as complex as that "in corporate annual reports, legal contracts, and the professional medical literature."[11] IRB privacy forms in major health-care centers are (median) six pages of 10-point font. A median of 80 percent of their likely readers "would have difficulty understanding" them.[12]

Business disclosures are no better. The "literacy required to comprehend the average disclosure form and key contract terms simply is not within the reach of the majority of American adults."[13] Only 3–4 percent of the country can understand the language of contracts. Credit-card agreements typically run eight pages in 7-point font and have about eighty provisions. Many of their terms require specialized knowledge.[14] Consumer-credit disclosures come packed in long, dense pages. People misunderstand financial language. (Is a discount fee a discount or a fee? What is a balloon?) Many borrowers cannot identify basic terms, and confusion permeates both the prime and subprime echelons.[15]

Yet all this *understates* the problem. As Reid observes, "Even writing the material to match the reading level of the reader does not assure comprehension. It depends not only on such textual variables as word complexity and sentence length, but also upon text organization, syntax, and rhetorical structure." Managing such "textual variables" has challenged experts for decades. Furthermore, people taking a literacy test virtually must pay attention to a text; disclosees in the flow and independence of their lives need not. Yet the success of disclosures depends on readers' "interest, reading skills, prior knowledge, need for cognition, and experience."[16]

Disclosures can defeat even sophisticated readers. During oral argument one state supreme court justice said he couldn't "understand half of my insurance policies." Another justice thought that "insurance companies keep the language of their policies deliberately obscure." The chief justice concurred: "I don't know what it means. I am stumped. They say one thing in big type and in small type they take it away."[17] And a billionaire investor wrote about bank disclosures that "there is no major financial institution today whose financial statements provide a meaningful clue."[18]

NUMERACY

Innumeracy is worse than illiteracy. A standard test asks people (1) how often a flipped coin comes up heads in 1,000 tries, (2) what 1 percent of 1,000 is, and (3) how to turn a proportion (1 in 1000) into a percentage. You probably answered each question as you read it. But 30 percent of women of above-average literacy had *no* correct answers, 28 percent had one, 26 percent had two, and only 16 percent had three.[19] Although most people in another study had at least some college education, 40 percent "could not solve a basic probability problem or convert a percentage to a proportion."[20]

More broadly, the 2003 National Assessment of Adult Literacy described four levels of numeracy: (1) below basic (22 percent); (2) basic (33 percent); (3) intermediate (33 percent); and (4) proficient (13 percent). Below-basic means being able to locate numbers and perform simple operations (primarily addition) with very concrete and familiar information. Basic means "locating easily identifiable quantitative information and using it to solve simple, one-step problems when the arithmetic operation is specified or easily inferred."[21] Roughly a third of the students in two-year and a fifth of the students in four-year colleges have only basic skills or worse.[22] Yet patients, for example, are increasingly given numbers about risks for disease and benefits of treatment.[23] So after getting numbers about how well mammography reduces risks, most of the women in a study could not estimate their risks of dying from breast cancer with and without mammograms. Accuracy ranged from 7 percent to 33 percent.[24]

The evidence about numeracy and financial disclosures is also grim. Only 18 percent of survey respondents could calculate how much a $200 investment earning 10 percent interest annually would yield after two years ($242). Only half could answer two basic questions: (1) would $100 invested at 2 percent per year for five years yield more, less, or exactly $102? (more); and (2) when inflation is 2 percent and money is saved at 1 percent annually, would money saved for one year buy more, less, or the same as today? (less). And "a significant portion" of the thousands of adults tested could not "make the comparisons necessary to assess the cost of credit card debt."[25]

When new Fed regulations sought to make disclosures of credit-card costs clearer, only a few basic computations were needed to pick the best card, but fewer than half the students tested did so. Researchers simplified the choice to make math skills unnecessary; students only needed to understand "the tradeoff between interest rates and annual fees." Even then, only two-thirds chose correctly. "Apparently, almost one-third of the subjects did not understand this basic product information."[26]

Much disclosure warns of risks. Knowing that well-educated people can be poorly numerate and doubting people's ability to understand individualized risk data, Han et al. conducted a study that found that both confident and unconfident people "miscalculated frequencies, misunderstood proportions, overestimated average risks and confused different measures of central tendency." Some had trouble "converting percentages to frequencies—e.g., calculating that 9% of 100 people equaled nine people." Others thought "the 9% number was on a 10-point maximum scale." Participants tended "to base comparisons on the magnitude of the numerator instead of the ratio." Some "misinterpreted the 9% risk estimate as a percentile rank."[27] Thus beset by error, people in one study

who saw information about "a disease that kills 1,286 people out of every 10,000" judged it as more dangerous than people who were told about "a disease that kills 24.14% of the population." The first disease appears more threatening than the second, although the former risk is only half as large as the latter! In an even more direct demonstration of denominator neglect, "a disease that kills 1,286 people out of every 10,000" was judged more dangerous than one that kills 24.4 out of 100.[28]

But is the literacy cup at least part full? Effectively, no. Disclosures often demand *more* than basic skill in reading texts and numbers. Disclosees must negotiate unfamiliar and complex problems where mistakes are easy, a full and exact command of data is needed, and one misunderstanding can be fatal. The levels of innumeracy we have described mean that many disclosures do not help most of their audience.

SECTOR LITERACY

The Need for Sector Literacy

We have been arguing that disclosees cannot understand many disclosures because they cannot understand their numbers, words, sentences, paragraphs, or documents. But even quite literate and numerate disclosees struggle and fail. Why?

At base, because disclosures provide unfamiliar and complex information about specialized areas. Confronted with complexity, everyone simplifies. Experts can simplify well; novices cannot. By repeatedly solving problems, experts master a field's assumptions, issues, and solutions. They acquire practical experience and intuition and learn to recognize a situation "as typical and familiar" so that they can "understand what types of *goals* make sense (so the priorities are set), which *cures* are important (so there is not an overload of information), what to *expect* next (so they can prepare themselves and notice surprises), and the *typical ways of responding* in a given situation. By recognizing a situation as typical, they also recognize a *course of action* likely to succeed."[29]

Novices simplify complexity crudely. They lack the knowledge needed for "a mental representation of the information."[30] Novices need the "repertoire of expectations, images, and techniques" that help experts know what to look for and how to respond to it.[31] For example, Ho found that customers misread even the simplest of disclosures (restaurant hygiene grades) because they did not know how ratings worked or how unreliable inspections were.[32]

Crucially, this knowledge-in-action cannot be learned "just by being told." It needs "lots of experience, and lots of variety in that experience."[33] It is based on implicit, not articulated, knowledge.[34] Experts "usually know more than they can say. They exhibit a kind of knowing-in-practice, most of which is tacit."[35] So even a formidably educated patient like Gillian Rose concluded that medicine and she too little understood each other's language to communicate fruitfully. She learned "words and phrases, even sentences," but not "the underlying principles of grammar and syntax." So she could not "generate the grammar of judgments" needed to ask questions and reach her own conclusions.[36]

When people make ordinary decisions, they draw "on a rich store of general knowledge of objects, people, events, and their characteristic relationships." From this knowledge grow beliefs and theories that people use to organize and explain information.[37] In familiar realms these theories generally work well enough. But in unfamiliar realms people lack the rich store of knowledge and have no theories (or bad theories) for interpreting what they are told. They don't know what matters greatly and what matters little, they focus on the wrong data, they notice detail rather than patterns, and their judgment is clouded by irrelevancies.

So faced with complexity and information that they lack the background and skill to interpret, novices are driven back on the kind of heuristics (see chapter 7) that suffice in familiar and simple circumstances but that fail in unfamiliar and complex ones. As Kirsch writes, people experienced with a product can make good choices with fewer facts, but for people lacking "an adequate contextual framework, data remain data and consumers can often be heard to lament what they perceive of as 'inadequate information.'"[38]

How, for example, do health-illiterate patients choose a treatment for prostate cancer? It helps to know the basics of the organ and the disease. It helps to know that cancer is not a single disease and that ways of treating many cancers apply poorly to prostate cancer. It helps to understand the kinds of probabilities that pervade medical decisions. It helps to grasp the idea of baselines, the idea that side effects are not dichotomies but continuums, and the fact that medical uncertainty is pervasive.

The need for sector literacy may be most apparent when it is missing. For example, experts disagree about PSA screening for prostate cancer. The counterintuitive argument against screening is that (1) most men with elevated PSA have no cancer while biopsies are unpleasant, expensive, and fallible and (2) treating the cancer may be otiose. The contending experts recommend disclosure—offering patients evidence so *they* can decide. Schneider and Farrell informed men copiously, but they still had "considerable difficulty" making "well informed and well reasoned decisions."[39]

Lack of health literacy was an important reason. Dr. Farrell's disclosures came from the sophisticate's template; the men hardly had templates and were frequently "swayed by unexamined assumptions which led them to ignore or misunderstand the information." They often recruited "principles of folk wisdom." For example, they were health-literate enough to know the argument for cancer screening but not enough to know that screening is not always cost-effective. Nor were they health-literate enough to distinguish between screening and prevention. Some were not health-literate enough to understand the fallibility of tests and treatments. One said, "[I]f there's a test, or an exam, or something, I'm going to take it."

Other men thought that you "can take the statistics and bend them any way you want to." This could lead to a kind of battle of templates:

RESPONDENT: The numbers [don't matter]. . . . Either way, I got a fifty-fifty
        chance . . . !
FARRELL: Hmm. Remember those numbers here aren't exactly fifty-fifty . . . .
RESPONDENT: Yeah, I hear you. But I figure it's a gamble, an even chance either way,
        you know, fifty-fifty.

In short, Farrell presented data ordered by a standard medical template; the men interpreted it without a real template but often using aphorisms useful in daily life and generalizations too simple and inapt to be helpful. So they could not understand, or even hear, what Farrell labored long and lucidly to explain.

Evidence about Sector Literacy

Having described the need for sector literacy, we now assess it in two key fields. First, without health literacy, people cannot deal competently with doctors, hospitals, and treatments.[40] They cannot make sense of medical disclosures. Many patients not only lack the understanding needed for health literacy, they are misinformed. "No area has been more plagued by questionable, erroneous, and often harmful beliefs" than health.[41] Patients interpret information about CPR in light of TV fantasy.[42] Mistakes about how bodies work are pervasive.[43] In one study *everybody* overestimated lifetime colon-cancer risk. Most said 50 percent or more, a few 10 to 50 percent, and none got near the actual risk of 6 percent for people over fifty. This is part of a tendency to overestimate cancer risks and to suppose that one's own risk is 50 percent.[44]

The problem with sector illiteracy is not just that people don't understand disclosures; it is also that they misunderstand them. For example, people in one study often thought that a report card showing high hospitalization rates for pneumonia meant that the plan did not make it unduly hard to be hospitalized, not that the plan vaccinated too few people.[45] Or, a corrective-advertising experiment gave eighty-three people one of four advertisements for Listerine, two with an FTC-mandated disclaimer. Of the twenty-nine people who recalled a disclaimer, two-fifths were misled about topics the disclaimer did *not* address.[46]

Financial illiteracy is also damagingly common. As the Fed says, consumers cannot use disclosures effectively without understanding markets and products, but disclosures cannot practically provide that "minimum understanding for transactions that are complex and that consumers engage in infrequently."[47] Measures of *basic* financial literacy are low: studies consistently find that high-school students are poorly educated in personal finance, and even when asked elementary questions, college students' mean was about 53 percent. Nor did family members who made household financial decisions understand the task's fundamentals.[48]

Financial literacy means more than knowing terms. Even if you recognize a term like "sum credit life insurance," can you evaluate it? How many people know that to compare a lender's life-insurance policy with those sold in the general insurance market requires a separate medical screening for each policy? How many people know that creditors may not require borrowers to buy the (often overpriced) policy from the creditor's affiliate but that creditors can be pushy without crossing the line? How many people know that the policy their lender is offering may overlap with insurance they already have?

Likewise, people poorly understand prepayment charges and how they interfere with refinancing.[49] Two-thirds of the respondents in one survey did not know about a prepayment penalty,[50] yet because refinancing can considerably affect the cost of a mortgage, such ignorance can be expensive. Many people know that points lower mortgage interest rates but don't realize that they are a poor choice for anyone planning to refinance or to pay the loan early. Credit-card issuers must disclose much, but in one study many cardholders "did not understand how high the interest would be, some because they generally did not understand how interest was applied and others because they did not realize how quickly debt would accumulate when they paid only the minimum due." None understood the harder parts of card billing, like double-cycle billing and minimum-finance charges.[51]

Hu concludes that "many individual investors are virtually beyond redemption with respect to probabilistic and financial illiteracy" and that they are prone to "fundamental errors" when they assess the risks and returns of different kinds of assets.[52] Interviews with investors found only 18 percent financially literate.[53] Many people had little idea what returns to expect from the stock market or thought annual returns over 20 percent were plausible. People typically think their own company's stock safer than a diversified mutual fund.[54] These gaps and errors in knowledge make interpreting financial disclosures a dicey business.

We have offered a glimpse of a sliver of the evidence of broad and deep ignorance about health and money because they are the topics of so many disclosure mandates. But sector illiteracy plagues people elsewhere. Many disclosures are about legal rights, but legal literacy is rare (we can testify from fifty years of teaching first-year law students). *Miranda* warnings are empty if you don't know what happens if you give up your rights. Many disclosures describe your contractual relationship with the discloser, but contract provisions are opaque unless you know their alternatives. And when Rhonda Castellana spent several hours reading her contracts, she surely did not know that complex rules govern the interpretation of contracts, including the parole evidence rule, which in her state barred her from using the salesman's oral assurance to support her interpretation of the contract.

CAN THE LITERACY PROBLEM BE SOLVED?

So, illiteracy, innumeracy, and sector illiteracy prevent many people from understanding (or wanting to tackle) many disclosures. Many people are insufficiently literate to read a garden-variety disclosure; a tiny number are literate enough to master the masses of hard disclosures. And the problem is not just failing to gain knowledge. It is learning things that are wrong. Illiteracy not only leaves people ignorant, it leaves them misguided.

Disclosurites generally acknowledge the literacy problem, and some are aware of the problem of sector literacy. For example, Graham writes that "Congress and the FDA decreed a labeling system that relied on complex factual information for use by consumers who lacked the sophisticated knowledge to understand associations between heart disease and saturated versus unsaturated fats." The need for sector literacy was apparent, for as the "law worked its way through Congress, virtually everyone had emphasized the importance of consumer education." For instance, the Institute of Medicine wanted "a comprehensive effort to inform the public about the likelihood of certain risks and the possible benefits of dietary modification."[55]

Disclosurites seem less aware that in one way the literacy problem continually worsens: in most relevant fields, increasing complexity makes choices increasingly impenetrable. As Bernanke observed, "Some aspects of increasingly complex products simply cannot be adequately understood or evaluated by most consumers, no matter how clear the disclosure."[56] More generally, as financial institutions devise new ways to invest, people's choices will increase, along with their confusion.[57]

Disclosurites have two solutions to the literacy problem. First, simplify disclosures. That idea is so important and its challenges are so great
that we devote chapter 8 to it. (Briefly, the complex cannot be made simple enough that people with the literacy problems we have sketched can
understand it.) The second solution is education (particularly sector education). Education is the great solvent for washing away American social problems. As one typical committee said, every level of American
education from kindergarten to the university should be used to teach
health literacy.[58] Even disclosure skeptics can think Congress could make
people savvier with consumer-education courses in schools.[59] Education
is "a cornerstone of the defined contribution plan services offered to employers; it is also a focus of public policy at the Department of Labor, the
Securities and Exchange Commission, and now the new Office of Financial Education within the US Treasury."[60]

Yet the literacy, numeracy, and sector literacy we have described already reflect many discouraging decades of exhortation and effort. True,
other countries produce more literate and numerate students than ours,
but the American scores are not so much worse that catching up would
solve the problems we have surveyed. And these other countries wrestle
with failures of mandated disclosure just as we do. Nor does the record of
concentrated efforts to improve sector literacy justify much hope (as, for
example, Willis's detailed and damning review of financial-literacy education demonstrates).[61] Even intensive education aimed at small groups
actually facing decisions has had limited success at prohibitive expense.

Even were improvements possible, they could not come quickly and
surely enough to rescue mandated disclosure. Raising levels of literacy
and numeracy is an arduous business. People learn to read well and use
numbers comfortably over years of high school and sometimes college.
Sector literacy requires working in an area long enough to learn how it
functions and how to handle basic concepts and processes. Since sectors
change rapidly, even good sector education in schools can lose its usefulness. And after people leave school the educational challenge soars.
People would have to be convinced that they needed and would profit
from education. Their attention and cooperation would have to be won
and sustained long enough to achieve the great improvements needed to

make disclosures effective. In short, education as a solution to mandated disclosure's literacy problems would mean teaching many hard subjects to a student body with faint zeal and few resources.

Finally, disclosurites hope for salvation by education in *many* areas, including health care, health insurance, savings, financial investments, privacy, safety, nutrition, and legal rights. But so much education of so many kinds would stretch already overstretched resources absurdly. This is the accumulation problem, to which we now turn.

CHAPTER 6

THE QUANTITY QUESTION

> *In an information-rich world, the wealth of information means a dearth of something else: a scarcity of whatever it is that information consumes. What information consumes is rather obvious: it consumes the attention of its recipients. Hence, a wealth of information creates a poverty of attention and a need to allocate that attention efficiently among the overabundance of information sources that might consume it.*
>
> —Herbert Simon, *Designing Organizations for an Information Rich World*

Chapter 4 identified a principal obstacle to mandated disclosure: its false assumptions about what people think, do, and want. Disclosurism imagines *homo arbiter* gratefully using disclosures to make well-considered decisions. Yet people tend to be decision averse—to resist making the kinds of decisions mandates address and to resist making them in the informed ways disclosurites desire. So disclosures go unstudied and even unread. Chapter 5 continued by arguing that the gap between the literacy it would take to understand disclosures and the literacy disclosees have can make the learning from disclosures too wispy to justify the trouble.

Chapter 6 continues our defense of decision aversion by asking how well even the literate can use disclosures given the "quantity question." It has two aspects—the "accumulation" problem and the "overload" problem. The overload problem arises when a disclosure is too copious for the disclosee to handle well. Rhonda Castellana's disclosures took almost three hours to read. Few people would accept so revoltingly long and perplexing a task, and when Ms. Castellana did, her learning did not save her from error.

The overload problem is well known, so we start with the less discussed, but perhaps more fundamental, accumulation problem. It arises because disclosees are assailed with many disclosures in many areas. A single disclosure may be manageable, but en masse, disclosures are overwhelming, and people cannot hope to attend to more than a trickle of the flood.

THE ACCUMULATION PROBLEM

The accumulation problem is little noticed. When disclosures come single spies, some may be manageable; in battalions they are not. When we shifted our perspective in chapter 4 from seeing mandated disclosure as a problem of transmitting data about a choice to seeing it as part of how people organize their lives, it became obvious that disclosures compete with each other for people's time and attention, with other ways people learn, and with everything they do besides making decisions (like working, playing, and living with their families). In short, even if people *wanted* to read all their disclosures, they could not.

Rhonda Castellana's was the story of a woman who read what she received. What if someone followed her example across the board? The parable of Chris Consumer describes a day in the life of such a person, a hero from the moderately comfortable middle class who never met a disclosure he didn't read.

The Parable of Chris Consumer

Chris starts his morning recklessly, by hoping that the mandated warnings in the package insert and on the bottle of his daily vitamin have not changed since he last read them. He turns on the weather channel and gets a commercial for a vacation site. The picturesque scenes and low price attract him, but he notices a disclaimer. Finding the print too small to read, Chris replays the clip in slow motion on Tivo and finds the price pockmarked with conditions. Hmm. After reading the warning on the toaster cord he cautiously plugs it in. Chris likes toast with butter and jam, but after studying the nutritional data on the packages he scrapes on a micro-layer. He has time only to glance at the newspaper. It belabors several political candidates, and Chris makes a mental note to search the campaigns' disclosures to figure out who is disseminating these stories.

Chris's car won't start, so he calls a towing company, hears a pre-recorded statement, and sends for help. The driver presents a form disclosing the company's charges, policies, and insurance. Chris reads it carefully, signs, and directs the driver to the repair shop. There Chris receives a detailed disclosure of its repair and pricing policies. The repair, he hopes, is covered by the warranty, so he pulls it out of the glove compartment, reads it, and sadly sees that the repair is outside the "power train" and thus is his to pay for. He also checks the "Owners' Rights under State Lemon Laws" booklet in the glove compartment, flips through the sixty-one pages to the California section—itself over 2000 words—and learns that any statutory right has expired.

At the office Chris logs in to his computer. A software-update program announces that new versions of Microsoft Office and Firefox are ready to be installed. Didn't he just install an update last week? Or was it Adobe's? Chris needs to click "I accept" at the bottom of the end-user license agreements. Chris reads these agreements—4000 words for the Microsoft program and only 1100 words for Firefox (open-source software, after all). Chris reads newspapers at 250 words per minute, but these contracts are no easy chore; however, since he studied the previous versions of the terms and conditions—not identical but also not much different—his reading takes only forty-five minutes. With this accomplished, and to catch a moment of leisure, Chris switches to nytimes.com but remembers to click on the link to "terms of service" (2500 words) and the privacy policy (only 650 words). True, he's read them before, but they are unilaterally modified occasionally (as the terms posted on the Web site warn), and blessed are the prudent.

The car repair shop calls to tell Chris the charges for parts and labor. It also found problems with the ball joints and asks for Chris's fax number so it can send him (as a local ordinance requires) the report of its tests. The charges seem inflated, Chris thinks, wishing he had known this *before choosing the shop. But he can hardly tow the car to another shop, and so, saying he would ne'er consent, consents. He then calls his bank to transfer funds for this repair since he recently—after reading a bank communiqué about new regulations—opted out of the overdraft coverage. The transfer requires signing, which he does by completing an electronic form on the Web site and clicking to accept another set of terms, moderately brief legalese he nobly reads. While at the bank's Web site, he checks his account activity and opens an automated message from the bank touting a new "rewards" debit card.*

Fedex arrives. After reading the shipping form with its disclaimers, Chris signs it. The package contains custom-ordered labels and an invoice that memorializes terms from yesterday's phone order. The terms on the front are as agreed, Chris notes, and then he turns to the preprinted terms on the back and sedulously ploughs through them.

Chris lunches with colleagues at a diner where a sign warns against food that is not overcooked. The menu lists the calories in each dish—thanks to a recent municipal ordinance. Thus chastened, Chris orders cautiously. At the men's room a sign reminds employees—Chris too?—to wash their hands and recommends a six-step procedure ("1. Wet your hands with warm water; 2. Apply a generous amount of soap; 3. Rub hands together for 20 seconds . . . ."). Feeling wan after his virtuous breakfast and informed lunch, Chris stops at Starbucks for an eggnog latte (610 calories).

Returning, Chris passes a construction site where a notice tells him about the building project and how he can access the city hall Web page to learn more. He checks on his iPhone but is first invited to download an update to one of his apps. Not so simple: as he enters his iTunes user ID he is told that he must first accept updated terms and conditions. He starts reading them on his iPhone, scrolling down until a note says, "Page 1 of 55." A month earlier, he recalls, he read the previous version (then, only fifty-three pages). Rather than reading the miniature script, he emails himself the terms to read later.

That afternoon Chris picks up his car at the garage, reads and signs the invoice, and drives out. It's early November, so he goes for a flu shot at the drug store. At the automated entrance to the parking lot, he receives a parking slip that reminds him to lock his car and includes a 150-word license and disclaimer of liability, which Chris reads while cars behind him honk an impatient encouragement. At the drugstore counter a two-page form recites the risks of a flu shot, including Guillain-Barré syndrome (which he has a bad feeling about) and death. He glooms through the form and signs. Unfortunately, his one concern—a rumor his wife heard about an unsafe version of the immunization—is not discussed (as far as he can tell). He also refills a prescription after getting a form stating that HIPAA requires the pharmacy to provide a notice "that describes how we may use your information for treatment, payment and other purposes that details your rights regarding the privacy of your health and medical information." Chris pauses to parse this sentence, fails, and turns to the notice (2,023 words). As he leaves, he notices a waste basket the drug store has provided so that customers won't just drop the HIPAA notices on the floor.

Reaching home, Chris sorts the mail. A notice from his credit-card provider looks like junk but turns out to be privacy policy changes. Uncertain whether these are favorable, Chris opens his file of prior notices—a thick dossier, to be sure—and compares the terms. But the language is so vague he can't tell which parties might get information about him. The new language assures him that his information will be shared only when "it enhances the service" to him, but it then says that his information will also be shared with "other companies to provide services to us or make services and products available to clients." Could they be saying one thing and then the opposite?

Today's mail also contains the quarterly bill from his auto insurance company and a brochure about a change in the law affecting his coverage. Chris reads the brochure. Finally, he opens an explanation-of-benefits form detailing the bill for a recent visit to the dentist, the amount covered, and his co-pay. This visit was five weeks ago, and Chris strains to recall the assurance he received that his co-pay would be lower. He finds no documentation to support his recollection and pays up.

Before dinner his daughter hands him a day-trip permission slip from school and another slip authorizing the school to take her picture during the trip and listing the uses of that photography. At dinner his son extols a new movie he downloaded free through the Internet. Chris recalls the FBI warnings about copying that appear (often bilingually) anytime he plays a

DVD movie. Does this warning apply to streamed movies? Before dessert the phone rings. After a pause an unfamiliar voice asks him to donate to some cause. The Voice reads a script text flat and fast, so Chris asks the Voice to explain the gist. The Voice can't, and so Chris musters his assertiveness and says goodbye. The Voice is persistent, though, and convinces him to receive more information by mail.

After dinner, Chris looks forward to Monday Night Football, *but first he must buy a wedding gift through an online registry and order a new toner cartridge. He opens an account in the registry Web site—a quick choice of user ID and password and a slow read through terms and conditions and another privacy policy. He then Googles the cartridge model and finds a discount eBay seller. He knows nothing about this seller and its name is unnerving—tonerdude101. Strangely, there is no fine print or disclosure on the eBay page. No terms or conditions, no privacy statement. Nothing to read! Just a picture of the cartridge, its price, shipping charge, and return policy. However, Chris finds a 99.8 percent feedback score from over 50,000 sales. He clicks "Buy It Now."*

Still on his computer, Chris checks his email and finds the iTunes terms he had emailed himself. Oops, a little over 10,000 words. Too long to read, he concludes, but he spends fifteen minutes skimming the "topics covered" and decides to read just the text in ALL CAPS.

Chris at last joins the football game midway through the third quarter, only to hear that "[t]his telecast is intended solely for the private, noncommercial use . . . ." A time-out brings a familiar Cialis® commercial. During the last ten seconds the narrator's warm, confident voice changes and delivers a rapid-fire list of side effects. Brooding on the chance (odds unspecified) of blindness and what he doesn't know is called priapism, Chris watches the end of the game. And so to bed. Michael Crichton's Disclosure *is open, but Chris has read enough.*

Yet this was Chris's lucky day; he faced none of life's nastier choices. He did not refinance his mortgage, apply for a credit card, choose a health-care plan, or become a research subject. He did not buy a house, lease an apartment, or hire a real-estate agent. He did not get a new prescription, seek life insurance, or sign a living will. He did not buy, lease, or rent a car. He did not invest for his retirement. He did not choose a cell phone or a burial plan. He did not buy art, adopt a pet, or choose a college for his child. He did not visit a rent-to-own shop, buy a time-share, or install an alarm. He was not interrogated by police. Today was "disclosure lite."

The Proliferation of Disclosures

By now the accumulation problem should be no surprise. Chapter 1 showed how alluring disclosure is to lawmakers. Chapter 2 described the many unfamiliar and complex decisions people face and the correspondingly numerous and elaborate disclosures lawmakers have mandated. Chapter 3 reviewed the ways that disclosurite rhetoric and ideology promote a full-disclosure standard. (And chapter 10 will catalog the forces that drive lawmakers to issue new mandates and expand old ones.) In sum, as people's choices grow in number and complexity, and as problems with these choices inspire mandates, disclosures overwhelm people's attention, time, and energy. Schwartz hints at this:

> We go to the grocery and stop in the cereal aisle. Should we buy hot or cold? Should we buy sugarcoated or (relatively) unsweetened? Should we buy with or without bran? Should we buy all bran, oat bran, rice bran, corn bran, cracklin' bran, raisin bran, honey bran, or nut bran? . . . [E]ven for a choice among similar kinds of things, the task is daunting. When the possibilities include things with little or nothing in common, the problem is overwhelming.[1]

Not only are choices numerous, but disclosures are long. For example, "Americans today are drowning in financial choices and detailed information about every one of them."[2] Internet privacy disclosures follow this pattern. The FTC assumes that consumers will search multiple sites for the right privacy policies. An ordinary Internet user who reads policies yearly (since policies change) would have expended at least 244 hours, slightly more than half the time people spend altogether on the Internet.[3]

As this suggests, the accumulation problem is exacerbated by the need (on disclosurite principles) to examine many disclosures more than once. Sometimes people forget what they read previously. Sometimes data change. Sometimes the conventional wisdom changes. (As Graham writes of food labeling, "Advice changed frequently and became increasingly complex."[4]) Some contracts change often, like the iTunes contract and credit-card policies. Package inserts tell us to reread them at each refill, just in case.

Not only are people buried in information, but it competes for attention. "A pervasive finding is that cue competition occurs: more salient cues weaken the effects of less salient ones," and irrelevant cues teach people to ignore relevant ones. So adding even accurate information can produce worse results.[5] A homely example is the children-at-play sign. The Federal Highway Administration advises using as few warning signs as possible, since unnecessary signs tend "to breed disrespect for all signs." If you drive by children-at-play signs daily and rarely see children at play, how attentive can you be to the warning?[6]

The parable of Chris Consumer is the *reductio ad absurdum* of the accumulation problem. He read all the disclosures, fine print, notices, and warnings he met. He did not filter, skip, or skim. And in the day we invented Chris was confronted only with mundane disclosures, not the hard ones.

THE OVERLOAD PROBLEM

What Does "Overload" Mean?

The overload problem is created by mandates for full disclosure of information about unfamiliar and complex decisions. Complexity demands explanations long enough to cover its many aspects; unfamiliarity increases the number of aspects that must be covered. The overload problem is well known and ubiquitous. When mandates are too detailed, dense, and demanding, disclosees often won't read them carefully—or at all. If they read them, they struggle to understand, analyze, remember, and assimilate the avalanche of information. Disclosures can overburden the mind, both by offering too many options and by providing too much information about each option.

The burden of complexity is increased by the uncertainties infecting the decisions that are the subject of mandates, for uncertainty multiplies the factors to be remembered and assessed. Some facts are unknown or even unknowable, some information is unreliable, some data conflict with other data. Often the "fact" is a probability, so that disclosees must keep in mind not a datum, but a range. Choice is further complicated when goals are uncertain, conflicting, unrealistic, or changing.

At the heart of the overload problem is the unpracticed mind's struggle to learn, remember, and use data. Even willing minds ordinarily can retain only a few things. As Kirsch observes, "[A]lthough experts continue to debate the precise limits of information loads, there is a consensus that they are quite modest."[7] Simon's review of several experiments concluded that short-term memory may be able to manage five to seven factors at once, and Broadbent thought the number might be three or four.[8] Even experts helping people invest for retirement used an average of just six of the many variables.[9]

In one sense it hardly matters what the number is since so many disclosures exceed any plausible figure. Even a score like the APR becomes burdensome when accompanied by pages and pages of additional information. Nutrition data boxes can now contain a battery of numbers, and presumably consumers should be comparing products and thus reading several boxes at once. And in crucial areas few disclosures are not overloaded. For example, even after many rounds of reform, disclosures about health plans are overloaded. Under the Affordable Care Act, a benefits summary was heroically reengineered to help us "meaningfully" compare our options, but it contains dozens of items for each plan offered. An experimental study concluded that participants found the forms more obscure than they first looked, that participants continued to be overwhelmed, and that many participants rested their choice on a single factor, like the cost of co-pays or the simplicity of a co-insurance formula.[10]

Even *Miranda* warnings are overloaded. They average ninety-six words and can exceed 400 words. Rogers concludes that even with "verbal chunking" (combining data into a single item for easier storage), warnings of more than seventy-five words are probably too long. Even when cued, people with less than a high-school education recalled just a bit more than half of what they were told. And this overstates understanding, since "many suspects have cognitive deficits," since disclosees get warnings in stressful circumstances, and since being able to answer questions about what you heard is different from understanding it adequately.[11]

Overload worsens when people go from learning facts to reasoning with them. A "large body of empirical work suggest[s] that the integration of different types of information and values into a decision is a very difficult cognitive process."[12] As the number of attributes disclosed increases, people quickly reach saturation. "In one experiment, consumers given information about eleven attributes of six investment fund choices felt there were too many options to consider, found the decision to be overwhelming, stressful, and difficult, and said it was a relief to make a decision."[13] No wonder, since people were asked to manage sixty-six variables. But *many* disclosures provide variables in just such quantities, as the three examples in chapter 2 suggest. Reading one mortgage disclosure is bad enough; reading fifty beggars the imagination. The iTunes contract is so unending that comprehending all its terms would take novices not hours, but days. The California bed sheet has so many provisions that they jostle for attention. Our descriptions of the information needed to choose a loan or a prostate-cancer treatment only began to show how many factors swirl about the disclosee's head.

The overload problem's intractability is well illustrated by mortgage disclosures. The FTC has worked ably to simplify a key disclosure: the HUD good-faith estimate—three pages listing the mortgage's fees, interest charges, payments, and related obligations. FTC laboratory experiments find the new formats more readable, understandable, and effective in reaching consumers. But in a typical mortgage closing consumers get over thirty *more* documents and disclosures, sometimes more than fifty, which means reading almost one hundred hard pages and signing more than fifty times. Much of this material deals with privacy, waivers and disclaimers, conflicts of interest, the closing agency's role, escrow agreements and other incidental financial issues, and taxes. In this deluge making one form clearer hardly matters.

So, overload is caused not just by the complexity of one form but by the multiplicity of forms. Credit-card shoppers get a different agreement for each card.[14] The average family has six credit cards and an average credit-card debt of about $9,000. And presumably the thrifty shopper checks sometimes to see whether another card has better terms.[15] Not only is each card garlanded in disclosures, but major issuers typically "amend their agreements in important respects with remarkable frequency."[16]

Lawmakers implicitly acknowledge the overload problem when they try to manipulate disclosures to make the really important things really conspicuous, as the California bed sheet does. This may seem a promising way to solve the overload problem, but fine print is inherently inconspicuous, and lawmakers are sadly naïve about their task. They like ALLCAPS, which catch the eye but slow and discourage readers.[17] And ALLCAPS are overused (there are forms with several pages of ALLCAPS). Consumer contracts are ablaze with ALLCAPS. Like this:

> BY USING THE SERVICE, YOU AGREE TO INDEMNIFY AND HOLD US, OUR DIRECTORS, OFFICERS, EMPLOYEES, AFFILIATES, AGENTS, CONTRACTORS, PRINCIPALS, AND LICENSORS HARM-LESS WITH RESPECT TO ANY CLAIMS, ACTIONS, AND JUDG-MENTS ARISING OUT OF YOUR USE OF THE SERVICE.

Disclosurites today confidently propose to tame the overload problem by trimming and simplifying disclosures. Simplification is so obvious a response to complexity, and faith in it is so common and passionate that we devote chapter 8 to its challenges and limits.

The Effects of Overloading

Overloading people lessens their wish to make choices and impairs the choices they make. Overloaded people "tend to defer decision, search for new alternatives, choose the default option, or simply opt not to choose." They tend to consider fewer choices and to use less of what they are told.[18] A homely example is a store's two tasting booths, one with twenty-four flavors of jam, the other six. Three-fifths of the passersby visited the abundant booth, two-fifths the other. But only 3 percent of the abundant booth's customers bought jam, while 30 percent at the other booth did (even though jam shopping is familiar and fun).[19] Such studies find "fairly consistently" that people "given a moderate number of options (4 to 6) rather than a large number (20 to 30)" are likelier to make a choice and to be more confident and happier about it.

This can matter quite a lot. Increasing the investment choices in a defined-contribution plan can overwhelm employees; some avoid stock funds in favor of safer but unrewarding funds, others don't participate at all.[20] In a megastudy participation quickly fell from 75 percent when plans had four funds to 70 percent for plans with twelve or more funds. Participation sank to 60 percent when plans offered fifty-nine funds.[21] Similarly, too many choices hampered decisions about health-care plans.[22] As these examples suggest, overloading can lead people into worse choices. Investors who rejected stock funds simplified their choices but built retirement portfolios lacking a crucial investment. One reason people tend to borrow too much is that the calculations and tradeoffs required to borrow shrewdly are so many and knotty that it's easier just to ask, "Can I afford the monthly payment?" Or in choosing a health-care plan, to ask, "Can I afford the co-pay?" These questions are crucial and relatively easy, but they are poor paths to a sound loan or a good health-care plan.

Finally, overload may most harm those who most need help. They "may be more prone to limited attention and information overload: uninformed consumers tend to search less before making choices and are significantly more likely to report information overload when presented with asset allocation decisions similar to one faced by 401(k) investors."[23]

Overload and Mandated Disclosure

Overload is built into the goal of full disclosure of information about unfamiliar and complex decisions. Rhonda Castellana could never manage her three hours of hard reading. Our three graphic illustrations—the mortgage stack, the iTunes scroll, and the bed sheet—are patently too much. In clinical medicine, overload begins with the mandate—enough information to make a good decision. (In one study doctors and nurses so taxed patients that the investigators concluded that they had "an extreme tendency toward information overload."[24]) Health-care regulations increasingly require disclosure not only of a plan's benefits and costs, but factors like ombudsman services, government consumer assistance, rights of internal and external appeal of coverage denials, details about grievances and appeals, and more.[25]

Or consider retirement planning: The Department of Labor's *Taking the Mystery out of Retirement Planning* requires sixty-two pages and eight worksheets to tell you how much you must save to retire in ten years. The worksheets require you to find over 100 data, predict your expenses, identify "rates of return so as to select growth and income conversion factors for each" of your assets, and "repeatedly add, subtract, and multiply these figures."[26] Then you must figure out how to do the saving and investing.

One more example: The National Association of Insurance Commissioners requires the disclosure of "extensive amounts of complex information, expressed in unfamiliar, technical language and relating to obscure issues." The model regulation wants disclosure of at least a dozen technical facts "ranging from a description of coverages and contract premiums to the insurer's illustrated scale of non-guaranteed elements and surrender values." Another rule adds "renewability, policy limitations, benefit triggers, premium increase provisions, federal taxation, reimbursement definitions and the like."[27]

Finally, before getting disclosures, consumers get ads, product packages, sales pitches, and consumer reports. No wonder they sip, not sup: they let Google filter information for them and filter even more with the "I'm feeling lucky" option. Why change their parsimonious ways for disclosures?

CHAPTER 7

FROM DISCLOSURE
TO DECISION

*Most, probably, of our decisions to do something posi-
tive, the full consequences of which will be drawn out
over many days to come, can only be taken as a result
of animal spirits—of a spontaneous urge to action rather
than inaction, and not as the outcome of a weighted average of quantitative benefits multiplied by quantitative
probabilities.*

—John Maynard Keynes, *The General Theory of
Employment, Interest and Money*

We have now asked what disclosees want, perceive, accept, understand,
and remember. Failure at any step can defeat disclosures, and at each step
failure is common. Decision aversion can make audiences inattentive and
reluctant. Illiteracy renders many disclosures useless. And the overload
and accumulation problems discourage and stop many disclosees. But
there is more. We have concentrated on cognitive problems with information. But solve them and other barriers to better decisions remain.

First, people making decisions often need information about themselves that mandated disclosure cannot provide. Second, disclosure's usefulness is limited by problems other than ignorance. People err because
they distort, filter, and misinterpret information, as a great and growing
literature in social psychology and behavioral economics is showing. This
literature is too large and unwieldy to summarize neatly and is accessibly
reported elsewhere.[1] (Following common if inaccurate practice, we will

refer to it as behavioral economics.) Yet because the literature shows how minds distort the decisions to which mandates are directed, we will draw several lessons from it.

Sophisticated disclosurites think this literature can rescue mandated disclosure.[2] They advocate a choice architecture (a legal framework intended to shape people's choices) that uses better-designed disclosures to improve disclosees' decisions. We are skeptical. First, the literature is too immature to provide insights reliable enough for choice architecture. Second, people interpret and use information so variously and unexpectedly that nobody can anticipate reactions well enough to write mandates that account for the variety and uncertainty.

KNOW THYSELF

However copious disclosures may be, disclosees need to know more to make decisions—they need to know themselves. Autonomists and free-marketers alike want people to make their own decisions because they should understand their own situation and preferences. Often, however, this knowledge is less thorough and accurate than good decisions require. For example, decisions commonly oblige us to predict how we will behave and feel about our choices in possible future scenarios. As Bar-Gill observes, knowing a credit card's terms doesn't help you if you wrongly expect never to borrow.[3]

A considerable and bemusing literature reveals the elusiveness of self-understanding. For example, many people know little about how they spend money.[4] Two-fifths of the people investing in pension plans did not know where they had put their funds.[5] People can think they know such things while tests show they do not.[6] People notoriously compare themselves to others inaccurately. (For example, most professors think they are more productive than their colleagues.)

If people don't know their current situation, imagine how accurately they predict their future. They go on dates determined to be chaste, begin foreplay expecting to use a condom, and start sex planning to stop in time. "Sexual arousal is familiar, personal, very human, and utterly commonplace. Even so, we all systematically underpredict the degree to which arousal completely negates our superego, and the way emotions can take control of our behavior."[7] In less familiar situations the problem worsens. Many cell phone users anticipate how they will use their phones or want to switch services; many people joining health clubs pay a flat rate because they overestimate their use by more than 100 percent.[8]

Then, preferences: Disclosees are supposed to use information to find the choice that best serves their preferences, but when issues are unfamiliar and complex, people often lack preferences considered and precise enough to guide them. Imagine a choice between a treatment with a low chance of success but a low risk of death and a treatment with a high chance of success but a high risk of death. Patients have relevant preferences—avoiding death and avoiding side effects. But here they conflict, and few patients have calibrated their values delicately enough to decide what risk of death is worth what chance of success.

Less dramatically, most people value privacy and might prefer that Google or Facebook not store their search histories, yet they would cheerfully trade some privacy for better search results or free services. But whose preferences are fine-grained enough to benefit from detailed disclosures in making the trade? Similarly, even if you understand arbitration clauses (often part of the "I agree" click), how do you feel about them? Some experts think they limit your ability to vindicate your rights; others think it matters little.[9]

Preferences are unhelpful guides when they are conflicting, incomplete, and labile. Klein calls these "wicked problems" common.[10] People have poorly defined goals about most problems, and no plausible amount of thinking will define them sharply. You must be content with developing rough goals as you go.[11]

Finally, it is hard to predict your reactions to a choice that is unfamiliar and complex. Even in ordinary circumstances people tend, for example, to overestimate how unhappy a bad outcome will make them and to underestimate their ability to cheer themselves up. So the ill react to their disease less despairingly than they had anticipated. They evaluate their lives more favorably than people around them, and despite the "quality trumps quantity" mantra they often give up buckets of quality for thimbles of quantity.[12] More prosaically, people mispredict the long-term costs and benefits of saving, for who can answer the right question—how much worse off will you be now and how much better off will you be in twenty years if you put an extra thousand dollars in your savings monthly?[13]

BOUNDED RATIONALITY: DISTORTED PERCEPTIONS, DISTORTED DECISIONS

We have been saying that even suffocatingly thorough disclosures can leave you short of information. But suppose this problem away. Disclosures are still impaired by the way people receive and use information. Even if people are literate, numerate, and knowledgeable, and even if they get and read full disclosures, systematic features of human thinking can distort their perception of what they read and how they handle it in making decisions.

Rational-choice theory teaches that people try to maximize their utility (or, faced with uncertainty, their expected utility). But the literature that we are (for simplicity) calling behavioral economics is identifying ways (in rough shorthand, heuristics and biases) in which people's choices systematically diverge from rationality. This includes ways that people interpret, reinterpret, and misinterpret information.

We begin with two classic examples that affect the kinds of decisions to which mandates speak. First, decisions are shaped by how information is framed. This presents well-studied challenges for informed consent. In one study some subjects were told the chance that they would be alive a year after surgery, others the chance that they would be dead. The risks described were identical, but not the reaction. Of the former subjects, 42 percent chose surgery; only 25 percent of the latter did.[14] The framing problem is widely recognized; Anspach quotes a doctor who says that "having the parents well informed is always well informed on your grounds."[15]

The second classic example is the availability heuristic: things vivid and disturbing are more readily remembered than things drab and routine. This difference in salience slants perceptions, reasoning, and decisions. So, for example, people are likelier to buy insurance if they've had damaging floods or know people who have, "quite independently of the cost/benefit ratio which they can calculate."[16] And some people will pay more for insurance against terrorism than for insurance against a slate of risks that includes terrorism.

Habits of the mind can also lead people to ignore disclosures or to read them inattentively. For example, the way people use evidence depends on their confidence in it. But "neither the quantity nor the quality of the evidence counts for much in subjective confidence." People's confidence "in their beliefs depends mostly on the quality of the story they can tell about what they see, even if they see little. We often fail to allow for the possibility that evidence that should be critical to our judgment is missing—what we see is all there is."[17] Even when we know evidence is unreliable, we have trouble ignoring it. So even when "stock traders rate rumors as low in credibility, they continue to trade on such information as if it were more reliable news."[18]

The quality of decisions turns partly on how accurately people judge their knowledge about a choice and their skill in making it. But evidence is ample that people tend to assess their "abilities, traits, and prospects" optimistically.[19] Because people tend to overestimate how much they know and underestimate how hard it is to learn enough, disclosures become easier to ignore or dismiss. The "illusion of knowing" (falsely thinking you understand something) can lead you to dismiss disclosures or read them carelessly.[20] Thus three-fifths of readers thought a pamphlet was easy but could recall little that it said. Similarly, "[o]veroptimism and overconfidence in personal-finance decisionmaking is widespread." Two-thirds of the people queried in one survey thought themselves "'very' or 'highly' knowledgeable about personal finance," but "they performed abysmally on objective questions."[21]

If people tend to misjudge the quality of the evidence they use and the knowledge and skill they have, care and caution seem to be called for. But, Kahneman and others say, the mind is disinclined to such restraint. They distinguish two styles of thinking. "*System 1* operates automatically and quickly, with little or no effort and no sense of voluntary control. *System 2* allocates attention to the effortful mental activities that demand it, including complex computations."[22] System 1 thinking is quick and easy; System 2 thinking is slow and painful.[23] So System 1 does much of the work but is apt to underweight disclosures. For example, many people do not think carefully about how much to save. Their practice "is largely cued by different institutional and mental frames. And on average, as a result, most people undersave."[24] Problems saving are exacerbated by a tendency to underestimate "contingent, long-run costs." Such "myopia is attributed to the triumph of the affective system, which is driven primarily by short-term payoffs, over the deliberative system, which cares about both short-term and longer-term payoffs."[25]

Much disclosure describes risks: of taking medicine, borrowing, investing, chatting with police, using products, and revealing personal information. People notoriously misgauge risk. Accurate risk disclosures are distorted by false assumptions. For example, although "the market rewards risk," people tend to believe the opposite. Told that an activity has great merits, they are apt to assume it has low risks.[26] So investors "tended to judge unfamiliar assets as either globally 'good,' low risk and high return, or as globally 'bad,' with high risk and low return."[27] Could disclosers overcome these problems with precision in stating risks? Frustratingly, disclosees reading precise statements often translate them into vague ones: "perceptions of risk are not merely cognitive appraisals of numeric risk (e.g., 6% vs. 7%). They include intuitive and emotional reactions which translate being 'high' or 'low' into 'something to worry about' or 'something to be relieved about.'"[28]

We have sampled only a few items from the hefty catalog of ways people misperceive, misinterpret, and misuse disclosures. This is (we reiterate) not to say that people can't adroitly handle familiar decisions. People do not "hold questionable beliefs simply because they are stupid or gullible." Some heuristics and biases work handily in making familiar decisions.[29] But in the areas in which mandates are most used, these habits of mind are common and can defeat even disclosures that lawmakers have mandated appropriately, that disclosers have disclosed effectively, and that disclosees have seen, read, and tried to use.

IS BEHAVIORAL ECONOMICS
A PROBLEM OR THE SOLUTION?

We have argued that the literature of behavioral economics describes ways of thinking that make disclosures less helpful. Yet some disclosurites think that literature is the "open sesame" to successful mandates. Why do they think so? Why do we doubt it?

Hopes for Behavioral Economics

Sophisticated disclosurites see the behavioral economics literature as (one critic suggests) generally favoring greater "regulation to address a wide variety of business practices that exploit the bias of consumers."[30] That is, they conclude that regulation focused on choice, especially disclosure, is *more* needed than had been appreciated. The literature identifies ways people are vulnerable in unfamiliar and complex transactions to manipulation and to their own misunderstandings. This lets regulators understand people better so that they can regulate better. As Sunstein puts it, the literature's findings "offer useful insights for thinking about regulation and its likely consequences. They also offer some suggestions about the appropriate design of effective, low-cost, choice-preserving approaches to regulatory problems, including disclosure requirements, default rules, and simplification."[31] Of the four approaches that Sunstein thinks particularly promising, three feature mandated disclosure: "(1) using disclosure as a regulatory tool, especially if disclosure policies are designed with an appreciation of how people process information; (2) simplifying and easing choices through appropriate default rules, reduction of complexity and paperwork requirements, and related strategies; (3) increasing the salience of certain factors or variables."[32]

Thus Thaler and Sunstein invoke psychological biases like anchoring, framing, loss aversion, and more to craft "nudges," including improved disclosures. Fung, Graham, and Weil believe that understanding people's errors and biases makes possible a superior disclosure that they call "targeted transparency." Cooley et al. think a better way to prevent misuse of financial products "might be to mandate information disclosure designed to improve decision making by overcoming cognitive biases."[33] In short, in several significant areas much recent academic work on disclosure (and, increasingly, lawmakers' beliefs) sees behavioral and cognitive biases as a key to understanding how mandates work, why they fail, and how to use them to promote "active choosing."

This is done nicely in Bar-Gill's *Seduction by Contract*.[34] He shows how sellers in several markets exploit buyers' irrationalities and how myopia and optimism mislead people choosing cell phone plans, credit cards, and mortgages. He carefully constructs disclosures that account for these irrationalities. He recommends innovative disclosures like "use-pattern" disclosure, in which businesses tell a consumer what they know about the consumer's behavior and how that behavior would affect a product's cost. This important idea might help people select cell phone plans and constrain credit-card debt.

Bertrand and Morse's study of payday borrowing is often invoked to illustrate the literature's promise. They designed three disclosures using the literature about cognitive lapses to which payday borrowers might succumb and about ways of de-biasing the borrowers. This meant getting borrowers to think about how the cost of borrowing added up over time, making the loan easier to evaluate by comparing it with other loans, "and, to a lesser degree, disclosing information on the typical profile of payday loan refinancing." This reduced borrowing 11 percent.[35]

Doubts About Behavioral Economics

However insightful the psychological literature is, it cannot equip law-makers to mandate or disclosers to design disclosures that will rescue mandated disclosure. First, the literature does not address most of disclosure's problems. As chapter 4 argued, decision aversion is common and rests on reasonable choices about how to live life and make choices. As chapter 5 argued, limited literacy keeps people from understanding disclosures. As chapter 6 argued, the overload and accumulation problems are implacable. And as chapter 8 will argue, the unfamiliar and complex cannot easily be made familiar and simple.

Furthermore, distortions in perception and reasoning are not so easily overcome. The great figure in their study—Nobel laureate Daniel Kahneman—says that except for some effects that he attributes mostly to his age, "my intuitive thinking is just as prone to overconfidence, extreme predictions, and the planning fallacy as it was before I made a study of these issues." He has improved only in his "ability to recognize situations in which errors are likely."[36] If *he* can't surmount these frailties . . . .

Nor is the literature strong enough to bear the weight disclosurites place on it. Much of its work is done in laboratories, not the messy real world. Even so, scholars have identified over sixty biases and heuristics and dispute their definition, description, mechanisms, causes, incidence, and cures. One decision may be affected by many distortions. For example, Stark and Choplin think mortgage decisions face "numerous cognitive and social psychological" problems, including "(d) availability heuristics, . . . (f) biases in attribute estimation and evaluation, (g) positive confirmation biases, . . . (i) argument immunization, (j) sunk cost effects, (k) endowment effects, (l) temporal and uncertainty discounting, [and] (m) a strong motivation to trust, that is exacerbated when the consumer is of a lower socioeconomic status."[37]

Furthermore, disclosees' reactions to disclosures depend on temperament, baseline knowledge, skills, and more. Shopping for credit cards is shaped by traits like a propensity to seek information,[38] financial decisions by factors like one's willingness to trust people and the seller's extroversion.[39] In short, since biases and heuristics are so many and since people respond so variously, nobody could write mandates that can account for that chaos of thought and passion, all confused. Mann correctly writes, that "departures from rationality are so unpredictable and contextually specific that intervention designed to remedy one departure without accounting for the others has little chance of a beneficial result."[40]

Consider Bar-Gill's use-pattern disclosure, which we admired earlier. Even its proponents say that people would have to see the need for the information—a need, we have argued, that people often do not recognize. Consumers with incorrect beliefs especially need help, yet they are the least likely to recognize their need. Even people who know they need information must overcome the procrastination common in these areas. *And* "someone will have to warn consumers that past usage data will not be a reliable indicator of future consumption."[41]

Mortgagors especially need to know whether they can afford the house they want. Would the many who cannot (by some measures, 30 percent of U.S. households[42]) listen to the unwelcome news? Would the many buyers who don't understand basics like the difference between adjustable and fixed-rate loans[43] understand use-pattern disclosures? If the quantity problems that chapter 6 reviewed meant that use-pattern disclosures had an entourage of other disclosures, would any of them be heeded?

For such reasons, Stark and Choplin doubt that reshaping disclosures can help people "make truly informed decisions" on the complexities of mortgages or can "mitigate the 14 psychological barriers" they identify.[44] They prefer mortgage counseling. But even it "would have to be carefully designed to explain risks, explain multiple characteristics to reduce reason-based decision making, evaluate attributes to reduce reliance on heuristics, overcome confirmation biases, senseless explanations, temporal and uncertainty discounting, and argument immunization." And even with the effort that individual counseling requires, improvements have been measurable but modest.

The unpredictabilities of designing disclosure to overcome biases are tellingly illustrated by conflict-of-interest mandates. They are intended to tame psychological biases, like advisors' subconscious or deliberate distortions and advisees' gullibility and naïveté. But they can have the opposite effect. Chapter 3 described the experimental studies showing that advisors who are compelled to disclose conflicts give *more* distorted advice than those not compelled to. Those studies also showed that the disclosees relied on advice *more* and made worse decisions than those not told.[45] To everyone's surprise, in addressing advisors' conflicts and advisees' susceptibility, new distortions (like an "insinuation bias" and a "strategic exaggeration" effect) were introduced.

Even the Bertrand and Morse study of payday borrowing is doubtful evidence of behavioral economics' ability to revitalize mandated disclosure. As they comment, if you think "that close to all payday borrowing is irrational," you might think an 11 percent reduction in borrowing is "a disappointing effect," especially since "the information disclosure interventions" were "quite powerful" compared with "more standard Truth in Lending Act-style disclosure."[46] In addition, while at least fifteen states have banned payday lending, scholars disagree about how irrational it is to borrow at the astronomical interest rates these lenders charge. Morse finds, for instance, that "the existence of payday lending increases welfare for households that might face foreclosures" and other troubles "even at a 400% APR."[47]

Finally, experience with other attempts to encourage rational and careful decisions suggests that even modest results require epic effort, ingenuity, and persistence. For example, educational programs designed to change how people manage retirement plans "have a poor track record."[48] And the campaign (partly through mandated disclosures) against smoking is still far from won, even with a social and legal full-court press.

If behavioral economics is to improve regulation, it is by teaching the futility of persisting in regulation intended to get people to make well-informed and well-considered decisions about unfamiliar and complex issues. As our last chapter will argue, that literature better teaches the lesson that lightening information burdens and replacing mandated disclosure with other regulatory techniques is the best, if still troubled, approach.

CONCLUSION TO PART II

Part I reviewed evidence that mandated disclosure fails so often that it is a suspect regulatory form. Part II asked *why* it fails. It found that the reasons run so deep that mandated disclosure cannot hope to succeed often.

Part II abandoned the assumption that mandated disclosure is the answer to the question of what information someone would have needed to make a better decision. Instead, it asked how mandated disclosure looks to disclosees. In short, it ill fits the way people live their lives and make their choices. People do not seize decisions with the eagerness disclosurites suppose, nor do they make decisions in the fully informed way disclosurites assume. Rather, people tend to leave disclosures unused, defeating disclosure before it starts. This produces some poor choices, yet people have good reasons for rejecting the gift of disclosure. Briefly, they don't think the game is worth the candle. It means taking on unpleasant work and giving up more pleasant work. And on assessing the educational labor mandated disclosure offers, people reasonably fear sowing much and reaping little.

Specifically, chapter 5 showed how illiteracy can keep people from using disclosures well, can cause people to use them poorly, and can keep people from using them at all. Illiteracy is protean. It includes the inability to understand words, sentences, and paragraphs and the inability to understand even quite simple numbers. Sector illiteracy can defeat even people who read without difficulty. And even the sector literate may be insufficiently specialized within the sector to profit from disclosures.

Chapter 6 reviewed another cognitive barrier to mandated disclosure—the quantity question. Disclosures are often more overwhelming than helpful. And the parable of Chris Consumer taught a related lesson—people are daily so assailed by information that they cannot attend to most of it and still have a life. Decision aversion then seems prudent, not feckless.

Finally, chapter 7 looked at writing in psychology and behavioral economics. For disclosurites, the study of how people misperceive and misapply information opens the door to disclosure that works. For us, however, the lesson is that nobody can write mandates that account for the many unexpected ways people read disclosures.

We have never argued, we repeat, that all disclosures fail. But we do argue that while some disclosures sometimes do some people some good, they cannot reliably achieve their goal of improving decisions in the way that disclosurites wish. Part II has described problems with disclosures too profound to be solved. You can't get rid of decision aversion because it makes too much sense in people's lives. You can't fix illiteracy without titanic social efforts to move the populace to unrealistic levels of skill and understanding. You can't get rid of the quantity question because unfamiliar and complex issues keep arising. You can't get rid of the things that distort people's handling of unfamiliar and complex decisions because those habits serve them well in most of their lives.

We have not exhausted the defenses its proponents mount for mandated disclosure. We have not dealt with proposals for fixing it (primarily by simplifying disclosures). We have not dealt with arguments that it's worth keeping despite its faults because, whatever its faults, its costs are low. To such arguments we now turn.

CAN MANDATED DISCLOSURE BE SAVED?

Part III asks whether disclosurism can be rescued from the problems cataloged in parts I and II. The story has several twists, but the *deus ex machina* is simplification. Chapter 8, however, finds that simplification helps only sporadically and feebly. Some simplifications substitute one complexity for another; others achieve simplicity by omitting or distorting information. Chapter 9 suggests that even if simplification worked better, it would often be defeated by the political dynamics of regulation: First, mandates expand, exacerbating the overload problem. Second, new mandates proliferate, exacerbating the accumulation problem. Mandated disclosure is a regulatory hydra: cut off one of its heads, and two grow back.

Chapter 10 addresses another reason that simplification cannot save mandated disclosure. That regulatory method depends on disclosers, but the core problem of complexity makes it hard for lawmakers to give disclosers good instructions and for disclosers to carry them out effectively.

Disclosurites might try to save mandated disclosure in one last way. Even if its benefits are small, it could be justified if its costs are smaller. Chapter 11 shows that not only can its operation be costly but that it can inflict unintended harms.

CHAPTER 8

MAKE IT SIMPLE?

Et surtout, faites simple! (And above all, make it simple.)

—A great chef

INTRODUCTION

If disclosure is defeated by complexity, can simplicity save it? For disclosurites, *faites simple* is almost as axiomatic as full disclosure, for it seems to respond so directly to so much of the critique of disclosure. If words are polysyllabic, be monosyllabic. If writing is jargon ridden, free it. If presentations are muddled, standardize them. If documents are long, shorten them. If disclosures describe too much, describe less. Unfortunately, simplification is a complex business, not readily mastered. And simplification is in tension with the full disclosure principle.

Put differently, simplification does not respond to many of our criticisms. Even a beautifully simplified form will fail unless the lawmaker mandates it perceptively, the discloser delivers it properly, and the disclosee reads and uses it perspicaciously. Simplification does not eliminate all the reasons disclosees skip or scan disclosures and make decisions incompletely informed. It can exacerbate sector literacy problems. It hardly budges the accumulation meter. It can be helpless before the cognitive and psychological challenges of turning data into decisions. Nevertheless, simplification of many kinds increasingly feeds disclosurite hopes for mandated disclosure and particularly inspires sophisticated disclosurites.

The Appeal of Simplification

Disclosurites have long understood the importance of *faites simple*. Sunstein writes that disclosure "may not be enough," that it matters "*how, not only whether, disclosure occurs*."[1] Many lawmakers agree. The SEC acknowledges that its requirements have encouraged mutual fund prospectuses that investors find too long, complex, confusing, and legalistic.[2] So disclosurites demand simpler language, numbers, and forms. Insurance documents are notorious for their unreadable language; disclosurites want "relatively simple transparency-oriented reforms" to "make insurance understandable."[3] Lawmakers require simplicity by fiat, by demanding simply written forms.

Do disclosurites recognize how hard simplicity is? Lawmakers often speak with disturbing confidence. In the Plain Writing Act of 2010, Congress blithely told federal agencies to be "clear, concise, [and] well-organized."[4] The Dodd-Frank Act placidly directs disclosers to give consumers "timely and understandable information to make responsible decisions about financial transactions."[5] The director of the federal office that supervises human-subject research airily says that disclosing conflicts of interest is "easily accomplished."[6]

Less naïve disclosurites know that simplifying is hard but still are eerily confident. The Obama administration is embracing smart disclosure that is empirically based. Sunstein says that "[p]roperly designed disclosure requirements can significantly improve the operation of markets, leading consumers to make more informed decisions."[7] The beau ideal of this is the summary disclosure that is "concrete, straightforward, simple, meaningful, timely, and salient."[8] And experienced commentators recognize disclosure's failures but advocate "meaningful," "honest and comprehensible," but still "heightened" disclosures.[9]

Simplified disclosures have been mandated and sometimes implemented in crucial areas. The SEC has a new summary prospectus, the Fed new mortgage disclosures. Under the new Consumer Financial Protection Bureau's auspices, newly simplified mortgage disclosures have been generated, tested in labs for readability and efficacy, and launched under the slogan "Know before you owe."[10] Federal law demands simplified credit-card disclosures. The Affordable Care Act requires simplified health-insurance disclosures. The Department of Education has simplified schools' disclosures to applicants. Regulators urge Web sites to post simplified privacy policies. Commentators proffer simplified insurance disclosures.

The Limits of Simplification

Simplification cannot rescue mandated disclosure. Years of urging, demanding, trying, and retrying leave effective disclosures elusive. Ever since TILA's salad days, for example, Congress and the Fed have labored to simplify consumer-credit disclosures. They labor still today. Much effort and intelligence has been lavished on the problem. Nor is empirically informed disclosure new. For example, the 1980 TILA simplification round drew on "testimony from a leading psychologist who has studied the problem of 'informational overload.'" The 2008 simplifications were based on much laboratory testing of new forms by FTC social scientists.[11] Informed consent has occasioned numberless empirical studies.

At base, simplifying fails because the complex isn't simple and can't easily be made so. Simpler words mean more words and longer (hence harder) documents. Formatting information better, standardizing its presentation, or summarizing it ordinarily means distorting or omitting information. Good compromises between adequate and accessible information are few. The Treasury says: "Reasonableness includes balance in the presentation of risks and benefits, as well as clarity and conspicuousness in the description of significant product costs and risks."[12] But balancing tends to mean omitting information that some disclosees find material. So less may be more, but less may not be enough.

Barr et al. seek salvation in having courts decide whether a "disclosure would have, under common understanding, effectively communicated the key terms of the mortgage to the typical borrower."[13] But courts are more the problem than the solution. Interpreting the informed-consent and failure-to-warn doctrines, they have swollen, not simplified, disclosures. Working case by case, courts dramatically see how withholding facts seems to hurt but cannot easily see the costs of additional disclosures.

Disclosurites yearn to simplify another complexity—contractual fine print. One solution is to replace iTunes scrolls and California bed sheets with simple pacts: "I will buy the bike for $120."[14] But even in the Edenic days before boilerplate, contracts were far richer than they looked. True, these village contracts could be briefly stated—the good (the bike), the price ($120), and the consent (I will buy). The sentence is boilerplate-free. But the contract—the obligations the parties accepted—abounds in unstated terms found in default principles of contract law, local customs and market norms, and regulations governing trade in a good.

The village contract has no boilerplate warranty, but disputes over a product's defects are governed by the intricate law of implied warranties. (The leading sales-law treatise spends 254 pages on product warranties.[15]) The village contract says nothing about breaches of contract, but it incorporates the law's default remedies. While boilerplate remedies are often simple (repair or replace; return the money), default rules are complex, since liability for consequential damage is famously uncertain. (Is the seller liable for injuries caused by a carelessly attached wheel? What if the bicycle is delivered late and a messenger loses income?) Boilerplate is swollen because it anticipates so many contingencies. The village contract is slender because it leaves them unresolved, relegating the parties to a maze of laws, regulations, precedents, norms, and customs. Which is simpler?

Such challenges do not diminish disclosurite faith in simplification; they stimulate disclosurites to crack the puzzle. Fung et al. propose targeted disclosure, Sunstein advocates empirically based simplification. Ayres and Schwartz find new "remedies for the no-read problem in consumer contracting." Big firms should survey their consumers and "substantiate" which contract terms most surprise them. Those terms would go into a standardized warning box. To avoid overload, boxes could have only a few terms; all else could be buried.[16]

We doubt the Ayres-Schwartz premise that contract terms are what people want to be warned about, rather than unexpected product features. Would you rather know that the keys in your pocket will scratch your iPhone's screen or that contract disputes are resolved in California courts? We also doubt that surveys can identify the worst contract terms. And that consumers have expectations about things like choice of law or modification clauses. But most telling is the authors' implicit acknowledgment that for pared-down warnings to work, all other disclosures must go. Each clause of fine print competes with the often numerous disclosures about a transaction (the overload problem) and with disclosures about other transactions (the accumulation problem). The irony is that the remedy for the failure of one disclosure is to eliminate most of the others.

In sum, forms are complex because so much affects a well-considered choice. You can simplify by eliminating factors. But the more you eliminate, the likelier you are to omit things that would have improved a decision; the fewer factors you eliminate, the more disclosees must struggle to understand, remember, and manipulate. This is the cleft stick in which lawmakers and disclosers are caught.

Simplicity, then, is usually in tension with full disclosure. Yet disclosurites seem often not to notice. The White House (we saw in chapter 3) says that "consumers have a right to easily understandable and accessible information about privacy and security practices" but then presents a string of complexities to be described with particularity.[17] The Institute of Medicine wants "clear, simple, unclouded, unhurried, and sensitive disclosure that gives the potential [research] participant all the information a reasonable person would need to make a well-informed decision."[18] But the disclosure must ensure "that research participants fully understand the nature of scientific rationale and procedure; have insight into a set of risks of various types that might be identified on their behalf by ethicists or regulators; and have motives for participation that are not 'false.'"[19]

Simplification is also illusory if you simplify one form in a transaction requiring many. The mortgage disclosure that the empirically informed regulators simplified is ingenious, but it is one of thirty or even fifty disclosures plopped before the mortgagor. Similarly, the simplified "TILA disclosure form usually is not furnished as a single document." Rather, a "large stack of documents, many containing very peripheral information, must be sifted through in order to find the one or two pages that contain key information."[20]

Another false simplification is ignoring significant factors that cannot be disclosed because they are unknown. As chapter 2 said, for example, even if you understand mortgages, uncertainties assail you (Will the housing market go up? Will interest rates go down? Will you have to sell soon? Will your income rise or your expenses fall?). The subprime borrowing that led to the recent mortgage crisis was partly caused by borrowers who inadequately understood what could happen to the economy and credit markets, their jobs, and housing markets. How do you simplify these topics?

Finally, as chapters 9 and 10 explain, simplification is inhibited by the way mandates are produced and implemented. The political dynamics of lawmaking propagate and swell mandates. The practical dynamics of carrying out mandates give disclosers incentives to offer more, not less, information.

Simplification is complex. We examine three kinds. First, simplifying words. Second, presenting data simply and selectively (e.g., in standardized formats). Third, abbreviating information sharply, as with a single score.

SIMPLIFIED LANGUAGE

The most straightforward form of *faites simple* is simpler language. Simpler writing should address many of the problems identified in part II, especially the literacy barrier. That in turn might incline people to read disclosures. Simpler writing also seems compatible with full disclosure: information isn't lost, it's just phrased more accessibly. Both naïve and sophisticated disclosurites advocate it; lawmakers require it.

Disclosurites are right: after years of reading disclosures, we can testify that they are often written so turgidly that they (and we) cry out for a good edit. They grossly flout Mark Twain's "eschew surplusage" rule. But good edits can carry you only so far.

First, simplified language simplifies words, not ideas. If a choice is complex, the complexity remains. It's just put into more common words. This is good, but many, perhaps most, of the problems raised in part II remain. As White and Mansfield say, "While design and readability experts could improve contracts and disclosure forms, the terms of modern consumer contracts are so complex that legal mandates to make contract forms readable may be futile."[21]

Second, easier language is hard to write. Disclosers are rarely *trying* to write unreadably. Experts have certainly tried intelligently and earnestly to present complex information simply. Advocates of medical decision aids have certainly tried to make their tool accessible. Financial regulators have certainly tried to produce more readable mortgage forms. But improvements are marginal, and forms remain at lofty reading levels. For example, a "'simplified' *Miranda* warning backfired when several *Miranda* components were included in a 32-word sentence."[22] To write simply you have to be a skilled writer *and* understand your subject. Writing well is hard; good writers are few; knowledgeable good writers are fewer yet and have many bidders for their services. Tellingly, the reports, regulations, and statutes that demand simple language are chronically stuffy, stilted, and stultifying. If the physicians can't heal themselves . . . .

The third problem with simplifying language to rescue mandated disclosure is that often it just transforms one kind of complexity into another. Disclosures often use words disclosees don't know. You can eliminate them, but they summarize complicated ideas. If you can't use them, you must explain the ideas they summarize, which takes sentences and even paragraphs. So here is another cleft stick: shorter words mean more words. Many words make forms repellently long and cognitively overwhelming.

Consumer financial disclosures illustrate this cleft stick. They are the achievement of many simplification reforms. They use readable sentences of low complexity. But string the sentences together and "the complexity and document density of the TILA disclosure form, together with the reference of other contract documents, pushes the form" to a level at which more than half the population cannot reliably understand it. Not to mention the numeracy and sector literacy needed to understand the numbers disclosed in the four boxes—"finance charge," "amount financed," "total of payments," and "APR."[23]

In short, sophisticated vocabularies and professional languages encapsulate complex thoughts. Use only simple words and everything must be spelled out. Robert Levine, a father of the IRB disclosure system, thinks it "necessary to use polysyllabic words in consent forms." Thus, "[i]f we want to invite someone with systemic mastocytosis to participate in a controlled clinical trial of cimetidine versus disodium cromoglycate, we must say so."[24] But can you say so in simple words? Wikipedia is written for a general audience; how does it manage? "Mastocytosis is a group of rare disorders of both children and adults caused by the presence of too many mast cells (mastocytes) and CD34+ mast cell precursors in a person's body."[25] So what is a mast cell? Back to Wikipedia: "A mast cell (or mastocyte) is a resident cell of several types of tissues and contains many granules rich in histamine and heparin. Although best known for their role in allergy and anaphylaxis, mast cells play an important protective role as well, being intimately involved in wound healing and defense against pathogens."[26] And down the rabbit hole to Wonderland you go.

Or consider a contract drafted in lay language—eBay's user agreement that we mentioned in the introduction, which affects millions of people.[27] Our version was 3500 words long (the privacy policy is a separate 3700 words). Many terms seem comprehensible, but they describe things that people may already know, like fees and services. In unfamiliar areas, like data policy and copyright, even the lay language is tough going. Like this: "When providing us with content or posting content on eBay's sites, you grant us a non-exclusive, worldwide, perpetual, irrevocable, royalty-free, sublicensable (through multiple tiers) right to exercise any and all copyright, trademark, publicity, and database rights you have in the content, in any media known now or in the future." In this syntactical tangle, ten modifying words come between the article ("a") and the noun ("right"). Those ten words mean little until you reach "right" and find out what they are modifying. Almost all the terms require special knowledge: "Content," "non-exclusive," "perpetual," "irrevocable," "royalty-free," "sublicensable," "tiers," "copyright," "publicity," "database," "rights," and "media" are words that people don't use in the contract's sense, if at all. We have yet to meet the nonlawyer who can decipher this sentence (or the lawyer who cares to try).

In sum, everybody likes better writing, but were it easy, there would be a lot more of it. And even were there a lot more of it, the underlying complexity that defeats so many disclosures would remain.

SIMPLIFIED PRESENTATION

If simplified words carry you only a short way, what about simplified presentations? Literacy problems arise not just from small vocabularies but from trouble interpreting complex presentations. Many hopes for *faites simple* lie in better forms and formats. One method is just to omit information. This returns us to the fundamental tension between full disclosure and simplification. And as chapters 9 and 10 show, regulatory dynamics push lawmakers and disclosers toward thorough, not thrifty, disclosure.

Another way to simplify formats is to standardize them and substitute generalization for detail. Because this method is in vogue, we examine several examples. First, the SEC has authorized a summary prospectus with basic information about a fund's objectives, strategies, risks, costs, and performance. It will have an opening summary with "key information" about the fund, including "its objectives, strategies, risks, costs, and performance." This information would speak "in plain English in a standardized order" and "succinctly, in three or four pages."[28] The SEC expects this to "improve investors' ability to make informed investment decisions" and "revolutionize the provision of information" to investors.

If "standardized and succinct" work anywhere, it should be here. Investors have strong incentives to understand disclosures and are better educated than average disclosees. So Beshears et al. tested the summary prospectus on a group—"Harvard non-faculty, white-collar staff members"—especially likely to understand it. They were better educated even than the average retail investor: almost all were college graduates; over half had graduate education. They were more sophisticated: a fifth knew what securities a money-market fund holds, while only 8 percent did in a survey of retirement plan members.[29] If these relative sophisticates could not benefit from *faites simple*, who could?

The Harvard staff group chose from two portfolios (one bonds, one equities) of actively managed mutual funds, and their compensation depended on how well their selections performed. However, the SEC's summary prospectus did "not alter subjects' investment choices. Dollar-weighted average fees and past returns of mutual fund choices [were] statistically indistinguishable." The staff members did not "respond sensibly to loads and redemption fees." Even when investing for just one month, they chose funds with loads and fees averaging 200 basis points more than funds with the lowest fees (rational only if, miraculously, the former funds did twenty-four percentage points better than the latter).[30] Worse, those given the simplified prospectus paid more attention to past returns (unwise in the circumstances). But at least people spent less time reading the new prospectus.

Our second standardized format is the CFPB's dedicated and expert effort to improve mortgage disclosures. The mortgage crisis and behavioral research inspired a three-page application form and a five-page closing form. In laboratory tests, people showed modest improvement using their information. But people seemed to do better when loan costs were itemized, not lumped, even though itemization is the opposite of simplification. And apparently subjects thought "the higher level of itemization signaled a higher level of disclosure."[31]

Third, the Affordable Care Act requires simplified "summary of benefits and coverage" disclosures. The government developed a form (now used in open enrollment); a consumer group tested it. The goal was to make health plans comparable by standardizing information, as nutritional labels do. While respondents thought the simplified form "helpful," when they tried "to estimate their out-of-pocket costs for a specific service or common scenario," they found the forms less helpful than they had thought. The "vast majority" had trouble with these tests, and "nearly all were confused" because they did not understand concepts like coinsurance, deductibles, allowed amount, and annual limits. "For example, they were not sure how 'screenings' differed from the 'diagnostic tests' referenced on the table of covered services." All this "not only frustrated respondents, but could lead them to select a plan that was not actually in their best interest."[32]

The study's authors—otherwise apostles of simplification—thought the forms were "not sufficient to alleviate respondents' confusion" and should be *amplified*. Some definitions, for example, might have been unhelpful "because they lacked concrete, numerical examples." The authors advised including *lots* more detail and used phrases like "[a]dd numeric examples," "explain the term," "[a]dd terms," "[l]ink to standardized medical scenarios," and "[s]trengthen instructions." In the next iteration, they said, details should be "spelled out unambiguously."[33] So the solution to simplicity's failure is—complexity. *Plus ça change* . . . .

Fourth, insurance policies surely need succinctness in standard formats. "It's like reading a book," complained an auto dealer who did not read his policy. "No other product in our economy that is purchased by so many people for so much money is bought with so little understanding of its actual or comparative value," an FTC chairman said of whole-life policies (that combine insurance and savings). Here too disclosurites want "relatively simple transparency-oriented reforms" and laboratory-tested lay language that would "make insurance understandable."[34] But examining recent efforts, we find again long documents requiring improbable sophistication and concentration.

SCORES

The acme of *faites simple* is reducing complexity to a datum—a number, a rating, a grade, or at least an index. We will call such a summary a score. Scores are not utopian. Unmandated scores are common. Some are given by raters: Zagat scores restaurants, AAA scores hotels, *U.S. News* grades universities. Many businesses invite customers to score products. Netflix and Amazon ratings are cleverly supplemented by other forms of evaluation. But how usefully can scores be mandated as replacements for complex disclosures?

The Example of the APR

The star score is the annual percentage rate. The APR, the centerpiece of consumer-credit law, helps disclosees compare the cost of loans. Consider a loan of $10,000 with three options:

- Option 1: you pay back $2000 each year over 10 years for a total of $20,000.
- Option 2: you pay back $20,000 in a lump sum after 5 years.
- Option 3: you pay back $200 for 100 months for a total of $20,000.

Which is cheapest? At a naïve first look, none: you borrow the same amount ($10,000) and pay back the same amount ($20,000). But because you pay in different ways, the costs differ (nonintuitively). For loans this simple, the APR accurately states the costs of borrowing, here 18.2 percent, 14.9 percent, and 23.7 percent. As we saw in chapter 2's example of borrowing, costs can be affected by fees as well as interest rates, but APRs can incorporate many of these.

The APR excellently simplifies some crucial information, but it has limits. It often cannot incorporate *all* credit's costs and burdens. If, for example, the APR excludes third-party costs and junk fees (like appraisal, credit-report, and title-insurance fees and prepayment penalties), it distorts choices. Thus proposals to make APRs more inclusive are common.[35] But mandates date easily because, for example, lending practices change and lenders undercut the APR by devising fees it does not cover.

APRs have other problems. First, mortgage costs vary and are not always predictable. The list of fees is long, but not all will be incurred. And factoring prepayment penalties into an APR requires information about the borrower's propensity to prepay in varying market conditions. Furthermore, interest rates and fees cannot always be known in advance—most obviously, in adjustable-rate mortgages. Also, much besides a loan's cost affects its appeal. Even in the simple case we just described, borrowers might not choose the cheapest loan. They might prefer monthly payments to a single large payment or prefer lower monthly payments to a lower interest rate. And borrowers must decide how many points to buy for a lower APR, a decision inexperienced borrowers often make poorly.

Finally, APRs often cannot overcome the several kinds of illiteracy we have discussed. Many studies show people misunderstanding APRs, confusing them with the interest rate, and preferring other information. Some people are not even sure whether a high or a low APR is preferable.[36]

The Example of the Prepaid Debit Card

An APR is a score summarizing a product's costs. Its calculation is simplified by its common unit of measurement—money. So, can complex prices always be scored? Consider another financial product with obscure costs—prepaid debit cards. They give people without bank accounts a way to get cash (ATMs) or to shop without it. But their cost is obscured by an army of fees, including application fees, activation fees, ATM fees, balance-inquiry fees, fees for using the card, fees for not using the card, maintenance fees, reloading fees, replacement fees, overdraft fees, and fees for calling customer service.[37] Walmart's MoneyCard, one of the cheapest and friendliest prepaid cards, charges $3 monthly and $2 for using an ATM. One study found that fees made cards 87 percent more expensive than consumers expected.[38]

Florida's attorney general makes the disclosurite response—penalizing issuers for not divulging all fees clearly and conspicuously, since not disclosing fees "is essentially stealing."[39] So can the fees be made simple enough that the unsophisticated can understand them? For instance, could customers be told how much of their deposit the fees would consume?

We are back to the problem we had with APRs—individualization. The amount of the fees depends on what fees users incur. The fees are numerous and various; so are users.

Similarly, reducing a checking account's cost to a score would mean calculating the value of overdraft protection, which depends on how often you use it. In short, the closer you come to a single score for a complex product, the less accurate the score is for individual disclosees. The score then must be complemented with information about particular populations. And the more unpredictable factors that the score incorporates, the less accurate the score and the more vital the complementary information.

Scores, Individualization, and Generalization

If scores are weakened by differences among consumers and by the unpredictability of the factors they incorporate, why not generalize? For example, calculate fees for prepaid debit cards by consulting market data and using algorithms that weight commonly incurred fees. Or use ranges. The new mortgage disclosures must deal with variable interest rates; their solution is to state a range of payments (unfortunately, a large range).

Weighted averages and ranges are ways to assign scores to products that can be bought and used in many combinations of prices and features in uncertain circumstances. But their generalizations are too vague and inaccurate for many disclosures. This brings us to our old friend smart disclosure.[40] Sunstein describes it as "the timely release of complex information and data in standardized, machine readable formats in ways that enable consumers to make informed decisions."[41] How would this help with the problems of individualization and unpredictability in scoring? Businesses might tell people not only about the product but about how the customer would use it.[42] Software would provide a score or other summary. When buying printers, people would be told about their total cost, including predictions about what the customer would spend on toner cartridges. When selecting a credit card, people would be told all the costs (including late fees and finance charges) that they were likely to incur.

Hopes for smart disclosure soar yet higher, to an era of personalized disclosure. Using mountains of data that allow computers to identify patterns that predict behavior, disclosures might be individually tailored. Shoppers might scan a product and see only the disclosures relevant to them. Deaf apartment hunters would not be warned "about a noisy rock band drummer who lives next door," but "noise-sensitive tenants" would be. Or "pregnant women would be shown prominent warnings" they needed; septuagenarian men would just be told what those of us approaching old age must hear.[43] Personalizing disclosures would reduce irrelevant disclosures and make relevant ones easier to spot.

Perhaps such devices would help with some products, including cell phones, credit cards, and printers. Perhaps they would moderate some overload and accumulation problems. But we doubt that most disclosures, including the major ones, would profit greatly from this technology. The decisions that people make often enough to generate useful data for the smart-disclosure algorithms are decisions people can master from their own experience. The problem for both people and software is the infrequent but momentous decision, like mortgage borrowing or agreeing to surgery. Besides, how many borrowers would walk into pawnshops with iPads armed with apps to scan disclosures and compare credit costs? And who would want to read even one personalized sentence for each of the policies on the Web sites they visit? The charm of total-cost disclosure is based on creative insights worth pursuing. But the great mass of modern complexity cannot be reduced to a few digits or words.

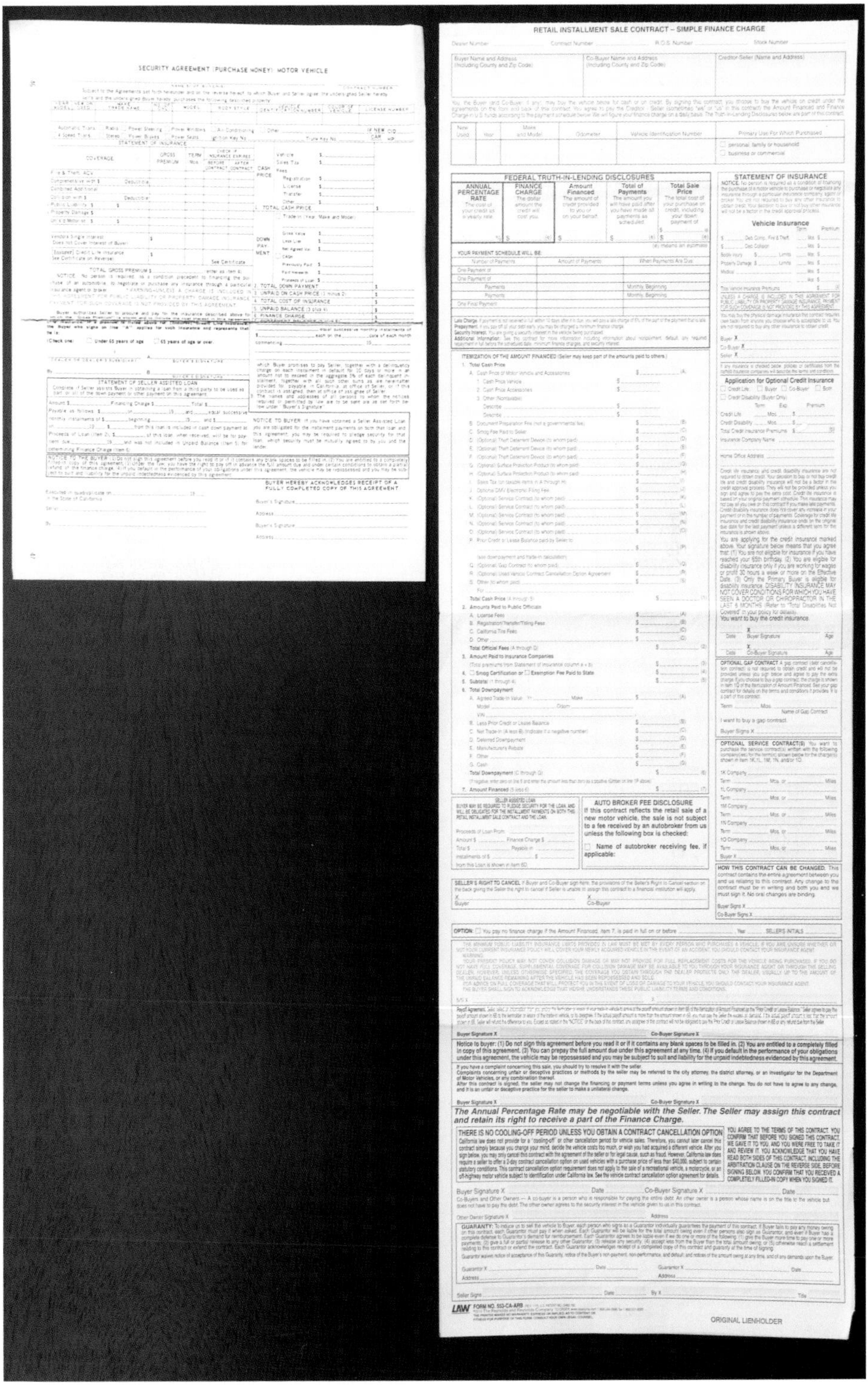

PLATE 3. *The California bed sheet, now and then*

2011

Offense	On-Campus Property			Non-Campus Property			Public Property			On-Campus Residence Halls†		
	Reported to UM DPS	Reported to Other Police	Reported to Non-Police	Reported to UM DPS	Reported to Other Police^	Reported to Non-Police	Reported to UM DPS	Reported to Other Police^	Reported to Non-Police	Reported to UM DPS	Reported to Other Police	Reported to Non-Police
Murder/Non-negligent Manslaughter	0	0	0	0	0	0	0	0	0	0	0	0
Negligent Manslaughter	0	0	0	0	0	0	0	0	0	0	0	0
Forcible Rape	1	0	5	0	0	2	0	2	0	1	0	4
Forcible Sodomy	2	0	0	0	0	0	0	0	0	1	0	0
Sexual Assault With An Object	1	0	0	0	0	0	0	0	0	1	0	0
Forcible Fondling	4	0	1	0	2	1	0	0	0	1	0	1
Incest	0	0	0	0	0	0	0	0	0	0	0	0
Statutory Rape	0	0	0	0	0	0	0	0	0	0	0	0
Robbery	4	0	0	0	0	0	5	5	0	0	0	0
Aggravated Assault	6	0	2	0	5	0	10	7	0	0	0	2
Arson	4	0	0	0	1	0	0	0	0	1	0	0
Burglary	25	0	12	1	22	0	0	0	0	14	0	12
Motor Vehicle Theft	12	0	0	0	2	0	1	1	0	0	0	0
Liquor Law Arrest/Citations	314	0	N/A	0	0	N/A	44	0	N/A	193	0	N/A
Liquor Law Violations Referred for Disciplinary Action	0	N/A	855	0	N/A	2	0	N/A	0	0	N/A	854
Drug Law Arrests	102	0	N/A	0	0	N/A	17	7	N/A	9	0	N/A
Drug Law Violations Referred for Disciplinary Action	0	N/A	202	0	N/A	0	0	N/A	0	0	N/A	199
Weapon Law Arrests	3	0	N/A	0	0	N/A	1	0	N/A	0	0	N/A
Weapon Law Violations Referred for Disciplinary Action	0	N/A	6	0	N/A	0	0	N/A	0	0	N/A	6

2010

Offense	On-Campus Property			Non-Campus Property			Public Property			On-Campus Residence Halls†		
	Reported to UM DPS	Reported to Other Police	Reported to Non-Police	Reported to UM DPS	Reported to Other Police	Reported to Non-Police	Reported to UM DPS	Reported to Other Police	Reported to Non-Police	Reported to UM DPS	Reported to Other Police	Reported to Non-Police
Murder/Non-negligent Manslaughter	0	0	0	0	0	0	0	0	0	0	0	0
Negligent Manslaughter	0	0	0	0	0	0	0	0	0	0	0	0
Forcible Rape	2	0	0	0	1	3	0	1	0	1	0	0
Forcible Sodomy	2	0	0	0	0	0	0	0	0	2	0	0
Sexual Assault With An Object	3	0	0	0	0	0	0	0	0	1	0	0
Forcible Fondling	8	0	1	0	1	1	0	1	0	0	0	1
Incest	0	0	0	0	0	0	0	0	0	0	0	0
Statutory Rape	0	0	0	0	0	0	0	0	0	0	0	0
Robbery	7	0	0	0	0	0	0	6	0	0	0	0
Aggravated Assault	10	0	0	0	0	0	1	0	0	2	0	0
Arson	1	0	0	0	4	0	0	0	0	1	0	0
Burglary	27	0	0	2	25	0	0	0	0	15	0	0
Motor Vehicle Theft	10	0	0	3	1	0	0	12	0	0	0	0
Liquor Law Arrest/Citations	391	0	N/A	0	15	N/A	5	38	N/A	224	0	N/A
Liquor Law Violations Referred for Disciplinary Action	0	N/A	483	0	N/A	0	0	N/A	2	0	N/A	479
Drug Law Arrests	116	1	N/A	0	0	N/A	0	4	N/A	19	0	N/A
Drug Law Violations Referred for Disciplinary Action	0	N/A	208	0	N/A	0	0	N/A	0	0	N/A	206
Weapon Law Arrests	2	0	N/A	0	0	N/A	0	0	N/A	0	0	N/A
Weapon Law Violations Referred for Disciplinary Action	0	N/A	1	0	N/A	0	0	N/A	0	0	N/A	1

2009

Offense	On-Campus Property			Non-Campus Property			Public Property			On-Campus Residence Halls†		
	Reported to UM DPS	Reported to Other Police	Reported to Non-Police	Reported to UM DPS	Reported to Other Police	Reported to Non-Police	Reported to UM DPS	Reported to Other Police	Reported to Non-Police	Reported to UM DPS	Reported to Other Police	Reported to Non-Police
Murder/Non-negligent Manslaughter	0	0	0	0	0	0	0	0	0	0	0	0
Negligent Manslaughter	0	0	0	0	0	0	0	0	0	0	0	0
Forcible Rape	1	0	4	0	0	6	0	0	0	1	0	4
Forcible Sodomy	0	0	0	0	0	0	0	0	0	0	0	0
Sexual Assault With An Object	1	0	0	0	0	0	0	0	0	1	0	0
Forcible Fondling	5	0	0	0	0	0	0	0	0	1	0	0
Incest	0	0	0	0	0	0	0	0	0	0	0	0
Statutory Rape	0	0	0	0	0	0	0	0	0	0	0	0
Robbery	1	0	0	0	0	0	0	5	0	0	0	0
Aggravated Assault	9	0	1	0	1	0	0	8	1	4	0	1
Arson	10	0	0	0	1	0	1	2	0	4	0	0
Burglary	13	0	2	1	24	0	0	0	0	5	0	2
Motor Vehicle Theft	5	0	0	2	7	0	0	5	0	0	0	0
Liquor Law Arrest/Citations	324	0	N/A	0	6	N/A	0	35	N/A	156	0	N/A
Liquor Law Violations Referred for Disciplinary Action	0	N/A	655	0	N/A	0	0	N/A	0	0	N/A	655
Drug Law Arrests	54	0	N/A	0	2	N/A	0	8	N/A	9	0	N/A
Drug Law Violations Referred for Disciplinary Action	0	N/A	77	0	N/A	0	0	N/A	0	0	N/A	77
Weapon Law Arrests	1	0	N/A	0	0	N/A	0	0	N/A	0	0	N/A
Weapon Law Violations Referred for Disciplinary Action	0	N/A	0	0	N/A	0	0	N/A	0	0	N/A	0

† Residential Facilities: These statistics are included in the On-Campus statistics; they include only incidents which occurred in residence halls and Northwood Community Apartments.
^ Other Police reports: the 2011 statistics are from Ann Arbor Police reports. Other law enforcement agencies contacted for other Non-Campus properties included:
- Southfield Town Center, 3000 Town Center, Southfield, MI – 2 motor vehicle thefts
- Biological Station, 9133 Biological Rd, Pellston, MI – 0 crimes
- Camp Davis, 13405 S Bryan Flat Rd, Jackson, WY – 0 crimes
- CS Osborn Preserve, Sugar Island, Sault Ste. Marie, MI – 0 crimes
- Detroit Center, Woodward Ave, Detroit, MI – no report

PLATE 4. *A Clery Act Report*

PLATE 1. *The iTunes "scroll"*

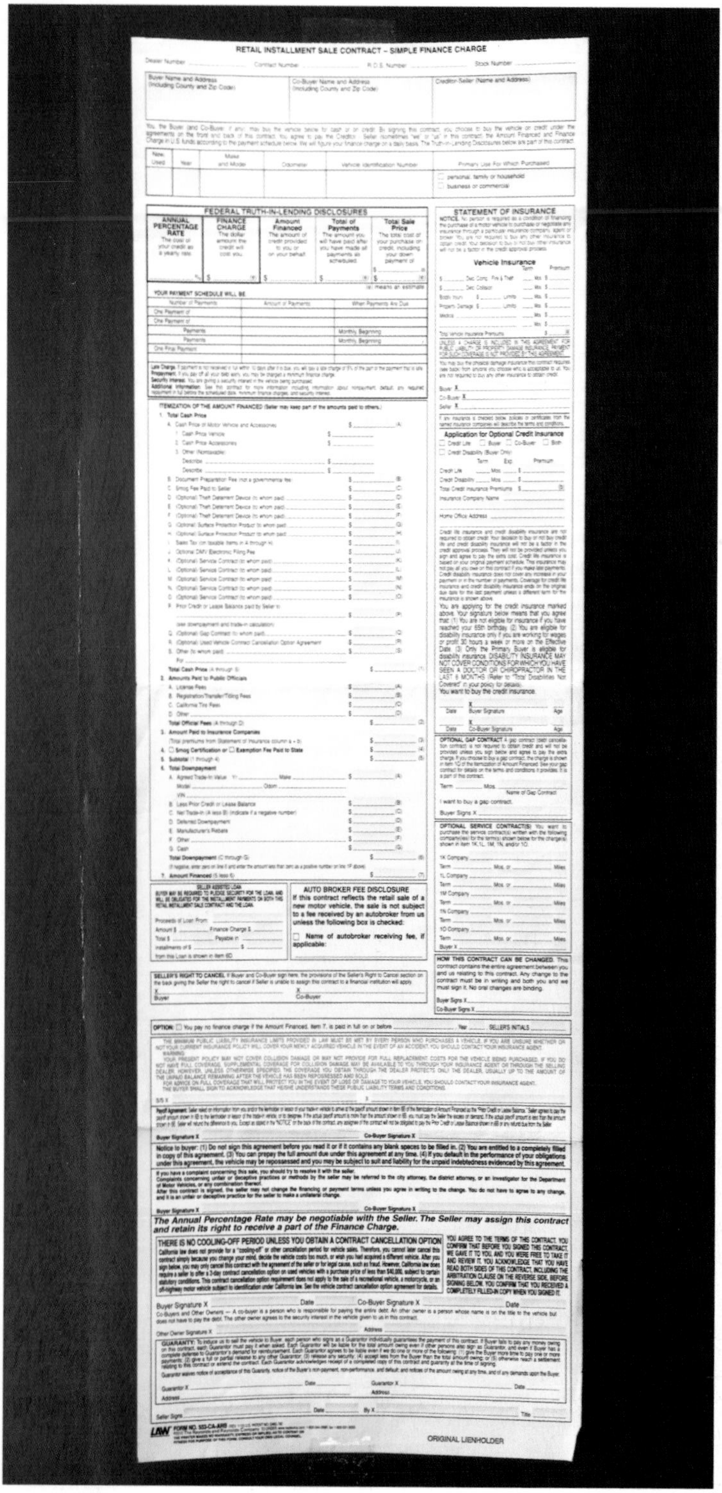

PLATE 2. *The California "bed sheet"*

Scores for Nonmonetary Choices

We have been discussing scores that primarily summarize numbers, especially prices. Assigning scores to qualitative information is far harder. There is rarely a sound way to score privacy policies, or medical treatments, or nursing homes, or warranties, or conflicts of interest, or contract boilerplate, or *Miranda* warnings. Consider privacy policies: HIPAA requires that patients be told what information is kept, how it is protected, how it is used, with whom it is shared, how to object to some uses, how to get it, and how to demand its amendment. We take this to be an area in which scores are a nonstarter. Or take medical care: Scores reporting the quality of hospitals have been essayed (chapter 11 discusses them), but quality comprises many elements, most hard to assess, interpret, and weight. So hundreds of subscores are given for various kinds of treatments and various aspects of quality (mortality, readmission, infections, safety, satisfaction, length of stay, staffing). Efforts have also been made to evaluate treatment choices numerically, but in ways too speculative and elaborate to help patients facing decisions.

Other problems in scoring qualities are presented by the hygiene grades that some cities require restaurants to post in the window. An influential study estimated that this decreased food-related hospitalization in Los Angeles by 20 percent. This is phenomenal but perhaps plausible, for who wants to eat where cockroaches cavort, flies infest, and salmonella spreads? But (as chapter 10 will report), later, more thorough research finds that these beautifully simple scores do not reduce illness but do misinform customers. The factors they aggregate are so varied, subjective, and volatile that the scores, alas, mean little.

THE EXAMPLE OF FOOD LABELING

The 1990 Nutrition Labeling and Education Act mandates a standardized label intended to make basic facts about many foods easy to find. Restaurants increasingly must post nutritional information. These mandates simplify in several ways. Labels on packaged foods are standardized and selective. Restaurants often need disclose only the calorie count.

Nutritional labeling may be mandated disclosure's easiest test. Mandates usually address unfamiliar and complex decisions; choosing meals we do daily. People have many chances and many years to learn to use labels. Learning is aided by a social campaign to change eating habits. The labels address a relative simple decision—should I buy this cereal or order that sandwich? Decisions to order a Big Mac are richly informed by experience and can be improved by even one datum (usually calories). People might *want* to read the labels, since so many of us want to eat wisely and lose weight.

If you ask people whether they use, like, and learn from labels, many say yes. Many testify that they know more about foods and that this changes their purchases. Attention to nutrition boxes may be increasing, although it is hard to know whether this is caused by mandates or by increased voluntary nutrition claims on packaging and in advertising. Studies of restaurant disclosures sometimes report some improvements and include research finding that people consume fewer calories at restaurants with posted calories. For example, after Starbucks began listing calories, calorie consumption declined 6 percent (because of prudence in choosing food, not drinks).[44] Other studies report slightly larger effects.

But there is reason for skepticism even about food labels. One influential study found that people rarely consult them and struggle to understand and use them or even find a single item (like fat). For most categories people have trouble gauging whether quantities are low or high.[45] A review of 103 studies found that while people grasped some of what the labels said, they generally thought "food labeling confusing, especially the use of some technical and numerical information."[46] Food labels are best used by the literate and numerate (so our colleagues, who are food-labeling fans, report greater benefit from food labeling than the general population).[47] Some experiments assigning subjects randomly find that menu labeling does not decrease calories ordered or eaten, even among those who noticed labels.[48] Other studies suggest that calorie labeling does not affect low-income people and might have perversely affected some populations.[49]

The ambiguity of this research is heightened by the way mandates coincide with social trends. Changing eating patterns, especially a rising demand for low-fat foods and a declining demand for high-fat foods, may have set a trend that mandated disclosure and voluntary advertising merely track. In any event, while labels may influence people, few change their overall diets. They may eat less of one high-fat food (like red meat) but more of another (like dairy products).[50] Or they may order less from a menu with calorie labels but eat more later. Meals may shrink while snacks increase. Over the past generation the median American's "eating occasions" rose from 3.5 to 5 per day, while calories increased by 400.[51] With many labeling laws a generation old, this hardly spells success.

We take seriously the hope that labels can inform choices. But even if they do, will success spoil food labels? Success, the next chapter finds, often inspires lawmakers to broaden mandates. Nutrition data, ingredients, and calorie labeling are now common. A country-of-origin label has been recently mandated, as well as organic, allergenic, trans-fat, and safe-handling information. Proposed mandates include information about choking, genetic modification, fair trade, caffeine content, and much else. All that, plus the labels, seals, and health claims manufacturers splatter on food packaging. This is disclosure's oft-traveled route to complexity and failure.

CONCLUSION

When everyone wants simplicity, when laws require it, when experts seek it but progress is scant, we should stop demanding success and start explaining failure. Simplicity's failure grows out of mandated disclosure's concern with complex and unfamiliar issues. Complexity can rarely be described simply to people unfamiliar with it. There is no *deus ex machina*.

CHAPTER 9

THE POLITICS OF DISCLOSURE

I would rather disclose than be regulated.

—Robert F. Elliott, president,
Household Finance Company

Parts I and II analyzed mandated disclosure's failure to achieve its goals. Part III is asking whether it can be rescued. Chapter 8 found simplification unsuited to the task. This chapter argues that even if simplification could be achieved, it would often be defeated by the irrepressible expansionism of mandates. That expansionism has two forms. First, ever more social problems are regulated through mandated disclosure. Second, once mandated, disclosures tend to grow to cover more aspects of an issue in more detail. The politics of lawmaking, then, helps explain why *faites simple* fails. The remedy for failed disclosure is more disclosure (exacerbating the overload problem). The response to successful disclosure is to extend mandates (again exacerbating the overload problem) and by expanding them to new areas (exacerbating the accumulation problem).

If mandates are so unreliable, why do so many kinds of lawmakers routinely impose and extend them? To use an evolutionary metaphor, we have a puzzling species—a regulatory technique that spreads prolifically in all kinds of environments. Yet the species' members rarely achieve its purpose. How can the *un*fit survive?

Disclosure mandates are driven by several forces that shape their creation and perpetuation. Crucial is disclosure's plausibility: *surely* information improves decisions. That plausibility is intensified—and distorted—by the way trouble stories frame the problem. Furthermore, mandated disclosure is largely unfalsifiable; failures, if recognized, are attributed to mismanaged implementation, not a misconceived method. Also crucial is the intuition—however illusory—that mandated disclosure is all benefit and no cost. Its direct costs are rarely paid by the government, while alternative forms of regulation must be governmentally funded. Disclosure's costs (direct and indirect) are borne by others, are often obscure to lawmakers, and seem distant and debatable. Because lawmakers address problems one at a time, they overlook the accumulation problem and overgraze the disclosure commons. Finally, mandated disclosure (more than its alternatives) is feasible. Legislatures pass disclosure laws overwhelmingly, partly because they please the whole political spectrum. So inappropriate disclosures are mandated, and appropriate mandates become morbidly obese.

THE AXIOMATIC EFFECTIVENESS OF MANDATED DISCLOSURE

The case for mandated disclosure has long seemed obvious. The more-information-is-better mantra seems axiomatic, and full disclosure follows from it. The *homo arbiter* view of human nature is well ensconced in policy making. Disclosure axiomatically gives people making unfamiliar and complex decisions what they need—information. Obviously, properly informed people must make better decisions.

This has all seemed plain for a century. In 1914 Louis Brandeis, the "people's lawyer" and later a Supreme Court justice, said that it was "now recognized in the simplest merchandizing, that there should be full disclosures." Federal law did not guarantee quality or prices, but it helped "the buyer to judge of quality by requiring disclosure of ingredients." Brandeis wanted "full disclosure to the investor of the amount of commissions and profits paid," not only because investors would "be put on their guard, but bankers' compensation will tend to adjust itself automatically to what is fair and reasonable."[1]

Mandated disclosure is the god that cannot fail. Failure only means that the mandate should be reengineered: expanded, modified, simplified, tightened, emphasized, shifted, repeated, supplemented. The pattern is now familiar. The first reaction to apparent failure is that too little disclosure has been mandated. But fuller disclosure creates the overload problem and inspires calls for simplification. As failure persists, other tactics are tried: mandating earlier disclosures to give people time to read them; mandating real-time disclosures to reach people when they act; designing new formats; aggregating information into scores; unifying separate disclosure forms to reduce paperwork; separating unified disclosure forms so that each gets individual attention; requiring simpler language; harnessing technology; and more.

The unfalsifiability of mandated disclosure is illustrated by lawmakers' invincible conviction that disclosures will preserve borrowers from irrational and destructive debt. Despite a consensus that TILA and its satellites did not protect borrowers in the subprime-mortgage debacle, disclosure is still the philosopher's stone. Secretary of the Treasury Geithner called it "one of the most powerful tools we have for getting people better information so they can make better choices about how they borrow, how they use credit, how they invest their savings."[2] The Director of the CFPB plans to "issue new disclosures for hybrid adjustable-rate mortgages."[3]

THE AXIOM MADE FLESH: THE TROUBLE STORY

Intuitively obvious as mandated disclosure generally seems, it is more so in the context of a "trouble story"—a tale of individual misfortune that apparently represents a systematic problem: the family made homeless by foreclosure, the patient who dies on the table, the doctor who sends patients to his own laboratory for tests, the child with food poisoning, the farmer injured by a tractor. Trouble stories seem to present a common problem (ignorance) and a common solution (information).

Trouble stories fall into several rough categories: narratives, scandals, and crises. The narrative trouble story is exemplified by Jeanne Clery's rape and murder in her Lehigh dorm room. Clery's parents "discovered that violence on college campuses was a widespread problem and devoted the rest of their lives to making campuses safer." This led to the Clery Act, and "for the first time institutions of higher education across the United

States began the process of consistently releasing crime statistics and security policies to their current and prospective students or employees."[4]

The scandal trouble story is exemplified by Public Health Service research at Tuskegee, where African American patients who had contracted syphilis were studied but not treated, even when medication became available. Tuskegee was the trouble story that remains the primary justification for the university and hospital committees (IRBs) that now mandate elaborate disclosures for human-subject research.

The crisis trouble story is exemplified by an apparent plague of consumer-credit misfortunes. Mary and Earl Ranson, an elderly couple, refinanced their home to pay medical bills. Confused about points, good-faith estimates, appraisal fees, and escrow, they ended up with a 19 percent mortgage when cheaper credit could have saved them $37,000. Congress's response? "We in Congress have to look out for the Ransons and for all Americans by providing simple and easily understood disclosures."[5]

Trouble stories (like trouble) flow unceasingly. They drive lawmakers toward mandated disclosure partly by creating urgency to do *something*. "Our political system is extremely sensitive to new calamities, real and imagined. The media thrive on stories of deaths and disasters; lobbying organizations, struggling to attract members and defeat opponents, have every incentive to exaggerate."[6] Such "[c]atastrophes are probably the most important catalysts of new regulation." Legislators in our "media-oriented" world "transform individual acts of malfeasance into social problems requiring society-wide solutions."[7] Even courts are swayed by trouble stories; a case can evoke as much indignation in judges as in the public and as violent a desire for action.

Trouble stories also tend to make mandated disclosure plausible. In them, the weaker party in a relationship made a decision that led to misfortune. The stronger party had information that the weaker party presumably lacked. Had the weaker party had it and used it properly, misfortune could have been averted. Q.E.D.

Making law from trouble stories is hazardous. Trouble stories are anecdotes seen through the distorting lens of hindsight. Good policy comes from understanding social problems; anecdotes are rarely representative enough to provide that understanding. To evaluate representativeness, we need to know how many decisions in a category are made and how many are made badly. If only a few are, regulation will rarely be cost-effective. Trouble stories, then, may tell us something about the numerator but not the denominator.

Even if the trouble story is true and representative, was the bad decision caused by a lack of information? Would supplying the information have improved the decision? In hindsight it may seem so. Had you known that Superstorm Sandy would wash away your house, you would have bought insurance. But analytic questions are rarely asked about trouble stories, for as Holmes said, "Most people think dramatically, not quantitatively."

To make our generalizations more concrete, here is a trouble story—*Truman v. Thomas*[8]—that led a lawmaker to mandate disclosure. Dr. Thomas was Mrs. Truman's primary physician. He urged her to have a Pap smear but never explicitly told her the risks of *not* having one. She died of cervical cancer. An expert testified that had she been tested, "the cervical tumor probably would have been discovered in time to save her life." Informed consent required doctors to tell patients about treatment's risks, but (it was then generally thought) not the consequences of failing to act.

Mrs. Truman made a decision—not to be screened—that, made differently, might have kept her alive. Her doctor had not expressly said that death was a risk of her choice. In response to this trouble story, the California Supreme Court expanded doctors' duty to inform people like Mrs. Thomas so that they would "appreciate the potentially fatal consequences of [their] conduct." The court clearly thought what a lower-court judge said: "Can it be doubted that, had the decedent in this case known that for $6 and mild discomfort she could discover the existence of cervical cancer and thus survive, she would have taken the test? Central to her failure to take the test was a clear lack of understanding of the significance of the doctor's recommendation."

Does this trouble story justify expanded disclosure? How many women are advised to have a Pap smear (the denominator)? How many decline (the numerator)?[9] How much of the court's reaction was biased by its knowledge of the story's end? In fact, Dr. Thomas campaigned valiantly to get Mrs. Truman to accept the Pap smear and other screening. When she came to him with an upper respiratory infection, he suggested a Pap smear, "but Mrs. Truman said she did not feel like it." More than once he threatened not to prescribe birth control pills "unless she had 'a pelvic and a pap smear.'" She promised to, but she kept putting him off. He offered to defer his fee. She still declined. Nor was Dr. Thomas the only doctor who failed to persuade Mrs. Truman to accept medical care. When she finally saw a urologist, he explained her grave situation and told her to see a gynecologist, but she did not. The urologist saw her three more times, but she put him off. Finally, the urologist himself arranged for Mrs. Truman to see the gynecologist, who diagnosed her disease.

In hindsight, a simple warning—you could die—seems so valuable that it overshadows all else. But what difference would it have made? Did Dr. Thomas truly fail to give Mrs. Thomas the information? Would a correct statement (in a preprinted form) of the odds of the Pap smear saving her life have changed her mind when so much else did not? And is a mandate to disclose screening statistics the best way to regulate doctors' dealings with recalcitrant patients? To help patients act providently?

In the trouble story of *Truman v. Thomas*, the court had naïve ideas about the value of information and failed to recognize its hindsight bias. But even sophisticated lawmakers who recognize the numerator and denominator problems can succumb. For example, the Federal Trade Commission has an expert staff and commissioners who serve long enough (seven years) to acquire real experience. The FTC regulates both "deceptive" and "unfair" practices, which gives it authority over warnings for products like vehicles, cosmetics, and tools. In a famous ruling[10] it examined the warnings and instructions International Harvester gave tractor users. Removing a hot engine's fuel cap can cause geysering—an eruption of burning hot fuel. In its early models IH did not warn about this, and some people were badly hurt. Later, IH added warnings to the operator's manual, though geysering was not fully explained even then. Was IH's failure to spell out the hazard "deceptive" or "unfair," and was more disclosure warranted?

The Commission decided (over vigorous dissent) that IH's failure to state the geysering risk was *not* deceptive because geysering was rare and injury rarer. The FTC knew the trouble stories of horrible injuries to operators removing sizzling fuel caps. The FTC (optimistically) assumed that a warning could have prevented the injuries. The FTC also saw the denominator: Over 1.3 million tractors had been driven millions of times over forty years with only twelve serious geyser-related injuries (including one death).

The FTC understood the denominator problem. Tractors cause bad but rare injuries in *many* ways. Warning about all the risks would deluge drivers in writing. The FTC recognized that people "may have erroneous preconceptions about issues as diverse as the entire range of human error, and it would be both impractical and very costly to require corrective information on all such points." Consumers might err about many things. Since the seller can't know where a particular consumer will err, it would have to provide full disclosure to everybody. "For example, there are literally dozens of ways in which one can be injured while riding a tractor, not all of them obvious before the fact, and under a simple deception analysis these would presumably all require affirmative disclosure."

So despite the more-information-is-better mantra and hindsight's distortions, the FTC calculated the denominator, recognized the rate of risk, and held that failing to disclose the hazard in the manual was *not* deceptive. But the FTC was not finished; while the failure to disclose was not deceptive, it was, the FTC said, unfair. The FTC described eleven victims' burns, suffering, and disfigurement. Sympathy trumped sense. The overload problem vanished: "the consuming public has realized no benefit from Harvester's non-disclosure that is at all sufficient to offset the human injuries involved." So even a sophisticated lawmaker that saw the denominator problem and the microscopic chance of harm (less than one one-thousandth of one percent) mandated disclosure, even after saying how ineffective it and similar disclosures were.

In sum, trouble stories help explain not only why disclosure is often mandated, but why it often fails. They create pressure to act even when action is unwise and to act quickly rather than well. They lead lawmakers to imagine that disclosure will work even when disclosure has failed before. They draw attention to sympathetic victims, not the social problem.

And while trouble stories could inspire *any* kind of regulation, they bias lawmakers toward disclosure.

THE AXIOM AND THE FISC

Mandated disclosure's effectiveness seems axiomatic, and trouble stories animate the axiom. But mandated disclosure has another attraction—the fisc goes unmolested. For the government, it's *really* cheap. It requires minimal budget, bureaucracy, or oversight—perhaps a small agency writing and interpreting regulations. The government does not usually pay for writing, distributing, and using disclosures. The story's villain, the stronger party who withholds information, seems to pay. TILA obliged the Fed only to clarify the law occasionally, while the daily burden of interpretation and implementation fell on creditors. Even enforcement was largely delegated to private parties.

In contrast, the regulatory alternatives can burden the government. In consumer-credit regulation, for example, the government has a toolbox for repairing market failures and protecting consumers. It can improve access to credit, enforce usury statutes, prohibit discrimination, punish abusive collection, regulate credit data and privacy, license lenders, and regulate mortgage terms. It can use fiscal measures to affect interest rates. But these strategies are expensive to set up and run, and they can fail painfully. In short, mandated disclosure is usually cheap, the alternatives often costly.

Mandated disclosure's fiscal attractions are suggested by lawmakers' reaction to the trouble story of Jeanne Clery's campus rape and death. They should first have asked whether campus safety is a bigger problem than safety elsewhere. If so, they could have required or helped schools to make campuses safer. But this could mean government expenditures. Police might have been hired, prisons built, safety standards set and enforced, subsidies provided. Lawmakers treated the trouble story as a problem not in campus safety but in choosing what school to attend or work for, an information problem solved by disclosure. A small federal agency publishes a large handbook—200 pages of instructions on safety reports. Compliance may cost schools something—a typical disclosure is over 10,000 words and requires managing much information—but costs government trivially.

THE AXIOM AND THE ART OF THE POSSIBLE

Politics is the art of the possible. Mandated disclosure is more possible than most alternatives. Sometimes its plausibility makes it lawmakers' first response to a problem. And it is the path of least resistance, for who could oppose it? Often, it is the result of dwindling ambition, of a failed attempt at better regulation.

Disclosure is politically attractive partly because lawmakers rarely assess its benefits or burdens. Congress passed the Patient Self-Determination Act—a disclosure statute intended to induce people to make advance directives—with only limited discussions of the problems the statutes sought to address.[11] The courts that primarily created the duty of informed consent barely asked whether patients wanted to make medical decisions, whether doctors could provide and patients could comprehend disclosures, whether patients would make better decisions with them, whether the mandate could be stated comprehensibly, or what informed consent would cost—despite empirical grounds for expecting troubling answers to each question.

We have already explained another reason for mandated disclosure's political success: it does not offend and generally appeals to the two fundamental political ideologies, the free-market principle, laissez-faire, and deregulation on one hand and the autonomy principle, consumer protection, and human empowerment on the other. Disclosurism also has occupied the ethical high ground (so conflict-of-interest disclosure is "a basic requirement of the fiduciary nature of the treatment relationship").[12] Disclosure might deter corruption, hence Brandeis's dictum that "sunlight is said to be the best of disinfectants." Disclosure is what's left of campaign-finance regulation because it "permits citizens and shareholders to react to the speech of corporate entities in a proper way."[13] Disclosure builds "civic empowerment" by allowing people to use knowledge to shape society. Its ecumenical appeal is nicely summarized by Sunstein and Thaler's libertarian paternalism. Libertarians should like mandated disclosure because it blocks no choices. People can eat Big Macs or take on big mortgages. Paternalists should like it because disclosures channel people in desirable directions. Lawmakers can require that Big Macs be wrapped in death skulls or that APRs be put in OVERSIZED ALLCAPS framed by green exclamation marks. Sunstein and Thaler call libertarian paternalism "a promising foundation for bipartisanship," for it is "neither left nor right, neither Democratic nor Republican."[14]

Mandated disclosure's catholic appeal is shown not only by the cornucopia of disclosure laws, but also by the margins by which statutes are enacted. TILA passed the Senate 92–0 and the House 382–4. It was preceded by similarly popular state TILA statutes (in Illinois the act passed the Senate 56–1). The Fair Packaging and Labeling Act passed 72–9 in the Senate and 300–8 in the House. The Clery Act went through the House "without objection." The Real Estate Settlement and Procedure Act (RESPA)—an important 1974 supplement to TILA and the ultimate mortgage-disclosure statute—passed both houses unanimously. The Magnusson-Moss Warranty Disclosure Act, which requires standard disclosures and clear language in product warranties, squeaked through the House 381–1. The Credit CARD Act of 2009 (simplified disclosures to protect card users) passed 90–5 and 357–70. We could go on.

Mandated disclosure tames even health-care reform. The Patient Protection and Affordable Care Act of 2010 provoked brawls. But mandated disclosure of drug companies' payments to doctors for research and consulting brought sweet peace. Both parties backed legislation to give patients more information for choosing doctors, for that "let the sun shine in" and fostered accountability.[15]

This is not normal. Legislation is contested. Even consumer protection gets, at best, partisan majorities. The Dodd-Frank Wall Street Reform and Consumer Protection Act of 2010, which created the CFPB and a framework for prohibiting abusive credit practices, passed along party lines: 223–202 and 59–39. The Home Mortgage Disclosure Act, which is not just a disclosure statute but also a reporting tool that government uses to distribute funds and identify discriminatory practices, passed 45–37 and 177–147. Business interests often resist regulations, but as the creditor in our epigraph said frankly, "I would rather disclose than be regulated. Everything you want me to disclose I can accommodate."[16] As Willis observes, in 2003 legislators considered lending regulation. Bills protecting home buyers from predatory lending or capping the price of payday loans never got to subcommittee, but the Financial Literacy and Education Commission was created in under three months.[17]

A similar dynamic operates outside legislatures. Take the battle over the reform of software licenses and downloads. Users pay for software on conditions that they may learn about only after their purchase. Since the 1990s legislators have introduced bills enhancing software users' rights, but either lobbyists weakened them or they were not enacted. Finally, an American Law Institute initiative to state the "Principles of the Law of Software Contracts" succeeded, but only with more disclosure: contracts may regulate licensees' rights quite freely if the fine print is disclosed before the transaction. The ALI probably wanted to do more, but facing strong opposition, it fell back on the feasible, reciting the standard disclosure rubrics: "economic efficiency," "fair" prices, "sharing," "autonomy," and "right and wrong."[18]

THE DISCLOSURE RATCHET

With mandated disclosure, nothing fails like success. Some disclosures initially seem to work. But lawmakers tend to broaden the mandate's scope past the point of usefulness by requiring that more data be disclosed and that data be explained more thoroughly. Mandates rarely shrink; they often grow. Chapter 2 introduced California's 5400-word bed sheet. In 1961, it had only 740 words (see plate 3).

In fifty years of disclosure ratcheting, four disclosure frames ballooned to sixteen. Two signatures grew to eight. Four fonts became twenty-two typefaces. Eleven spaces for explaining prices soared to sixty.

A more systematic illustration of the ratchet comes from human-subject research regulation. The regulator (the IRB) approves the exact words of every consent form given to every prospective subject. The literature, government agencies, and elite commissions decry long forms, but in the decades of IRB operation, forms have lengthened implacably. In one study forms grew "roughly linearly by an average of 1.5 pages per decade. In the 1970s, the average consent form was less than one page long and often only a paragraph or two," but by the mid-1990s, it was over 4.5

pages. In another study the mean length of consent forms nearly doubled in seven years. The universality of disclosure dynamics is suggested by an Australian finding that the median length of forms went from seven to eleven pages in five years.[19]

Why the ratchet? If a disclosure looks successful, lawmakers hope that it can be recruited to do more. If a disclosure fails, the social problem persists, trouble stories recur, and pressure builds. Because mandated disclosure is unfalsifiable, more disclosure looks reasonable. So mandates ratchet up toward more language, more items, more detail, more often. New problems and new injuries inspire new disclosures and new versions of old ones.

In a symmetric world problems that receded, circumstances that improved, and injuries that ceased would lead lawmakers to repeal mandates. But social problems and trouble stories attract attention; what would attract attention to their absence? What would be evidence that a problem was too rare and minor to regulate? Which interest groups would push to repeal mandates? The pressure for more is urgent, politically charged, and plausible; the pressure for less is feeble. The numerator of twelve fuel-geysering injuries provoked trouble stories; the denominator of 1,299,988 tractors that caused no such injuries faded. Even if new fuel caps reduced the numerator to zero, would the FTC revoke its mandate? Noninjury has no moment.

Finally, lawmakers that mandate disclosures run faint risk of political harm. But lawmakers that have trimmed or revoked a mandate must explain why they left unprotected the consumer who might in hindsight have benefited from the additional disclosure (as Congress had to do after the mortgage crisis). Who will reward the lawmaker who repealed an obsolete mandate or punish the lawmaker who failed to?

LAWMAKERS' COLLECTIVE ACTION PROBLEM

Lawmakers have a collective action problem: Everyone would benefit if lawmakers coordinated and constrained mandates, but the structure of lawmaking prevents it. This injures a public commons—people's attention. Each new disclosure draws a bit more of this resource, degrading the effectiveness of other disclosures. The accumulation problem, in other words, is the lawmakers' dilemma.

If all mortgage disclosures were mandated by one regulator instead of dozens, it could prioritize disclosures. But American law is divided into federal, state, and local jurisdictions and into legislatures, administrative agencies, and courts. Consumer lending is regulated by multiple agencies, including those concerned with finances, privacy, real estate, tax, safety, and insurance. Overlapping jurisdictions let one lawmaker act even if other lawmakers think action is unneeded, undesirable, or unsafe. For example, the FDA must approve the content of drug labels, yet a drug company may be liable for injuries attributed to labels the FDA approved but a state court jury thought insufficient.[20]

Lawmakers hear trouble stories and confront social problems piecemeal, in specialized legislative committees, in administrative agencies, and in courts hearing particular cases. Nothing highlights the accumulation problem, nor would raising it be politically attractive or (often) legally relevant. And even if the accumulation problem were recognized in the literature, even if lawmakers assimilated the literature, and even if lawmakers wanted to prune the disclosure thicket, they would have neither the incentives nor the occasion to do it effectively.

In sum, however committed disclosurites and lawmakers may be to simplification, the dynamics of mandated disclosure impede it. For reasons embedded in the structure and processes of lawmaking, new mandates are recognized, and old mandates expand whether they have failed or succeeded. Faced with such imperatives, simplification rarely prevails. Mandated disclosure is a species that serves lawmakers even if it does little for disclosees, and it is a species without natural enemies. Its evolutionary status seems secure.

CHAPTER 10

PRODUCING DISCLOSURES

[W]hat about the option of disclosing this type of conflict . . . ? This is . . . easily accomplished. It would not take much work to add a brief paragraph in the consent form mentioning, for example, that the researcher . . . owns stock that may be worth millions of dollars if the research is successful.

—Jerry Menikoff (director, Office for Human Research
Protection), *What the Doctor Didn't Say*

In part III we have been asking whether mandated disclosure can be saved from the evidence of failure in part I and from the reasons for its failure in part II. Chapter 8 concluded that, whatever its occasional merits, simplification could not rescue mandated disclosure as a regulatory method, largely because the complex is *not* simple and can rarely be made so well. In chapter 9 we saw simplification undercut by lawmakers that create new mandates and expand old ones.

Part II primarily discussed disclosees' problems with disclosures, and chapters 8 and 9 asked whether simplification could diminish them. But since the quality of disclosures depends on how they are produced, we now examine the producers. Lawmakers presumably know what information disclosees need. How hard can it be to tell disclosers to provide it? Disclosers presumably have the information and use it themselves. How hard can it be to pass it on to those who need it?

Chapter 9 has already begun our work, for it described the lawmaker's problems deciding what must be disclosed. Disclosers must interpret lawmakers' edicts and implement them. In these often challenging tasks their incentives make disclosing too much the course of safety, since disclosing too little can excite the ire of regulators and inspire lawsuits from disclosees. "Firms may potentially incur tort liability penalties for underwarning. Yet there are no penalties levied for overwarning."[1] (Another nail in simplification's coffin.)

In every chapter we have found that mandated disclosure's deficiencies do not lie primarily in the failings of lawmakers, disclosers, or disclosees but in the nature of the regulatory device. At every stage looms the problem of reducing complexity to useful form. In this chapter we see that while disclosers often have reasons to fudge and smudge the data, their essential problem is that complexity makes it hard for lawmakers to write clear instructions and for disclosers to understand and obey them.

The discloser's most basic task is determining its duty: what should be included in the disclosure? Another task is assembling the data. They are not always at hand, and collecting them can be costly and fraught with troublesome judgments. Further, disclosers must usually decide how to present the information, a process we already know to be pocked with pitfalls. When decisions are complex, disclosers' capacity to collect, process, and deliver information can be more wish than reality.

Finally, disclosers may have incentives and even good reasons to resist mandates and to manipulate disclosures. To disclosers who want to obey the mandate's letter but flout its spirit, much is possible. They can heighten chapter 5's literacy problems. They can flood disclosees with information, exacerbating chapter 6's overload problem. They can exploit chapter 7's biases and heuristics.

THE DISCLOSER'S PERSPECTIVE

You are the president of Holystone College, a college in Houston. You are one of the great majority of colleges operating on the financial edge, competing for students and fighting to control expenses. For many reasons you want faculty, staff, and students (not to mention yourself) to be safe. Congress does too, but it treats safety as a problem of disclosure. The Clery Act (recall chapter 9), requires you (and some 6600 other colleges and universities) to publish an annual report including crime statistics for three years, policy statements, descriptions of crime-prevention, and procedures for handling sex offenses. And you must keep a public log of reported crimes and warn of crimes that threaten safety. This, the Department of Education says, will "provide students and their families, as higher education consumers, with accurate, complete, and timely information about safety on campus so that they can make informed decisions."[2]

The DOE warns ominously that "compliance with the Clery Act is not simply a matter of entering statistics into a web site or publishing a brochure once a year. Compliance is a whole system of developing policy statements, gathering information from all the required sources and translating it into the appropriate categories, disseminating information, and, finally, keeping records. Many people at your institution—from the president on down—should be involved."[3] The DOE has just sent you more than 300 pages of instructions in the new amendment to its "Handbook for Campus Safety and Security Reporting." At wealthier schools, you hear, trained staff interpret these oft-amended instructions but still "routinely struggle with the crime classifications." No surprise, since crime statistics are infamously hard to collect, categorize, and analyze. The DOE's instructions puzzle you. Aggravated assaults are reported by victim, but robberies are counted by incident. And what's a reportable campus crime? A crime committed on campus that harms someone unaffiliated with the college? A crime against a student seven miles off campus? One expert fields "five or six calls a week from colleges that need help figuring out what to report." She "always turns up errors in the way they are counting crimes" and has never found a fully compliant campus.[4]

You observe that resources diverted to complying with the Clery Act cannot be spent making your campus safer. And you find the act's incentives perverse: the more policing you do and the more you encourage students to report crimes, the worse your report looks. So how should you respond to the DOE's instructions?

Apparently experts "suspect that many institutions simply import numbers from the 'Clery complaint' software program sold to police departments and send off their reports," and "some colleges may manipulate

their numbers."[5] The complex instructions lead to long, technical disclosures. (The University of Michigan's report is forty pages for relatively safe
Ann Arbor.[6]) You are confident that nobody reads these reports anyway,
particularly not the potential students who are the ones with the real decision to make. Even if people did, what would they learn? They don't
know how crimes are reported and tallied, and since reports include total
crimes, not rates, the disclosures mean little to most readers. (Again, that
nagging denominator.) And if colleges interpret the instructions differently, reports cannot be used to compare colleges' safety, as the table from
Michigan's Clery Act report suggests (see plate 4).

FOLLOWING THE RULES

Mandates tell disclosers how to inform disclosees. Lawmakers write
mandates along a continuum from bright-line rules to discretionary
standards. At the rules end, mandates tell disclosers what to say; at the
discretion end, guidelines state a disclosure's general goals. Each end of
the continuum has virtues and faults. *Very* crudely, rules give lawmakers
more control, increase uniformity, and require less adjudication; discretion eases lawmakers' struggle to anticipate what situations will arise and
to determine how they should be handled (often leaving it to courts to
fine-tune mandates). For disclosers, mandates toward the rule end of
the continuum can be clearer (unless they get too numerous and complicated) but rigid; mandates toward the discretion end give disclosers
flexibility but may leave them uncertain how to give the mandate content.

At first glance rules look attractive, for they seem to tell disclosers
what is required of them so that they know what to do and cannot escape doing it. But the clarity of rules can be illusory. The Clery Act illustrates one way this can happen. There the discloser had to interpret
elaborate rules that seemed to require disclosures that made little sense
to the discloser. This is not uncommon, for complex social problems can
generate so many rules and amendments that confusion soon reigns. For
example, TILA and its implementing regulations turned out to be con-
tradictory from the start. They were gradually interpreted in countless
rulings (over 1500 official and unofficial interpretations from the Federal

Reserve) that left disclosers more befogged than before. Commentators thought compliance was "exceptionally difficult, perhaps even impossible."[7] Well-advised creditors could not comply. The Fed's own pamphlets for creditors did not comply. Many creditors found the Fed's Regulation Z "a conundrum too deep for either good will or high-priced intellect to solve."[8] Even after a simplification statute, TILA had a formidable body of "official staff commentary" that courts heeded and disclosers had to follow. And TILA is only one mandate in the area; other statutes add many more requirements.

What if a rule is truly simple? One such is the requirement we described in earlier chapters that restaurants post hygiene grades. Since the city inspects and issues the grade, disclosers need not interpret a mandate. As a "highly effective regime"[9] supposed to have reduced food-related hospitalizations by 20 percent,[10] it has been invoked and imitated. We once called it an apparent success for disclosure.[11] But Daniel Ho recently scrutinized restaurant grades in two of the largest cities using them (San Diego and New York). He found that grades have no discernible health benefits, distort the allocation of inspection resources, and mislead diners.[12]

One problem with this beautifully simple rule is that the disclosers (the restaurants) had enough influence to win the right to quick reinspections and to encourage grade inflation. New York restaurants scoring badly can reapply (and clean up) for a reinspection and meanwhile need not post the bad grade. On reinspection, a wonderfully high number of restaurants do just well enough to earn an A. In San Diego 99.9 percent of the restaurants get As. It takes a score of 90 or above to receive an A. Behold, 703 restaurants scored 90, only 2 scored 89.

But the more significant problem with this apparently simple rule is that the issues that complexity raises do not disappear. Rather, they must be resolved by the lawmaker itself. The goal is presumably not good decisions but safe restaurants, yet safety resists measurement. Cleanliness is a proxy, but a poor one. No method has "been found to summarize the factors in one score." New York's solution is to list about 100 kinds of violations with five severity levels and two to twenty-eight points per violation. New York "records separate violations for (i) '[e]vidence of rats or live rats,' (ii) '[e]vidence of mice or live mice,' (iii) '[l]ive roaches,' and (iv) 'flies,' each of which can be scored 5, 6, 7, 8, or 28 points, depending on the amount of evidence. Thirty 'fresh mice droppings in one area' result in 6 points, but 31 result in 7 points."[13] The grade is meaningful only if this elaborate grading scheme measures hygiene accurately, which would be a high intellectual achievement. Furthermore, the grade is meaningful only if the government's employees (the inspectors) can apply the criteria consistently. But they score "in drastically divergent ways." In one study mean scores (on a scale of 100) for experienced inspectors ranged from sixty-nine to ninety-two. And in New York "grades are not a particularly good predictor of future inspection scores."[14] The apparent objectivity of the scoring hides the discretion that inspectors have, for example, to decide how thoroughly to search for mouse droppings.

Sophisticated disclosurites hope for more reliable ways to collect and categorize information, thus easing problems of discretion. (Thaler and Sunstein propose a solution they call RECAP that is part of the federal smart-disclosure campaign.) Some product attributes (like miles per gallon) and even complex prices (like cell phone costs) can be managed in such ways, and we expect ingenuity and technology to make scores more accurate and give consumers better price information. But consistency is hard to achieve, as restaurant grading suggests.

A DISCRETIONARY MANDATE

Unhappily, there is no safety in the discretion end of the continuum. A doctor's duty to obtain informed consent typifies ways discretion can go wrong. Doctors need to know what is wanted of them and how to avoid tort liability. What happens when a leading case—*Canterbury v. Spence*—tries to answer those questions?[15]

Dr. Spence told Mr. Canterbury, a nineteen-year-old with severe back pain, that he needed spinal surgery (a laminectomy). After the operation and a fall Mr. Canterbury suffered from paralysis, which was a one-percent risk of the surgery but which (as he claimed in a suit four years later) Dr. Spence had not mentioned. What was the mandate? Disclosure, the court said, must let the patient "chart his course *understandably*," so he needed *"some familiarity* with the therapeutic alternatives and their hazards." (We italicize terms defining the legal standard.) "Full disclosure" is unrealistic, so the doctor should tell "the patient that which in his best interests it is *important* that he should know." That is, he needs *"enough information to enable an intelligent choice."*

What is "enough"? Well, *"adequate* disclosure." Or not *"unreasonably inadequate"* disclosure. Disclosure is "measured by 'good medical practices.'" It is measured "by the patient's *need,* and that need is the information *material* to the decision." So, *"all risks potentially affecting the decision* must be unmasked." The doctor should provide information "a *reasonable* person . . . would be likely to attach *significance* to."[16] With standards of understandability, reasonableness, materiality, significance, patient needs, good medical practice, adequacy, and inadequacy, no ascertainable line separates "the significant from the insignificant." So the answer "must abide a rule of reason."

Let's apply this rhetorical avalanche. You're the doctor. A drug's side effects include

> excess stomach acid secretion, irritation of the stomach or intestines, vomiting, heartburn, stomach cramps, bronchospasm, stomach ulcers, intestinal ulcers, hepatitis, stomach or intestinal bleeding, inflammation of skin, redness of skin, itching, hives, rash, wheezing, trouble breathing, life-threatening allergic reaction, giant hives, rupture in the wall of the stomach or intestines, hemolytic anemia, large skin blotches, decreased blood platelets, decreased white blood cells, and loss of appetite.[17]

You want to make "adequate" disclosure of the "important" risks, to "unmask" all the risks "potentially" affecting the patient's decision. Which side effects do you describe? All? The likeliest? The gravest? Which items meet your standard? Does your answer change if you know the drug is aspirin? Does it change again if you learn that NSAIDs like aspirin kill thousands of people yearly?[18]

All this grossly understates the mandate's obscurity. We have spoken only of describing risks of a specific treatment, but *Canterbury* requires disclosing "therapeutic alternatives and their hazards." What, then, to include? Don't forget that descriptions of illnesses and treatments "are necessarily incomplete, and patients and the public are likely to fill in the blanks idiosyncratically, with . . . personal experiences or stereotypes."[19]

It is tempting to blame disclosers for poor disclosures, especially since they may have reasons to undermine a mandate. But the same interpretive problems arise when a *regulator* is doing the interpreting. Every researcher working with human subjects must receive a license to conduct the experiment from a review committee called an IRB. The review is predominantly about disclosure, and IRBs have plenary discretion to decide what disclosure is needed. The result is that in multisite studies, when many IRBs review the same protocol, the regulators (IRBs) disagree wildly about what should be disclosed and how. When the same consent form was submitted to forty-four IRBs, more than 90 percent demanded revisions, but "the requested revisions varied widely from site to site."[20] In Green's forty-three-site study, IRBs reviewed identical forms, and a large proportion demanded revisions. But the revisions the IRBs wanted differed so much that the researchers could not detect any pattern; "they comprised a wide range of requests for deleting or adding sentences or paragraphs, phrasing, tense, and word choice."[21] As one study acidly concluded, when multiple IRBs review the same protocol, they treat it so disparately that "IRBs seemed to behave in ways that defied any pattern" except that they "approve inappropriate investigations and inhibit appropriate investigations."[22]

We have described problems at both the rules and discretion ends of the continuum. The reason for these problems is a familiar one. Earlier chapters described the complexity of the problems that mandates address and the difficulties that disclosees have in understanding that complexity. Lawmakers and disclosers face these same problems when they present complex information to disclosees. Someone—the lawmaker, the discloser, or both—must analyze the complexity, must decide how to aggregate, filter, sort, average, weigh, rank, and repackage the disorderly data. Whoever does the work, the problem is the same: when the data's complexity is preserved, disclosees struggle. But when the complexity is simplified (as in the restaurant-grading regime), accuracy is sacrificed. There is no happy solution to the problems of rules and discretion. Regulators can choose their spot on the continuum, but when they walk toward one blessing, they walk away from another.

DELIVERING DISCLOSURES

Even under the sweetly optimistic assumption that disclosers truly understand and truly try to comply with mandates, much will affect the quality of their disclosures. They face challenges in collecting information, presenting it, and disclosing it through agents, and they have reasons both good and bad to manipulate and resist disclosures.

Collecting the Information

If the discloser can tell what data to reveal, it must locate and assemble them. But much can go wrong. First, information is often inaccessible, or elusive, or scattered, or unknown, or overwhelming. In Illinois private business and vocational schools must disclose enrollments; students' graduation, licensing, and employment rates; and graduates' salaries.[23] How many universities have such information or can get it (from balky graduates)? Many businesses must post long lists of information. Rent-to-own laws require as many as seventeen items, used-car laws more than thirty.

Information must be monitored and updated. Disclosers must identify changes, revise disclosures, and try to contact past disclosees. In some areas disclosees need detailed updates often. For example, some disclosurites think consent to research expires when significant changes have occurred in "(a) the nature of the research itself, as determined by its purpose, risks, potential benefits, requirements, and alternatives; (b) the individual's personal and medical situations; and (c) the individual's preferences and interests."[24]

Problems of Presentation

Suppose the discloser can tell what to disclose, can assemble and process it, and now must present it. How? This question has looked easy to lawmakers and scholars. It is not.

First, complexity (again) creates dilemmas. Mandates in many areas—medicine, consumer credit, product warnings—warn of risks. The problem is not just the complexity of what you're describing; it's also the ambiguity of language. "Different people interpret given chance terms very differently," and even the same person may interpret the same term differently depending on its context.[25] Research in a medical setting found that even absolute terms were variously interpreted. Only four-fifths "agreed that *certain* meant 100 of 100 people," while only two-thirds "agreed that *never* meant zero of 100 people."[26] One study found doctors' interpretations of "likely" ranging "from 25 to 75%," and another study found interpretations of "very likely" ranging "from 30 to 90%, even when presented in a restricted medical context."[27]

Numbers offer no escape. For example, risks can be stated as rates or proportions. Genetic counselors (specialists in describing risk to the uninformed) have believed "that women understand proportions better than rates" even though there is "no scientific evidence" of it. But in a study, "more than three times as many women (151) judged risks correctly with rates alone, compared with only proportions (41)," and "many women (129) did not understand either format."[28] Presumably responding to such problems, two lawmakers—the European Union and a UK agency—proposed substituting words for numbers. But the EU's terms "lead to considerable overestimations of risk by patients, doctors and the general public." "Common" meant "side effects that occur in 1–10% of people," but patients thought the word meant around 45 percent and doctors thought it meant around 25 percent.[29]

Presenting ideas and concepts is hardly easier. *Miranda* looks straightforward: police must tell suspects in custody about several rights. But how? Two surveys "yielded 945 distinct Miranda warnings from 638 jurisdictions" and "122 juvenile English warnings and 121 general Spanish warnings." They ranged from 21 to 408 words and averaged 96. Reading levels differed remarkably; a fifth were written below a sixth-grade reading level, most at a sixth- to eighth-grade level, and 2 percent "needed at least some college education."[30]

Disclosers find that human situations are trickier than lawmakers anticipate. Disclosers with bad news tend to soften it, perhaps rightly: "Mildly but unrealistically positive beliefs can improve outcomes in patients with chronic or terminal diseases," and "unrealistically optimistic views have been shown to improve quality of life."[31] Thus cancer patients were even more optimistic about their prognoses than their optimistic doctors, partly because physicians avoided discussing prognoses, with-held prognostic information, or were unduly optimistic.[32]

Then there is the torrent of detail that mandates loose. Consumer-directed health care—that hopes to teach patients to use care better and buy it more shrewdly—must overcome the fact that health plans offer many kinds of care of differing quality and flexibility and have varying reimbursement rules, costs, and co-pays. Plans change often, sometimes annually, requiring disclosers to revise what they say. The Affordable Care Act, as we said earlier, has devised a summary of benefits and costs intended to be used easily. But when tested, "the vast majority of respondents" had trouble. As they worked with the forms, "the concepts they needed to estimate cost-sharing became much more confusing—terms like coinsurance, allowed amount, and annual limits, for example." This "not only frustrated respondents but could lead them to select a plan that was not actually in their best interest."[33]

In health care, disclosers interpret broad mandates and reasonably infer that they require—or that prudence demands—telling all. HIPAA obliges providers to describe possible uses of patients' health informa-tion. This produces detailed and deadly disclosures:

> We may make your personal health information (PHI) available electron-ically through health information exchanges (HIEs) to other health care providers, health plans and health care clearinghouses. Participation in HIEs also lets us see their information about you which helps us provide care to you. You have the right to opt out of participating in such efforts by contacting the person listed at the end of this notice.[34]

Can privacy practices be better described? Michigan's notice is rela-tively good, with lay language, a friendly tone, repeated instructions on opting out, and many examples. The problem is less the words than the lushness of legitimate uses.

As digital databases grow, their use of personal information has become a concern, but few people know how that personal information is collected, analyzed, stored, and sold. After deliberating several years, the FTC asked "companies providing mobile services to work toward improved privacy protections," including "short, meaningful disclosures." It "urges" companies to make practices "transparent" and to consider Web sites where data brokers describe how data are collected and used and what consumers can do about it.[35] But not even the FTC's experts could tell disclosers how to do it.

Disclosing Through Agents

Another presentational challenge is the agency problem. Lawyers write disclosures, but they are distributed by people who often know little. They may be bored, their audience alienated. Some agents deliver information like automata, radiating weariness and impatience, urging people to sign without reading, dismissing disclosures as just fine print. And rather than struggle to explain choices to patients, some doctors use forms delivered by subordinates (like nurses, technicians, and social workers). Furthermore, those forms may contain nonmedical material (like liability disclaimers and arbitration clauses) that even doctors can't explain.

Thus the weary car-rental agent points to the lines for your signature or initials, the weary flight attendant recites the safety liturgy, and the weary title-company agent quick steps through your pile of papers. One of us, refinancing his mortgage, paused in his work (which, thanks to the efficient agent, took less than forty minutes, despite 101 pages and fifty-three signatures) to ask about the "Borrower's Certificate of Net Tangible Benefits." Above the signature line were menacing words: IMPORTANT NOTICE TO BORROWERS: DO NOT SIGN THIS DOCUMENT UNTIL YOU READ IT CAREFULLY AND FULLY UNDERSTAND IT. YOUR SIGNATURES BELOW MEAN THAT YOU HAVE DONE BOTH. "Oh," said the agent, busily notarizing, "that's just some information your lender wants you to sign." Thus reassured, the law professor signed. The form said, "I understand that lender will rely upon this Borrower's Certificate of Net Tangible Benefit as an agreement and certification that this refinance transaction results in a benefit to me." How could the agent know this was a warning about loan-flipping scams?

Resisting and Manipulating the Disclosure

Even earnest disclosers can confront daunting problems informing disclosees, but disclosers may wish to resist the mandate. Police may question suspects "outside *Miranda*."[36] Financial and car-rental agencies may not say that their insurance is duplicative.[37] And lending-disclosure re-quirements may "create incentives for lenders to draft contract terms that evade current disclosure regulation and continue to obscure the actual contract terms."[38]

Still, policy ought not be driven by stereotypes about malign non-disclosers. Many disclosers are not evil; many disclosers have reasons to behave well; and many disclosers obey mandates. Furthermore, scrupu-lous disclosers may resist mandates for plausible reasons. The mandate is often one of many commands, incentives, and pressures in their work. Disclosers want to get that work done, and disclosures can be irrelevant to and even inconsistent with that. For example, doctors and hospitals swim in disclosure requirements. But they properly concentrate on cur-ing illness and soothing suffering, which alone wholly outstrip their available time. (A typical doctor cannot provide just the *preventive* care that guidelines prescribe, and "comprehensive high-quality management of 10 common chronic illnesses require[s] more time than primary care physicians have available for patient care overall."[39])

Disclosers may consider a mandate not only burdensome, but use-less and even pernicious (as Holystone College's president probably did). They know disclosures are unread and unheeded. They find that no mat-ter how precise they are, people give some information undue weight. For example, doctors may fear that patients' tendency to exaggerate risks of side effects will deter them from following treatment instructions, and doctors know that baseline noncompliance is woefully high. In a French study, "[o]nly 44% of the rheumatologists regularly told their patients about possible serious side effects and only 7% about life-threatening side effects." But patients were told about the consequences of not taking medication "all the time" or "fairly often" by as many as 88 percent of the rheumatologists. The researchers concluded that the physicians worried "that concern about side effects may cause poor compliance."[40]

Resisting mandates can be easy. They can be ignored. European leg-islation requires that patients be given "all the information that is pro-vided to health professionals in the summary of product characteristics, including all adverse effects, but in a form understandable to the patient." In a recent study, 40 percent of the leaflets "gave no indication of the like-lihood of any adverse effect."[41]

Or disclosers can dress up disclosures. They can beautify language. When health plans had to reveal how their doctors were paid, "almost none" mentioned that doctors' payment regimes might distort their judgment. They more often bathed incentives in positive language by saying, for example, that they rewarded better care.[42] Since there are so many interests that may affect doctors and so many ways for doctors to be compensated, HMOs can hardly escape obfuscation: "there are literally over 100,000 ways to pay, and these systems are very proprietary [and] the plans change them all the time."[43]

Or disclosers may put unpleasantness in fine print. True, this may make the disclosure inadequate, and securities law has developed a "buried facts doctrine" (violated by, for example, sliding a statement about directors' conflicts of interest into the appendix of a 200-page document).[44] But litigation is cumbersome, and outside securities law there is less attention to buried facts.

Finally, disclosers can disclose too much, exploiting the overload problem.[45] (This is common enough to have a name—overshadowing.) In consumer-debt collection, for example, swamping consumers with so many forms and words that they miss the four-paragraph description of some fairly powerful consumer rights is easy. One creditor put the disclosure on page eight of a sixteen-page letter.[46] Even a major bank hid a significant overdraft disclosure on page twenty-four of a sixty-page, ten-point-font agreement.[47] Congress responded with a law: "Any Collection activities and communication during the 30-day period may not overshadow or be inconsistent with the consumer's right to dispute the debt or request the name and address of the original creditor."[48]

AN ILLUSTRATION: PRODUCING A CONFLICT-OF-INTEREST DISCLOSURE

We have argued that unfamiliar and complex choices are hard to explain effectively. We now proffer an example of what happens when a discloser truly tries to do it. The regulator responsible for the committees that license research and researchers' disclosures thinks that disclosing conflicts of interest "would not take much work." Such disclosures are often mandated, since "the self-serving bias affects virtually every category of professional, including lawyers, physicians, auditors, . . . investment bankers, securities analysts, scientists, policy researchers, expert witnesses, judges, and, of course, stock brokers."[49] Disclosurites have been firm, even fiery; as we noted earlier, one conflict-of-interest committee chair said that the future of academic health centers depends on doing conflicts oversight "right."[50] So let's write it right.

Since we are writing for disclosees, we should ask what they need to know to make better decisions. Only a minority of them in one study "thought such financial information would influence their decisions about research participation in any way," and in two large studies of enrolling in "hypothetical clinical trials, most respondents rated financial disclosure as the least important factor in their decision about whether to participate."[51] They often did not want the information "because it did not matter to them or was perceived as a burden."[52] If we use *Canterbury's* reasonable-person standard, conflicts disclosure looks unnecessary, but our mandate requires it. So we begin.

First, where should we put the disclosure in our consent form? In one survey, some "investigators, IRBs, and conflict of interest committees" wanted it "early in the consent process," even "near the top of the consent document." Others wanted it highlighted but worried that this would imply "that the financial disclosure is more important than other components" of the form.[53] So we can't tell where to put this disclosure until we have prioritized the others.

Next, how do we describe conflicts? One study, we may recall, "went to unusual lengths to ensure that the essential information was conveyed. Information about incentives was disclosed by mail, followed by phone calls in which subjects' understanding was tested and reinforced through repetition and simple quiz questions." But even though the study "greatly increas[ed] knowledge of incentives," a majority still could not answer more than half the questions they were asked. So "even the extensive and [horribly] impractical methods used here to attempt to convey only limited knowledge of incentives" did poorly.[54]

And is "only limited knowledge of incentives" enough? Incentives can include awarding "stock contingent on certain occurrences, licensing rights, 'put' options, seed money for commercial start-ups, limited partnership and other joint venture opportunities, royalty-based payments, and specialized grant funding." Incentives "vary in intensity and impact depending on the overall context, such as the number of other investigators sharing the same incentive, how the incentive is actually calculated, the amount of money to be earned compared to an investigator's other compensation sources, the time period over which the incentive is applied, and whether the institution as a whole shares in the incentive."[55] No wonder one study found that "many people have trouble" understanding "financial relationships in clinical research" and that some focus group members "remained confused" about some interests "even after 2 hours of discussion."[56]

Well, assume we've succeeded where others fail. We now learn that some disclosees see no problem with researchers consulting for drug companies, holding drug patents, or owning stock in a company, and some—including educated people "with long term experience in research at the NIH"—think such interests "a *positive* sign" that researchers will be spurred to do good work.[57] These people thought "financial incentives for investigators were expected, integral to the research process, and deserved."[58] Should we respect their belief? Or disclose and disclose until they recognize their error?

But come closer, Starbuck; thou requirest a little lower layer. Suppose people understand the conflict. What are they to do? Having a conflict is not misbehaving; it is, perhaps, having an incentive to misbehave. Our disclosees need to know how likely the discloser is to succumb. How corrupt are our researchers? How tempting is the incentive? How will it bias what our researchers do? The real problem with conflicts is not "overt corruption," but "unintentional and unconscious" behavior.[59] If disclosees don't understand all this, our disclosure will help them little. So we'd better tell them.

Now—we'll recklessly suppose—subjects have read and understood the disclosure and understand the actual incentives and psychological mechanism of the conflict. Will they understand how it might affect them? For example, "few can imagine" their own doctor succumbing. Should you—can you—bring that danger home? Should you tell them that people "tend to overestimate their ability to evaluate 'trustworthiness'"?[60] That trust and a fear of offending the discloser tend to deter disclosees from taking conflicts seriously?[61] That disclosing conflicts can *increase* trust? "Research suggests that when managers offer negative financial disclosures about future earnings," they become "more credible agents, at least in the short term."[62] And in one study "insinuation anxiety" led disclosees to rely *more* on advice after a conflicts disclosure lest they seem insolently distrustful.[63]

The point of our disclosure is to help people make better decisions. But how *should* they respond to a conflict? Discount everything the researcher says by some percentage? Reject some information as false but accept some as true? Investigate further? Should you warn disclosees of the experiment finding "moral licensing"—a tendency to exaggerate advice when you are compelled to disclose your conflict?

In our epigraph an OHRP director says that disclosing conflicts is "easily accomplished," since it "would not take much work to add a brief paragraph in the consent form mentioning" the conflict. We have just spent several pages *beginning* that work. It is *not* "easily accomplished." Nor are thousands of other disclosures.

CONCLUSION

Mandated disclosure is supposed to improve disclosees' decisions by supplying information. The information's usefulness depends on how it is produced and presented. As we have just seen, both processes encounter our old problem—the complexity of the choices that mandates typically address. Lawmakers must sort through that complexity to see what disclosees need to know and then write mandates effectively instructing disclosers.

Law governing complex situations is written along a continuum from rules to discretion. Rules seem to give lawmakers more control over disclosers, but lawmakers cannot easily read the complexity, anticipate all the issues the rules present, or foresee how conditions will change. This leads to rules too elaborate or confusing to be interpreted, as the TILA and Clery Act experiences suggest. That leaves the earnest discloser unguided and the devious discloser free to manipulate the mandate. Yet discretion has just the same effect, as our discussion of informed consent showed. Failing to recognize their dilemma, lawmakers oscillate between the ends of the continuum. If TILA's rules fail, some disclosurites would give courts and experts discretion to decide whether a disclosure "effectively communicated" the "key terms" of a mortgage.[64] When discretionary standards for residential-sales disclosures leave disclosers unguided, states adopt rules intended to replace discretion.

So lawmakers struggle to instruct disclosers, and disclosers struggle to understand their instructions. And once disclosers think they understand the instructions, they must apply them, which can mean not just collecting information but presenting it effectively. As our attempt to write a conflict-of-interest disclosure showed, disclosers confront a long series of challenging choices. Ultimately, if disclosees are to be given complex information, somebody must reduce the complexity to useful form. That involves judgments that can defeat both lawmakers and disclosers.

CHAPTER 11

AT WORST, HARMLESS?

Disclosure is also inexpensive and, at worst, harmless.

—Robert Hillman and Maureen O'Rourke, Reporters,
ALI Principles of the Law of Software Contracts,
Defending Disclosure in Software Licensing

Hillman and O'Rourke recite a common and consequential idea about mandated disclosure—the harmlessness hypothesis. Justice Breyer thinks disclosure is popular despite frequent ineffectiveness because "at worst, too much information, or the wrong information, has been called for."[1] The harmlessness hypothesis goes without substantiating evidence; underlying it is probably both the more-information-is-better mantra and a rough judgment that disclosure's burden is so negligible that even slight and spotty benefits would outweigh it.

Mandated disclosure is not harmless if its costs outweigh its benefits. This chapter argues that mandates have costs, sometimes big ones. Mandates can do harm, harm that is disproportionately borne by exactly the people who most need protection. This harm is unintended and unnoticed, but harm it is—and in several forms: mandates can undercut other regulation, deter lawmakers from adopting better regulation, impair decisions, injure markets, exacerbate inequality, and in some important cases, cripple valuable enterprises.

Mandates impose various direct costs on both disclosers and disclosees. For example, disclosers expend resources in collecting elusive information. They pay someone (often lawyers) to draft the millions of words cast to the winds. Some disclosers must mail disclosures to thousands of disclosees annually or even more often. Many transactions are nontrivially prolonged by disclosure rituals. Doctors and hospitals must solicit signatures on (and store) billions of HIPAA, PSDA, treatment-consent, and research-consent forms. Lenders labor to interpret disclosure rules, present the disclosures, collect signatures, and store them. Furthermore, we all spend uncounted hours dealing with disclosures, sometimes even reading them. The time is spent intermittently in small doses and so is little noticed, but aggregated, "costless" is not the word that comes to mind.

MAKING REGULATION WORSE

Mandated disclosure can undermine other regulation and ease pressure on lawmakers to enact better but more controversial regulation. Thus bad law drives out better.

Undermining Other Regulation

It is little noticed that mandated disclosure can undermine other forms of regulation, so we give several examples. First, disclosures can diminish courts' ability to protect injured consumers. Manufacturers sometimes choose between avoiding liability by designing a safer product or warning users about the product's risks. As the Restatement (Second) of Torts says, "when adequate warning is given, the seller may reasonably assume that it will be read and heeded," and a product that is safe if the warning is heeded is neither defective nor unreasonably dangerous.[2]

Consumers should certainly watch out for themselves, but tort law expects us to read fine print, package inserts, and instruction manuals, even if the product is draped in cascades of warnings (like the famous aluminum ladder with forty-four of them).[3] For example, manufacturers can sell a lawnmower without a guard and escape liability for lost toes if the booklet warns of the danger. Why engineer costly precautions when lawyers can offer a safe harbor at a fraction of the cost? Thus product liability law, which protects people through incentives to produce safer products and compensation for injuries, is undermined by disclosure.[4]

Second, disclosure also displaces regulatory protection in consumer law. Consider loan flipping, which few of our readers but many poorer Americans have encountered. Loan flipping is inducing borrowers to keep refinancing a loan so that they incur repeated closing fees, buy unnecessary points, and even exchange a low-interest for a high-interest loan or an unsecured loan for one secured by their home. Verna Emery[5] borrowed $2000 from her bank, promising to pay back $1300 in finance charges over three years (36 percent interest). The loan was secured by household items. A few months later the bank's branch manager wrote her a letter:

> Dear Verna:
> I have extra spending money for you.
>   Does your car need a tune-up? Want to take a trip? Or, do you just want to pay off some of your bills? We can lend you money for whatever you need or want.
>   You're a good customer. To thank you for your business, I've set aside $750.00 in your name . . . . Just bring the coupon below into my office and if you qualify, we could write your check on the spot. Or, call ahead and I'll have the check waiting for you . . . .

Verna showed up with the coupon, and the bank *was* ready. But instead of getting an additional loan, Verna was induced to refinance her old one. The bank gave Verna $2400, of which $2000 paid off the prior loan, $200 covered new closing expenses, and $200 went to Verna as the "extra spending money." She agreed to pay $1200 more than under the old loan. When she sued for fraud, the bank showed it had complied with the truth-in-lending mandates—it had recited Verna's APR, her total payments, the finance charges, and the fees. She said that the bank did not tell her that she could have borrowed less calamitously. But citing the bank's compliance with TILA, the trial court dismissed the suit.

That is what most American courts do. But on appeal in Verna's case, Judge Richard Posner held that the bank's compliance with TILA did not bar Verna's claim. "[W]orking-class borrowers" like Verna don't understand the "computations necessary to determine the comparative cost" of loan flipping. They "do not read Truth in Lending Act disclosure terms intelligently" and are tricked into "overpaying disastrously for credit." Posner wrote:

> She is no "Dear Verna" to them; she has not been selected to receive the letter because she is a good customer, but because she belongs to a class of probably gullible customers for credit; the purpose of offering her more money is not to thank her for her business but to rip her off. . . . "I'll have the check waiting for you." Yes—along with a few forms to sign whereby for only $1,200 payable over three years at an even higher monthly rate than your present loan . . . , you can have a meager $200 now.

Suppose, he asked, "that Verna were blind. Or retarded. Would anyone argue that shoving a Truth in Lending Act disclosure form in front of her face would be a defense to fraud?"

Well, yes, consumer law would. TILA's shield is what the dissenting judge invoked: Defeating all Verna's arguments was the "simple and uncontroverted fact" that the bank "fully complied with the disclosure requirements of both the federal Truth in Lending Act and the Illinois Consumer Installment Loan Act."[6] By enacting TILA, Congress provided "all the protection it deems appropriate for borrowers, be they financially astute or ill-informed and gullible." Thus are sleazy practices washed clean by technically accurate disclosures.

Disclosure also undercuts rules against unconscionable contracts, as Hillman warned.[7] A contract is unconscionable if its terms are unfair *and* the bargaining was tainted. Taint is ordinarily proved by showing that the unfair term was hidden and thus not consented to. But how can you claim surprise if you got a PROMINENT DISCLOSURE in ALLCAPS and initialed it? An empty formality saves the unconscionable contract. Thus, a court upheld a one-sided and unfair arbitration clause in a cell phone contract because it was disclosed (in a thicket of fine print in a "welcome kit") prominently enough (it began with an "ARBITRATION" heading and came "early" in the long form) that the consumer was not "surprised." Other courts have agreed.[8] Similarly, disclosure of an advisor's conflict of interest could limit remedies for tainted advice, and disclosure of insider trades may impede suits alleging securities fraud.[9]

Mandated disclosure can also undermine people's ability to protect themselves. Voluntary disclosures can signal care, knowledge, experience, and even compassion. A doctor or banker who volunteers information seems trustworthy and dependable, but mandates obscure the difference between revealers (good guys who volunteer information) from concealers (bad guys who must be forced). Mandated disclosures can also be hijacked: some commentators believe police use *Miranda* to inveigle suspects into seeing the police as their friends. And Willis says that disclosures give mortgages a "veneer of legality" that makes consumers incautious.[10] The privacy policies of Web sites are not vows to protect privacy but announcements of plans to collect data, yet the disclosures' very presence soothes consumers' privacy worries and builds trust in the firm, however long and opaque the policy.[11] And recall the experiment that found that disclosing a conflict of interest tends to increase disclosees' trust of disclosers (and encourage disclosers to be especially emphatic when giving advice).

Precluding Better Regulation

Lawmakers beset by trouble stories have a repertoire of policies. They could protect Verna Emery by forbidding unfair practices, making unethical lenders liable in tort, authorizing regulators to enjoin deceptions, punishing misconduct civilly or criminally, or licensing lenders. But finding the right tools is hard, and regulation with bite usually brings out the lobbyists. So lawmakers must seize moments when urgency is felt, political agreement is possible, and funds can be found. Mandates virtually invite lawmakers to spare themselves this travail because (for reasons that chapter 9 described) mandates appeal to almost everybody and offend almost nobody. Even businesses often prefer disclosure to more restrictive regulation.

The Clery Act's campus-crime disclosures illustrate one way this works. The resources the Act commandeers for collecting and reporting crime data would be better spent making schools safer. One criminologist called the mandate "symbolic politics" and said that safety is likelier to come from installing blue-light telephones and security cameras. "That's just one fix, he says, for a system that revolves around complex annual reports, a huge investment with little return." He wants to give up "producing a bunch of statistics that are basically useless."[12] Similarly, Ho's meticulous study of restaurant-grading disclosures concluded that they shifted agency resources "from compliance inspections (generally at worse-scoring restaurants) to reinspections (generally at better-scoring restaurants)."[13]

A battle over contract-law disclosures also illustrates the tension between mandated disclosure and better regulation. Contract terms sometimes come inside shrink-wrapped boxes. In 1996 Judge Frank Easterbrook wrote an opinion[14] which many courts followed holding that consumers are bound by such terms if customers who disliked them could return the item. Under this rule the consumer gains a right—to return the purchase.[15] But the opinion incensed disclosurites, who believed that buyers should be able to read the terms first. Eventually the American Law Institute's Principles of the Law of Software Contracts announced a "preferred strategy"—"to promote reading of terms" before contracting and "to increase the opportunity to read." (The principles are not law but are influential.) This would "increase the number of readers of standard forms" and make assent more "meaningful" and "robust."[16] So the consumer would lose the right to withdraw from the contract and get another disclosure.

How will the CFPB protect people like Verna Emery? Will it prohibit such deceptive marketing? Institute harsher sanctions? Limit loan flipping? Revoke licenses? Forbid the risky loans common in the subprime market? Or will the mountain labor to produce useful reforms, only to bring forth the mouse of disclosure? Then-Secretary of the Treasury Geithner's announcement that the new bureau would "dramatically" improve disclosures fits this history. His subordinates have warned that "merely simplifying disclosure to those consumers unlikely or unable to shop for a loan . . . cannot be expected to protect them from abuse." They have warned that disclosure mandates "without other protections, can have the unintended effect of insulating predatory lenders."[17] But (as we saw in chapter 9) Geithner continued to chant the disclosurite creed.

MAKING DECISIONS WORSE

Not only do disclosures generally fail to improve decisions, they can make them worse. First, the more-information-is-better mantra is more appealing than true. More information is not better if it is wrong, or misleadingly incomplete, or irrelevant, or likely to lead people to over- or under-emphasize elements of a decision. Disclosure succeeds only if people get the right information at the right time in the right quantity in the right way with the right emphasis *and* interpret and use it in the right fashion. But this, we need hardly repeat, asks much of lawmakers, disclosers, and disclosees.

Second, drenching people in information is a poor way to improve their decisions. For example, consider the "crowding out" effect. As Craswell writes, disclosures may "reduce the attention consumers pay to other information, conceivably leading to worse decisions."[18] Craswell suggests, for example, that disclosing brokerage fees can lead consumers to overestimate a loan's cost. Similarly, pension-plan participants are awash in seas of disclosures with waves of data about defined-contribution plans, 401(k) enrollment, company-stock diversification, distributions, and rights-to-defer. And some disclosurites have urged disclosing yet more detailed information about fund-managers' fees. This heightens the overload problem, but it might also lead investors to give fees more weight than they merit. In short, brightly illuminating narrow slices of a problem can leave the rest of the picture darker.

Sometimes mandates reduce the likelihood that other information will be provided. For example, marginally useful medical disclosures can drive out necessary but unmandated information. Mandates oblige providers to tell patients about advance directives, privacy policies, risks and benefits of treatment choices, side effects, safety, cost, conflicts of interest, and sometimes insurance. After this, how much is left in the tank for literally vital information, like how to manage a chronic illness? People must be patiently taught and persistently prompted to fill the prescription, take the right dose at the right time, and not stop early. (About half the people who are prescribed medicine don't do all these things.) Thus overweening mandates crowd out essential but strenuous teaching.

Disclosures can also make people overconfident. In one study, for example, university staff members were given several hours of financial training alone or in small groups. Their ability to consider information and manage tasks improved modestly, especially among the least knowledgeable. But while skills improved, decisions didn't. People made errors that would have depleted their assets long before their (actuarial) demise. Yet they thought the training had improved their decisions. So "training may do more harm than good—individuals may feel confident that the quality of their financial planning efforts are sound, despite clear objective evidence to the contrary."[19]

MAKING MARKETS WORSE

Mandated disclosure is supposed to improve markets by improving information, but it sometimes impairs markets. For example, mandates can induce disclosers to direct resources toward what they must report and away from what they need not. In 2002 the Center for Medicare and Medicaid Services launched the Nursing Home Quality Initiative, which replaced an ineffective disclosure regime that reported more than 190 quality dimensions. The new report card began with only ten measures (e.g., "percent of residents with pressure sores") and grew to fifteen. There was encouraging evidence that clients were consulting report cards and that homes were making improvements in the areas measured. However, the number of deficiency citations from random inspections—the study's measure of a nursing home's quality—grew. So, nursing homes did better in the areas where they were scored and worse in other areas, with the losses more than offsetting the gains.[20]

When disclosures report overall customer satisfaction, there is less room for strategizing. People find such ratings more useful and rely on them more. This is true in a variety of transactions, from buying a $10 flash drive on eBay to choosing health plans. A study of 40 million Medicare enrollees showed a substantial shift toward health plans with better report cards. Enrollees did not respond to data about a plan's specifics; they listened to satisfaction ratings.[21]

Years ago, Easterbrook and Fischel argued that mandated disclosure benefits larger enterprises because disclosure's costs are generally the same whatever the enterprise's size.[22] For example, vocational schools in some states have disclosure burdens that require investments that small schools can ill afford. Even when disclosers do not compete directly, mandates can favor large, rich, and sophisticated endeavors and discourage small, poor, and unsophisticated ones. For example, the IRB system that regulates disclosures to prospective research subjects has grown so exigent that 15 percent of the research budget in multisite studies can go to dealing with the regulators. Well-funded researchers can afford to pay for this; poorer researchers cannot. Long-term projects may be able to spend months getting IRB agreement on disclosures; if short-term projects cannot get approval quickly, they must be curtailed or abandoned.

We argued that mandated disclosure is too weak to constrain unscrupulous lenders, but occasionally it is too powerful. John Dalton and Arnold Lowery bought cars they financed through the dealer.[23] They paid $4 for license and title fees, which the dealer forwarded to the DMV, but the dealer did not itemize these charges on the disclosure statements. Dalton and Lowery each sued to recover $2000 in statutory damages under TILA for that failure. The court complained about the shakedown but obediently found for the plaintiffs. (Lowery similarly sued at least two other creditors.) More commonly, debtors invoke disclosure violations as a defense against creditors. A debtor in arrears can often find some technical failure to comply with the elaborate disclosure requirements. Since violations are easy to prove and trigger automatic statutory damages and attorney's fees, the creditor cannot recover the debt and might even have to recompense the consumer. One commentator called this the "disclosure defense game."[24] And sometimes home buyers invoke disclosure technicalities to renege on home purchases (because prices have dropped).[25]

Such tactics harm creditors and markets. They do not discriminate between good and bad creditors or meritorious and frivolous consumer complaints. They waste resources by "transforming loan documents into contest puzzles in which prizes are awarded to those who can uncover technical defects"[26]—all of which makes credit more expensive and obliges honest debtors to subsidize the unscrupulous.

EXACERBATING INEQUALITY

Disclosurites say that mandates honor human dignity and protect the weak. But mandates tend to help least those who most need help and help most those who need help least.

Helping the Rich

The poor and ill educated generally have fewer and worse choices than the prosperous and well educated. They have harder decisions and, living on the economic precipice, more to lose from bad ones. They pay higher interest rates, deal with shadier lenders and vendors, and lacking other resources, must rely on them more. They can afford only inferior and riskier products. They have worse health plans, more risk, and less insurance. They rarely consult professionals, much less the ablest ones.

These are, then, the people regulation needs most to help, but the reasons they lack information and expertise also diminish their ability to use disclosures. They are ill informed because they cannot read easily or use numbers well. Yet reading and numbers are what mandates supply. They misunderstand information because they lack a baseline understanding of problems and the sector literacy necessary to interpret them. But disclosures generally assume that disclosees have that baseline understanding and that literacy.

So even though the poor and little educated need more aid in dealing with stronger parties, the help they get from mandated disclosure is the kind least likely to assist them. This is not only a logical supposition, it is supported by empirical evidence. Poor consumers are less helped by some kinds of educational campaigns. Low-income parents are more fatalistic about children's exposure to hazards and less influenced by safety warnings, even though their children are disproportionately exposed to hazards.[27] Financial education helps the prosperous more than the poor. Older and wealthier shoppers are likelier to benefit from disclosures because they read them more easily. Information disclosed in the sale of used cars—the car's safety and repair history, odometer readings, and warranties—seems not to help the poor, who continue to pay more for worse cars.[28] This problem also affects nutrition data, hospital report cards, informed consent, vaccinations, preventive dental care, gun handling, and seatbelts.

Medical disclosures suffer from the same problems. As chapter 5 reported, ordinary people cannot read many consent forms. A study of the ten best resources for learning about prostate cancer—presumably developed by people skilled at their work—found that even though they did not give patients enough information to help them make decisions, all but one were too difficult for the average adult to read.[29] Another study examined the model HIPAA authorization forms of elite medical centers. "Nearly all of them had inappropriately complex language on all 3 readability scales."[30]

Furthermore, the choice of which disclosures to mandate appears to be influenced by upper-middle-class concerns about risk, health, privacy, finances, the environment, and accountability. Many educational disclosures—about retirement savings, Internet privacy, health-plan choice, mandatory arbitration in consumer contracts, college choice, restaurant patronage, and nutrition—particularly correspond to middle-class and elite concerns.

Anatole France wrote that the law, "in its majestic equality, forbids the rich as well as the poor to sleep under bridges, to beg in the streets, and to steal bread." Here, the law's mandates are offered to all, but the poor are least likely to use them. Disclosures are walnuts distributed to everybody, but only those with teeth can bite. The poster cases for disclosure, those whose hardships and trouble stories sparked the process that generated the mandates, gain least.

Taking from the Poor

If the prosperous benefit more from disclosures, they should pay more. But disclosure's burdens often fall disproportionately on those least likely to enjoy them. For example, hospital report cards may have made things better for the rich and worse for the poor. Healthier patients go to better-rated hospitals; sicker patients are treated in hospitals with worse grades. Thus Dranove et al. concluded that report cards led to "marginal health benefits for healthy patients, and major adverse health conse- quences for sicker patients." Overall, people were worse off.[31] Wealthier credit-card users get free cards and frequent-flyer miles while paying al- most no fees and lower interest. Poorer users carry higher balances; pay more interest, finance charges, and other fees—and get few perks. Dis- closures exacerbate the subsidy. Better-educated and wealthier users can read, understand, and exploit information in the Schumer boxes or the disclosures in monthly statements better than other users.

Contract boilerplate works similarly. For example, Comcast's residential-service contract includes a mandatory-arbitration provision and discloses that customers can opt out.[32] Those opting out can bring suits and perhaps class actions, as only the sophisticated know. This cre- ates a higher likelihood of suits and of greater liability for the firm. These benefits do not accrue to those who don't opt out (because class-action remedies have low redemption rates, they are unlikely to benefit the poorer members of the class). If opting out creates higher liability costs, Comcast must add the cost to the service charge all customers pay.

AT WORST, LETHAL

Finally, mandated disclosure can impede efforts to ease suffering, cure ill- ness, improve welfare, and prevent deaths. The principal example is the disclosure regime that IRBs administer. It may be the acme of mandated disclosure, for IRBs regulate and approve each word of every disclosure and consent form that researchers give subjects in medical trials and social- science studies. We leave aside the large (but little remarked) administra- tive costs of a system that uses thousands of doctors and other expensive folk to draft, review, and negotiate disclosures. We speak of the harm of making research more expensive, delaying it, and even preventing it.

Consider two research projects, both posing essentially no risk. In an "eight-site observational substance abuse treatment study," the cost of re- view "*after* the home IRB had approved the project" was 17 percent of the research budget, in significant part because the IRBs "frequently disagreed on the formatting of consent procedures and patient survey forms." Yet the study's essential procedures were never substantially altered, even after 15,000 pages were exchanged.[33] And in a mailed survey and medical-records review on repairing ventral hernias, IRB issues cost roughly 13 percent of the thirty-month budget and a quarter of the first year's budget.

Disclosure requirements can, for example, slow research by making it hard to recruit subjects. A striking instance comes from an international study on treating heart attacks. The study showed that blood thinners reduce the mortality of hospitalized heart-attack patients. About 20,000 American patients are eligible for this treatment every month, and about 75 percent of them now receive blood thinners. This reduces mortality 5.6 percent, which means that over 800 lives are saved every month. To comply with their consent regime, American researchers had to use more elaborate disclosures (1750 words) than researchers in other countries. This delayed the American part of the study eight months, which meant that some 6400 lives were lost in the United States alone due to the delay.[34]

Disclosure requirements also keep research from being conducted at all. For instance, nobody knows when to clamp the umbilical cords of extremely low-birth-weight babies, so doctors must decide arbitrarily. The time of clamping may make a life-or-death difference to these human beings who may weigh one pound. However, prominent researchers have concluded that the consent forms IRBs would require are impractical during these emergency deliveries and therefore have not sought IRB approval to randomize patients and keep track of the results. In the absence of such research, treatment continues to be just as arbitrary as if patients were randomized, but lessons from it cannot be extracted.

Finally, disclosure itself can fatally delay the treatment of research subjects. Thus, in one study of head injuries, centers that did not make disclosures treated patients seventy-two minutes sooner than centers that did. The researchers estimated that even a shorter delay (of an hour) reduced "the proportion of patients who benefit from the trial treatment from 63% to 49%," which meant "avoidable mortality and probably morbidity." So "far from protecting the interests of patients participating in research, requirements for written informed consent and the resultant delay in starting treatment could be lethal."[35]

Even if the risks of unethical research were substantial and insufficiently deterred by tort, criminal, administrative, and professional sanctions, how much could informed consent diminish those risks? Given everything we have said about mandated disclosure generally and given the length and complexity of research consent forms particularly, a generous answer is "trivially, at best."[36] Nobody has undertaken a cost-benefit analysis of the IRB system, but whatever benefits it offers are bought at a price, for this disclosure regime is far from harmless.

CONCLUSION

Most of this book has analyzed mandated disclosure's ineffectiveness. We have argued that disclosures are chronically ignored, unread, and misunderstood. In other words, we have presented extensive evidence that their benefits are exiguous. This chapter has looked at mandated disclosure's costs. It began with the harmlessness hypothesis (that disclosure is "inexpensive and, at worst, harmless"). We argued that the direct costs of operating and using mandated disclosure vary widely but are in many areas significant. And we said that mandates can forestall better regulation in common and costly ways, undercut better regulation, crowd out more useful information, foster opportunism, be anticompetitive, be inequitable, and damage enterprises that can save lives and health. The harmlessness hypothesis needs to go; the cost-benefit analysis that has become a norm for regulation should come.

It is a particularly unhappy irony that mandated disclosure's costs tend to help the impoverished less than the prosperous. Many of the reforms that mandates preempt matter most to the poor. So does much of the consumer-protection law that mandates undercut. The vulnerable suffer more from the bad decisions that mandated disclosure can lead to. The research that the IRB disclosure regime most impedes is the research likeliest to help the ill and weak. But for this to change, the people who most influence lawmaking must be convinced, and they are the people best placed to use and benefit from disclosures and the people to whom they make the most sense.

CHAPTER 12

CONCLUSION: BEYOND DISCLOSURISM

The definition of insanity is doing the same thing over and over again, but expecting different results.

—Attributed to Albert Einstein

We end as we began: If mandated disclosure is everywhere, if it fails widely, if it cannot be fixed, and if it can do harm, lawmakers should stop using it, commentators should stop proposing it, and interest groups should stop advocating it unless they can convincingly show that this time it *really* is different. Disclosure is not always useless. Information can be vital. Mandates may sometimes help. But mandated disclosure is so indiscriminately used with such unrealistic expectations and such unhappy results that it should be presumptively barred. This would spare the world much pointless regulation and might help drive lawmakers—legislatures, administrative agencies, and courts—to search harder for solutions actually tailored to problems.

In writing this book, we have spoken with many colleagues, critics, students, judges, and regulators about our ideas. They are rarely surprised by our evidence or our argument that disclosures commonly fail to achieve their purposes. But then they ask what should replace mandated disclosure. That is the wrong—indeed a bad—question. It implies that mandated disclosure was doing something that needs to be replaced. Our argument has been that it accomplishes so little that eliminating it would deny few people anything.

This book was written to persuade lawmakers not to use a failed regulatory method. That is surely a sufficient goal for any book. If regulation does not work, if it does more harm than good, it should not be used even if you have no better alternative. If disclosees do not benefit from disclosures, it is a regulatory error to pay for mandating and administering the regime. For two thousand years, bloodletting was physicians' panacea. When its failures (and worse) became clear, most of the ailments it was used to treat could not be cured. That was, however, no argument for persisting in bloodletting. So it is with mandated disclosure.

What should we do instead is the wrong question for another reason. It seems to (and usually does) imply that we should find another panacea to replace the one that cures few ills. Panaceas work no better in public policy than medicine. One of disclosure's faults is exactly that it has been asked to do so much that it cannot do. And one of its great costs has been that it helps lawmakers avoid working toward effective regulation. We realize that that work is politically difficult, sometimes even impossible. But that does not justify perpetuating pointless policies.

However, it is hardly surprising that living in a constant drizzle of disclosures makes people suppose that they are needed and will be missed. But disclosures will rarely be missed because they are little used. This is the lesson of the Chris Consumer parable. This is the lesson of the study of online privacy disclosures, which found that *nobody* reads them and that it would take weeks annually to try. This is the lesson of the iTunes scroll, the kind of document we daily click yes to and never think about.

Of course mandated disclosure is sometimes employed for graver purposes. It is a terrible thing when, for example, unsophisticated people are inveigled into an unaffordable mortgage on unconscionable terms. But this happens (and the mortgage crisis occurred) *despite* the magnificent edifice of disclosures that was conscientiously debated when it was adopted, that has been repeatedly revised and expanded, and that has been supervised by an agency that has poured effort and expertise into it.

Were mandated disclosure scaled back to an appropriately modest role, how would people learn about the choices they make? The news here is good; the knowledge is strewn richly before us. And its availability and usefulness do not depend—*pace* many disclosurites—on mandates.

Never has so much information been so easily available in such helpful forms—and not because government requires it. In this chapter we review some sources of helpful information and show that they do not need mandates to work well.

INFORMATION WITHOUT MANDATES: THE ROLE OF INTERMEDIARIES

When we abandon the unreal world in which people tirelessly sponge up disclosures and diligently make informed decisions and instead ask how people really make choices, we see that they are likelier to want opinion than data. Faced with the unfamiliar and complex decisions that disclosures are intended to inform, people don't want to be educated, don't want spreadsheets, and don't want scrolls. They want advice.

Advice is (usually) not just simpler and shorter than disclosures—it offers a different kind of help. Successful advice does not teach fundamentals or facts. It answers the real question: how likely are you to be satisfied? Many markets voluntarily provide advice in the form of ratings, rankings, scores, grades, labels, warnings, and reviews. A company like EBay uses ratings of sellers (the percentage of satisfied customers) to get millions of bidders to pay anonymous sellers before the bidders see, much less receive, the goods. People turn to CNet.com and Amazon for product reviews, to Yelp for merchant recommendations, to Expedia for hotel scores, to Netflix for movie ratings, and to Angie's List for local-services evaluations. Similarly, Zagat rates restaurants, US News rates colleges (maybe not our finest example), AM Best rates insurers, Consumer Reports and the insurance industry rate cars, AAA rates vacation spots, and the NRA rates politicians. Nonprofits award seals to alert people to particular concerns—unsafe data, unhealthy food, or unsavory movies. Professionals offer advice to clients or strangers, free or for a fee, often in a simple recommendation. In short, innumerable activities are rated by consumers and experts. Some raters even ask people to rate the ratings, thus—without anything more than well-behaved software—improving and individualizing their advice.

Most of this advice emerges without government instruction. But disclosurites often claim that these intermediaries need mandated disclosures to generate the information that they acquire, read, filter, and repackage. This conjecture is commonly invoked, for example, to justify securities disclosure: brokers employ analysts who read financial disclosures, rate them, and recommend stocks to investors. Without mandates, wouldn't intermediaries be disabled?

We take this claim seriously, even though it conflicts with disclosurite assumptions. (Why simplify disclosures for sophisticated intermediaries? Why give disclosures to disclosees instead of directly to intermediaries?) The three kinds of intermediaries—consultants, aggregators, and savvy consumers—can all succeed without mandated disclosure.

Consultants

People need consultants. Doctors acquire information about treatments and interpret it to patients. Brokers and analysts give investment advice. Real-estate agents, insurance agents, lawyers, accountants, bankers, and even Web sites counsel people about their specialties. Do consultants depend on mandates for the information they analyze?

The first problem with the consultant thesis is that often there is no consultant. Lawmakers often mandate disclosures exactly because people make decisions alone. Many people arrive at a mortgage closing with nobody to translate the disclosures. Consumers get documents from credit cards, banks, stores, pharmacies, or manufacturers by mail or e-mail, which they must interpret alone (if at all). Users opening an "Important Notice Concerning Your Privacy" are on their own. Indeed, many disclosures tell people to consult an advisor. *Miranda* reminds people of their right to expert advice. Other disclosures tell people to see their doctor or to ask a lawyer to see "what legal or civil options may be available to you."

The second problem with the consultant thesis is that consultants can be unreliable. In fact, they often must disclose interests adverse to their clients'. Title IV of the Sarbanes-Oxley Act is about disclosing accounting conflicts; the 2010 health-care reform abounds in sunshine provisions about physicians' and drug companies' conflicts of interest; and insurance agents, financial brokers, real estate agents, and attorneys must make detailed conflicts disclosures. Such disclosures are imposed because disclosurites think advisors have reasons to be faithless. Instead of disclosure *through* agents who help people with information, we find disclosure *by* agents, or *about* agents.

The third (and related) problem with the consultant theory is that often the consultants aren't intermediaries: they are disclosers. Consumers getting mortgage and credit disclosures might rely on their broker, closing agent, or loan officer to explain things. But they are often agents for the disclosers or *are* the disclosers. They often lack the incentive, patience, and reliability to evaluate and warn borrowers of fine-print surprises and to provide good advice. Consumers receiving a bed sheet might consult the car salesman, but that's hardly safe. Your doctor is often a reliable agent, but disclosurism views doctors as disclosers with conflicts of interest and regulates the information they disseminate.

Information Aggregators

Information aggregators collect information and convert it into useful forms like price comparisons, ratings, labels, seals, and certificates. They often collect the information that is in mandated disclosures. Services like Creditcards.com compare the information about rates, fees, and much more that is in credit-card disclosures. Services like TRUSTe assess online privacy policies (and award a seal). And Web sites like WebMD. com aggregate information about drugs and treatments.

Information aggregators monitor disclosers. Some perform inspections and verify compliance. Others file class actions. News organizations investigate and expose trouble. Retailers can be aggregators; supermarkets sort through information from food producers and importers, choose items from reputable sources, and display products by categories, thus saying something about nutritional quality, about whether food is organic, imported, locally grown, homemade, or gluten-free.

Information aggregators are invaluable, but they do not need mandated disclosure. They often use information that disclosures do not provide. Rating agencies evaluate insurance companies without them. Product evaluators do not base their rating on warranty disclosures. Online privacy-certifiers do not just read privacy statements. What aggregators need is information about performance, about actual use, and about consumers' experience. They test products, collect data about risk ratios, measure consumers' satisfaction and complaints—in short, they aggregate knowledge of *practice*. This information generally comes from surveys and research, feedback and observation, expertise and judgment, not disclosures. Consumers need to know how businesses actually behave, which disclosures rarely teach. In fact, many disclosures resist aggregation. Some are individually tailored (like borrower-specific information about loans). Some are hard to transform into a rating (as chapter 10 showed).

Even if disclosures contain necessary information, intermediaries can usually get it without a mandate. Their very presence can induce companies to release it. Drug companies cheerfully tell intermediaries like hospitals and HMOs about their wares. Walmart solicits information about its suppliers' compliance with environmental and labor standards. And what automaker would deny Consumer Reports data (which it could get on its own anyway)?

Finally, requiring that information go first to consumers, trickle through to aggregators, and then bounce back to consumers through aggregators' scores is clumsy and inefficient. Why make aggregators assemble bits and pieces of information written for the untutored? Some disclosure regimes do require that information go directly to intermediaries. Hospitals make quality-of-care disclosures (through mandated report cards) that health plans use, employers make safety disclosures that labor unions use, and firms make environmental disclosures that government agencies use. And, as we've seen, most securities disclosures to investors are read and analyzed by professional analysts and eventually reflected in securities prices. Disclosures to these parties largely bypass the public. Read a typical report card or prospectus; it is not for Everyman. Mandated disclosure to eager and sophisticated intermediaries seems much more sensible than the present system.

Savvy Readers

Savvy readers study disclosures for their own use, to understand them and make rational choices. They spot the nasty fine print, scorn bad deals, and know what's worth paying for. While they benefit themselves first, they indirectly help everyone because they drive disclosers to provide better terms. That is, they impose market discipline. Since everybody—sophisticates and naïfs alike—gets the same disclosures, terms, and prices, the sophisticates who secure better treatment for themselves get it also for the rest of us. Restaurants may fear the critical palates of reviewers and gastronomes, but they cannot know when they will show up and so must serve everyone food fit for the discriminating. In like manner many businesses sell to everyone products designed to keep astute shoppers from going elsewhere.

This is a serious theory that has flourished in the literature.[1] Disclosurites claim that mandated disclosures work this way: nonreaders can accept a deal safely because savvy readers scrutinized it and would have rejected it if it displeased them, thus driving the company to shape up or go broke.

This theory works in some markets, but it is implausible applied to fine-print contracts and even odder applied to disclosure generally. First, the theory proves too much. If a few readers induce firms to improve terms for everyone's benefit, why mandate disclosures? Would not savvy readers demand the information anyway? Computer companies design products to please customers and happily disclose their pleasing features. If their sophisticated customers care about monitors, memory, software, and return policies, information about all that will be disclosed (even advertised). If customers start caring about things buried in fine print (like arbitration, remedies, warranties, and choice of law), they too will be disclosed.

The second problem with the savvy-reader hypothesis is that there aren't enough fine-print readers to influence sellers. Shoppers care about a product's attributes but not the legal details. People rarely buy a laptop without considering its weight, but they almost never notice or fret about the fine print, however conspicuously posted. As chapter 4 said, the savvy course is often *not* to read. Thus there are too few readers to affect sellers.

Moreover, savvy readers are not agents for the rest of us when they get their own sweet deals. Sophisticates can often be segregated from the naïve. They shop in different markets and for different products. How many savvy readers wanted a subprime, adjustable-rate, negatively amortized, pre-2008 mortgage? How many savvy readers want expensive teaser loans? And many businesses have tracks (regular or premium, standard or elite, household or commercial) that segregate customers. Finally, savvy customers often wait until a problem arises, complain, and get accommodations not granted naïfs.

Even in unsegregated markets, savvy readers are good agents only if they are reasonably typical. But anyone with the time, knowledge, skill, and fortitude, not to say paranoia, to plow through disclosures is almost weirdly atypical. Such readers may want idiosyncratic things. They may be too litigious. They may be reacting to a bad experience. But a credit-card user who cares about boilerplate arbitration clauses lacks the typical user's characteristics, concerns, and attitudes about price and quality.

In sum, the savvy-reader account militates in favor of mandated disclosure only in markets in which disclosers cannot distinguish readers from nonreaders and must give everyone the better deal that the savvy demand. But disclosure is often mandated in areas in which people use or enjoy information differently, as in medical situations like informed consent, in *Miranda* settings, and in warnings about products.

In short, we believe that information intermediaries of all kinds—consultants, aggregators, and even savvy shoppers—often do much better than mandated disclosures at giving people the advice they need to make unfamiliar and complex decisions. And, happily, intermediaries can prosper without mandated disclosure. They are largely substitutes for, not complements to, mandated disclosure. The services they perform, the information they use, and the advice they give, do not depend on mandated disclosure.

A WORLD WITHOUT PANACEAS

We are asking what a world without a kudzu-like mandated disclosure would be like. We saw that information would continue to circulate, and often in a more valued form. But this would be a world without panaceas. In such a world there would be no easy political consensus, regulation would have to be paid for, priorities would have to be set. This is the world that disclosurites hope to avoid when they find the holy grail of effective disclosure. But it is the world our conclusion forces us to confront.

It seems odd in a contemporary book about regulatory policy to be arguing that lawmakers should forswear panaceas. Systematic ideas about protecting consumers, patients, employees, or Internet users can address a spectrum of problems. But disclosure cannot be the key to such new designs. Some eminent commentators seem to agree and profess to offer alternatives to mandated disclosure. But on examination these alternatives reintroduce disclosure in another guise. Mostly prominently, Thaler and Sunstein represent a movement that believes that choice architecture, while not a panacea, can protect many consumers in many critical areas, including mortgages, retirement savings, health plans, and privacy.[2] At its core is the default: Government sets terms that people receive automatically but may opt out of. Like software defaults, they are supposed to be easy and cheap to change if you prefer different terms. Ideally the default is, in the current cliché, plain vanilla—a simple plan that is good value for most people. Thaler and Sunstein call defaults a nudge, a device that changes people's behavior, does not restrict their choice, and is easy to avoid. They acknowledge the paternalism of the device but think it is also libertarian because defaults can be rejected.

Barr, Mullainathan, and Shafir (professors of law, economics, and psychology at Michigan, Harvard, and Princeton) think the plain-vanilla default should be the regulatory, well, default. In a *New York Times* op-ed frankly titled "A One-Size-Fits-All Solution," they say that people make poor choices, err in assessing trade-offs, and are misled by sharp marketing. "While disclosure alone is unlikely to help," they write, "there's another option"—defaults. For example, the mortgage default would be a thirty-year, fixed-rate loan.[3]

No doubt defaults can do good in consumer protection and in regulation more broadly. One of us said as much many years ago.[4] Defaults can perhaps improve some transactions. For example, it is widely thought that automatic enrollment in 401(k) plans has increased participation rates and overall retirement savings significantly, since employees rarely opt out of the plans that defaults put them in. This has been an excellent thing for all concerned. People had been making bad decisions (not to have a pension) and are now making better ones. Employers had many employees without a major benefit (a pension) and now have fewer.

But default plans work only if nobody is luring people away from the default and into the mire. Defaults work for pension plans because employers want employees in them. But in many areas, including those where consumers are particularly vulnerable, many enterprises profit from seducing people away from the defaults and find the seduction easy. What protects consumers from seduction? Disclosure.

It is their libertarian veneer that makes opt-out plans so appealing to so many. Freedom of choice is the default regime's foundation (which is why it's called choice architecture). How is that freedom assured? Barr et al. understand that their one-size-fits-all solution depends on this. Opt-outs from the default plans would be valid only when preceded by "meaningful disclosures." These would have to be "honest and comprehensible disclosures" that "effectively communicate the key terms and risks of the mortgage to the typical borrower." Thus "people could raise the lack of reasonable disclosure as a defense" against attempts to hold them to improvident opt-outs.

Does this sound familiar? Recall that Barr et al. call defaults an *alternative* to mandated disclosure. They say that "disclosure alone is unlikely to help" and that they have "another option." But that option, we now learn, depends on our meretricious friend, the meaningful disclosure. So what will "effectively communicate the key terms"? How would they accomplish what two generations of TILA-mandated disclosures could not?

In the panacea world, opt-outs with meaningful disclosures will succeed where previous meaningful disclosures failed. But in the real world, default plans are just more disclosurism. Lenders will quickly figure out what formulas make a disclosure "reasonable," "honest," and "comprehensible" and use them to steer clients away from plain-vanilla products to more profitable ones. But if disclosures failed to make meaningful people's choice of plans from a menu, they will also fail when one of the menu options is preclicked. As long as it only takes another stack of forms and a few more signatures to make opt-outs "informed," cunning lenders will divert people into bad choices as easily as they do now. The voice is Jacob's voice . . . .

While they are novel in some circles, defaults have a long and discouraging history in contract law. For example, a contract for the sale of

goods comes, courtesy of the Uniform Commercial Code, with a generous warranty of merchantability guaranteeing consumers that the goods
are reliable and of fair value and assuring consumers adequate remedies.
This warranty is a default; the parties can modify or remove it if their
agreement is preceded by a "conspicuous" disclosure. Indeed, Barr et al.
think this example of an informed opt-out rule is so successful that all
consumer law should follow it.[5] But the reality is disheartening: practically every sales contract has boilerplate *disclaiming* the warranty, which
requires little more than writing (again, in ALLCAPS) that the product
is sold "AS IS." A well-intended, pro-consumer, plain-vanilla scheme is
trumped by disclosure. The same can be said of almost every other pro-
consumer default rule—it doesn't stick. Consumers have the (default)
right to file grievances in courts, but they click "I agree" to arbitrate. They
have (default) rights to generous damages, to privacy, and to the Web
content they generate, but they routinely sign them away through meticulously disclosed opt-outs.

Lawmakers have recently recruited defaults to protect people from
exorbitant overdraft fees. Banks can no longer just make overdraft protection (i.e., charging customers hefty fees for overdrafts) standard.
People must choose it. One of us logged into his bank's Web site recently to make a routine payment and was prompted to an e-disclosure
to which he had to consent to get into his account. On the disclosure
page he found prominent statements about the sanctity of informed
agreement and links to disclosures. He clicked and downloaded twenty-
eight pages of disclosure with 23,000 words in over 505 paragraphs. The
overdraft terms were part of the documents (albeit a separate page, to
comply with the government's mandate to make the opt-out disclosure
more meaningful), as were many other tidbits that lawmakers require
people to see before they opt in or out. He didn't much like them but
clicked "I agree" to get to his account. Did he opt out of the plain-vanilla,
no-overdraft default?

Banks make money from overdraft fees, lots.[6] Standing to lose it,
banks have contrived to lure people away from the no-overdraft default,
particularly heavy overdrafters (who tend to be their poorer customers).
And so a policy intended to replace mandated disclosure (but that relies

on disclosures to preserve individual choice) "appears to have dramatically failed to achieve this aim."[7]

Sometimes the choice between paternalism and libertarianism simply can't be avoided, and substantive regulation with no opting out is needed. Such regulation is already common. That's what usury laws are. It's easy to imagine that particular kinds of mortgages might be outlawed generally or that mortgages below a set amount might be prohibited. Some lawmakers favor minimum down payments on homes. In many areas contract terms are (and should be) truly mandatory. If sensible restrictions were mandated, many people might end up better off, safeguarded from ill-advised, disclosure-induced choices. But such protections have costs, since some people would have benefited from having a choice. It is beyond our writ to resolve such trade-offs or even to propose guidelines for paternalistic policies. But the trade-offs must be evaluated and not ducked with the painless panacea of mandated disclosure.

Plausible trade-offs are at least not hard to find. In a number of core areas of mandated disclosure, more paternalistic regulation may be desirable. Consumer credit and banking in the subprime market may well be such cases. The Dodd-Frank Act gave agencies the power to regulate some financial activities in ways that go beyond disclosure, and there are early signs that the SEC and the CFPB are ready for the challenge. Some states have interest-rate caps tailored to specific transactions (general debt, small loans, installment loans, pawn loans, farm loans, reverse-mortgage loans). Lawmakers do know how to get their hands dirty and address market failures.

At the other end of the regulatory spectrum are cases where disclosures are mandated but regulation is not needed, like the opportunity-to-read rule in contract law. The right to read boilerplate before a purchase, a right that recent reforms have strengthened, can be discarded and only a few eccentrics will notice. Academics write powerfully of the normative and democratic "degradation" that boilerplate causes as it "divests" us of our rights,[8] but the millions using Google and Facebook, booking seats on trains and planes, licensing software and music tracks, or buying iPhones and iPads seem not to feel degraded or even to notice.

About many of the trade-offs reasonable minds may differ. Some think *Miranda* a fig leaf for police coercion and want stricter regulation of interrogations. Some think doctors should be prohibited from having conflicts of interest, not just made to disclose them. Some think IRBs obstruct medical research without protecting research subjects while superior means of regulating research are already in place. And a fascinating debate is emerging about privacy—are people hurt or benefited by Web sites collecting personal data, and how might regulation secure the benefits while reducing the harms of these activities?

* * *

In the sixteenth century Spaniards arriving in the Americas found themselves greeted with villagers' "malice or ignorance." Hence *el Requerimiento*, the "Spanish Requirement," 400 words read to audiences who knew no Spanish: "We ask and require you that you consider what we have said to you, and that you take the time that shall be necessary to understand and deliberate upon it, and that you acknowledge the Church as the ruler and superior of the whole world. But if you do not do this, . . . we shall make war against you . . . [and] slaves of [you] . . . ."

So mandated disclosure has been with us for centuries. Telling people more than they want to know in language they don't understand should not have legal consequences. Happily, disclosures no longer excuse slaughter and slavery. On the contrary, their goals are admirable. The modern history of mandated disclosure is one of irrepressible hope, of the rise of a form of regulation perhaps unequaled in the extent of its use or the fervor of its proponents. But modern audiences blessed with disclosures are usually as uncomprehending and ungrateful as the ones who were read *el Requerimiento*. *¡Basta ya!*

NOTES

CHAPTER 1

1. Lauren E. Willis, *Decisionmaking and the Limits of Disclosure: The Problem of Predatory Lending: Price*, 65 Md. L. Rev. 707, 712 (2006).
2. National Research Council, *Protecting Participants and Facilitating Social and Behavioral Sciences Research* (National Academies Press, 2003), 2–3.
3. Clifford Winston, *The Efficacy of Information Policy: A Review of Archon Fung, Mary Graham, and David Weil's Full Disclosure: The Perils and Promise of Transparency*, 46 J. Econ. Lit. 704, 713–14 (2008).
4. Federal Reserve Board, *The Federal Reserve Board Consumer Handbook on Adjustable Rate Mortgages*, 4 (2006).
5. "eBay User Agreement," eBay, visited January 11, 2013, pages.ebay.com/help/policies/user-agreement.html?_trksid=m40.
6. Sheena Iyengar, *The Art of Choosing* (Twelve, 2010), 192.

CHAPTER 2

1. Oren Bar-Gill, *Seduction by Contract* (Oxford, 2012).
2. Federal Reserve Bank of Boston, *True or False? Know Before You Go to Get a Mortgage* (Federal Reserve Bank of Boston), 15, http://www.bostonfed.org/consumer/knowbeforeyougo/mortgage/mortgage.pdf.
3. Pew Charitable Trusts, *Checking Account Risks at a Glance*, visited January 11, 2013, www.pewtrusts.org/our_work_report_detail.aspx?id=85899359140.
4. Minnesota Department of Commerce, *Auto Insurance: What You Need to Know*, visited January 11, 2013, http://mn.gov/commerce/insurance/images/auto-insurance-brochure.pdf.
5. Alexi Madrigal, *Reading the Privacy Policies You Encounter in a Year Would Take 76 Work Days*, Atlantic, March 5, 2012, visited April 9, 2013, http://www.theatlantic.com/technology/archive/2012/03/reading-the-privacy-policies-you-encounter-in-a-year-would-take-76-work-days/253851/.
6. Michael O. Leavitt, *Building a Value-Based Health Care System*, Department of Health and Human Services, visited January 11, 2013, www.hhs.gov/secretary/prologueseries/buildingvaluehc.pdf.
7. ALI Principles of the Law of Software Contracts 2.02(c)(3) (2010).

CHAPTER 3

1.   15 U.S.C.A. § 1601(a) (2004).
2.   Federal Reserve Board, *The Federal Reserve Board Consumer Handbook on Adjustable Rate Mortgages* (2006), 4.
3.   Ezekiel J. Emanuel and Linda L. Emanuel, *Four Models of the Physician-Patient Relationship*, 267 J. Amer. Med. Assoc. 2221, 2223 (1992) (emphasis in original), (quoting the President's Commission for the Study of Ethical Problems in Medicine and Biomedical and Behavioral Research, *Making Health Care Decisions* (U. S. Gov't Printing Office, 1982)).
4.   Charles W. Lidz, *Informed Consent: A Critical Part of Modern Medical Research*, 342 Amer. J. Med. Sci. 275 (2011).
5.   John Hancock Financial Services, *Insight into Participant Investment Knowledge & Behavior*, visited January 11, 2013, http://www.jhancockstructures.com /gsfp/survey2002.pdf.
6.   FTC Telemarketing Rule, 16 CFR 310.3(a)(1) (2000).
7.   White House, *Consumer Data Privacy in a Networked World: A Framework for Protecting Privacy and Promoting Innovation in the Global Digital Economy* (2012), visited January 11, 2013, http://www.whitehouse.gov/sites/default/files /privacy-final.pdf.
8.   Department of Education, *The Handbook on Campus Safety and Security Reporting* (Washington, D.C., 2011).
9.   Philip Keitel, *Federal Regulation of the Prepaid Card Industry: Costs, Benefits, and Changing Industry Dynamics*, Conference Summary (Federal Reserve Bank of Philadelphia, 2010), 25.
10. Alan Meisel, *A "Dignitary Tort" as a Bridge between the Idea of Informed Consent and the Law of Informed Consent*, 16 L. Med. & Health Care 210 (1988).
11. Margaret Jane Radin, *Boilerplate: The Fine Print, Vanishing Rights, and the Rule of Law* (Princeton University Press, 2013), 15.
12. *ALI Principles of the Law of Software Contracts*, 137 (Robert Hillman and Maureen O'Rourke, Reporters, 2010).
13. Daniel Schwarcz, *Transparency Opaque: Understanding the Lack of Transparency in Insurance Consumer Protection*, 61 UCLA L. Rev. (forthcoming, 2014).
14. Department of the Treasury, Internal Revenue Service, Privacy Act Notice, Notice No. 609 (Rev. Sept. 2009).
15. *In Re International Harvester Co.*, 104 F.T.C. 949 (1984).
16. Donna Shalala, *Protecting Research Subjects—What Must Be Done*, 343 N. Engl. J. Med. 808, 808 (2000).
17. Cass R. Sunstein, *Empirically Informed Regulation*, 78 U. Chi. L. Rev. 1349, 1369 (2011).

18. Thomas A. Durkin and Gregory Elliehausen, "Disclosure as a Consumer Protection," in *The Impact of Public Policy on Consumers,* ed. Thomas A. Durkin and Michael E. Staten (Kluwer, 2002), 109, 127, 130.

19. Mary Graham, *Democracy by Disclosure: The Rise of Technopopulism* (Brookings, 2002), 139.

20. Ibid., 77.

21. Institute of Medicine, *Responsible Research: A Systems Approach to Protecting Research Participants* (National Academies Press, 2003), viii.

22. Mary Dixon-Woods et al., *Beyond "Misunderstanding": Written Information and Decisions About Taking Part in a Genetic Epidemiology Study,* 65 Soc. Sci. & Med. 2212, 2213 (2007).

23. Steven H. Woolf et al., *Promoting Informed Choice: Transforming Health Care to Dispense Knowledge for Decision Making,* 143 Ann. of Int. Med. 293, 295–96 (2005).

24. Marshall B. Kapp, *Patient Autonomy in the Age of Consumer-Driven Health Care: Informed Consent and Informed Choice,* 2 J. Health & Biomedical L. 1, 10 (2006).

25. Gail Geller et al., *"Decoding" Informed Consent: Insights from Women Regarding Breast Cancer Susceptibility Testing,* 27 Hastings Center Rep. 28 (1997).

26. On the attitudes behind such mandates, see Frank Anechiarico and James B. Jacobs, *The Pursuit of Absolute Integrity: How Corruption Control Makes Government Ineffective* (University of Chicago Press, 1996).

27. Kevin P. Weinfurt et al., *Disclosing Conflicts of Interest in Clinical Research: Views of Institutional Review Boards, Conflict of Interest Committees, and Investigators,* 34 J. Law. Med. Ethics 581 (2006).

28. Archon Fong et al., *Full Disclosure: The Perils and Promise of Transparency* (Cambridge University Press, 2008).

29. Daniel E. Ho, *Fudging the Nudge: Information Disclosure and Restaurant Grading,* 122 Yale L.J. 574 (2012).

30. Mary Graham, *Democracy by Disclosure: The Rise of Technopopulism* (Brookings, 2002), 82–83.

31. Ibid., 96–97.

32. Lauren E. Willis, *Decisionmaking and the Limits of Disclosure: The Problem of Predatory Lending: Price,* 65 Md. L. Rev. 707 (2006); Lauren E. Willis, *Against Financial-Literacy Education,* 94 Iowa L. Rev. 197 (2008).

33. Edward L. Rubin, *Legislative Methodology: Some Lessons from the Truth-in-Lending Act,* 80 Geo. L.J. 233 (1991).

34. U.S. Department of Housing & Urban Development & U.S. Department of Treasury, *Recommendation to Curb Predatory Home Mortgage Lending* 67 (2000).

35. See, e.g., Florencia Marotta-Wurgler, *Will Increased Disclosure Help? Evaluating the Recommendations of the ALI's "Principles of the Law of Software Contracts,"* 78 U. Chi. L. Rev. 165 (2011).

36. Barrie R. Cassileth et al., *Informed Consent—Why Are Its Goals Imperfectly Realized?*, 302 N. Engl. J. Med. 896 (1980).

37. Charles W. Lidz, *Informed Consent: A Critical Part of Modern Medical Research*, 342 Amer. J. Med. Sci. 273 (2011).

38. National Research Council, *Protecting Participants and Facilitating Social and Behavioral Sciences Research* (National Academy of Sciences, 2003), 2.

39. Margaret L. Schwarze et al., *Exploring Patient Preferences for Infrainguinal Bypass Operation*, 202 J. Amer. Coll. Surgeons 445, 449 (2006).

40. Angela Fagerlin et al., *An Informed Decision? Breast Cancer Patients and Their Knowledge About Treatment*, 64 Patient Education & Counseling 303, 309 (2006).

41. Mark A. Hall et al., *How Disclosing HMO Physician Incentives Affects Trust*, 21 Health Affairs 197, 203, 205 (2002).

42. David A. Herz et al., *Informed Consent: Is It a Myth?*, 30 Neurosurgery 453 (1992).

43. Joan H. Krause, *Reconceptualizing Informed Consent in an Era of Health Care Cost Containment*, 85 Iowa L. Rev. 261, 379–83 (1999).

44. Ann Butler Nattinger et al., *The Effect of Legislative Requirements on the Use of Breast-Conserving Surgery*, 335 N. Engl. J. Med. 1035, 1039 (1996).

45. Steven Joffe et al., *Quality of Informed Consent in Cancer Clinical Trials: A Cross-Sectional Survey*, 358 Lancet 1772, 1774–75 (2001).

46. FTC Report, *Protecting Consumer Privacy in an Era of Rapid Change*, (U.S. Federal Trade Commission, March 2012), 72.

47. Kesten C. Green and J. Scott Armstrong, *Evidence on the Effects of Mandatory Disclaimers in Advertising*, 31 J. of Pub. Pol'y & Marketing 293 (2012).

48. Richard A. Leo, *Questioning the Relevance of* Miranda *in the Twenty-First Century*, 99 Mich. L. Rev. 1000, 1012–13, quoting Patrick Malone, *You Have the Right to Remain Silent:* Miranda *After Twenty Years*, 55 American Scholar 367, 368 (1986).

49. William J. Stuntz, *Miranda's Mistake*, 99 Mich. L. Rev. 975, 976 (2001).

50. James J. Choi et al., *Why Does the Law of One Price Fail? An Experiment on Index Mutual Funds*, 23 Rev. Fin. Stud. 1405 (2010).

51. Ibid.

52. Daylian M. Cain, George Loewenstein, and Don A. Moore, *The Dirt on Coming Clean: Perverse Effects of Disclosing Conflicts of Interest*, 34 J. Legal Stud. 1, 22 (2005).

53. Ibid., 18.

54. Ibid., 6; see also Sunita Sah, George Loewenstein, and Daylian M. Cain, *The Burden of Disclosure: Increased Compliance with Distrusted Advice,* 104 J. Personality and Social Psychology 289 (2013).

55. 12 U.S.C. § 2601(a) (1974). ("It is the purpose of this chapter to effect certain changes in the settlement process for residential real estate that will result: (a) In more effective advance disclosure to home buyers and sellers of settlement costs.")

56. 15 USC § 1601 et seq. (1980).

57. Pub. L. 96–221, Depository Institutions Deregulation and Monetary Control Act of 1980, Senate Report No. 96073 (Apr. 24, 1979).

58. *RESPA Roundup Archive*, visited January 11, 2013, http://portal.hud.gov/hud portal/HUD?src=/program_offices/housing/rmra/res/resroundup.

59. 73 Fed. Reg. 14030 (2008).

60. Integrated Mortgage Disclosures under the Real Estate Settlement Procedures Act (Regulation X) and the Truth In Lending Act (Regulation Z), Proposed Rule by BUREAU OF CONSUMER FINANCIAL PROTECTION, 12 CFR Parts 1024 and 1026 [Docket No. CFPB-2012–0028], 3.

61. For an early discussion of improvement in TILA, see William N. Eskridge, Jr., *One Hundred Years of Ineptitude: The Need for Mortgage Consonant with the Economics and Psychological Dynamics of the Home Sale and Loan Transaction*, 70 Va. L. Rev. 1083 (1984).

62. Thomas A. Durkin and Gregory Elliehausen, *Truth in Lending: Theory, History, and a Way Forward* (Oxford University Press, 2011), x.

63. Samuel Issacharoff, *Disclosure, Agents, and Consumer Protection*, 167 J. Institutional and Theoretical Econ. 56 (2011).

64. Jeff Sovern, "Help for the Perplexed Homebuyer," *New York Times*, July 19, 2012.

65. Michael S. Barr, Sendhil Mullainathan, and Eldar Shafir, "A One-Size-Fits-All Solution?", *New York Times*, December 26, 2007.

66. http://www.healthcarereportcard.illinois.gov/, visited June 30, 2013.

67. David Dranove et al., *Is More Information Better? The Effect of "Report Cards" on Health Care Providers*, 111 J. Pol. Econ. 555, 556 (2003).

68. Leemore Dafny and David Dranove, *Do Report Cards Tell Consumers Anything They Don't Already Know? The Case of Medicare HMOs*, 39 Rand J. Econ. 790 (2008).

69. David Dranove and Ginger Zhe Jin, *Quality Disclosure and Certification: Theory and Practice*, J. Econ. Lit., 48, no. 4: 935–63 (2010).

70. Quoted in Durkin and Elliehausen, *Truth in Lending*.

71. Cathy Charles, Amiram Gafni, and Tim Whelan, *Shared Decision-Making in the Medical Encounter: What Does It Mean? (Or It Takes At Least Two to Tango)*, 44 Soc. Sci. & Med. 681, 689 (1997).

72. See, e.g., Daniel Schwarcz, *Reevaluating Standardized Insurance Policies*, 78 U. Chi. L. Rev. 1263, 1337 (2011); Oren Bar-Gill, *Seduction by Contract* (Oxford University Press, 2012); Jonathan H. Adler, "Labeling the Little Things," in *The Nanotechnology Challenge*, ed. David Dana (Cambridge University Press, 2011); Richard A. Epstein, *How Conflict of Interests Rules Endanger Medical Progress and Cures* (Manhattan Institute, 2010).

73. Robert A. Hillman, *Online Boilerplate: Would Mandatory Website Disclosure of E-Standard Terms Backfire?*, 104 Mich. L. Rev. 837, 849–50 (2006).

CHAPTER 4

1. Will C. van Den Hoonaard, *The Seduction of Ethics: Transforming the Social Sciences* (University of Toronto Press 2011), 118.

2. *Castellana v. Conyers Toyota*, 407 S.E.2d 64 (Ga. 1991).

3. Sheena Iyengar, *The Art of Choosing* (Twelve, 2010) (quoting Nikolas Rose), 84. For an analysis of "mandatory autonomy" in medical ethics, see Carl E. Schneider, *The Practice of Autonomy: Patients, Doctors, and Medical Decisions* (Oxford University Press, 1998).

4. See Barry Schwartz, *The Paradox of Choice: Why More is Less* (HarperCollins, 2004); Edward C. Rosenthal, *The Era of Choice: The Ability to Choose and Its Transformation of Contemporary Life* (MIT Press, 2005).

5. Jack Ende et al., *Measuring Patients' Desire for Autonomy: Decision Making and Information-Seeking Preferences Among Medical Patients*, 4 J. Gen. Int. Med. 26–27 (1989).

6. William M. Strull, Bernard Lo, and Gerald Charles, *Do Patients Want to Participate in Medical Decision Making?*, 252 J. Amer. Med. Assoc. 2990 (1984).

7. William Martin, *My Prostate and Me: Dealing with Prostate Cancer* (Cadell and Davies, 1994), 54.

8. Laurence D. Brown, *Management by Objection? Public Policies to Protect Choice in Health* Plans, 56 Med. Care Res. and Rev. 146, 151 (1999).

9. James J. Choi et al., "*Defined Contribution Pensions: Plan Rules, Participant Choices, and the Path of Least Resistance,*" in *Tax Policy and the Economy* 16, ed. James Poterba (NBER, 2002), 32.

10. George A. Akerlof and Robert J. Shiller, *Animal Spirits: How Human Psychology Drives the Economy and Why It Matters for Global Capitalism* (Princeton University Press, 2009), 122.

11. Ibid., 117.

12. Marlynn L. May and Daniel B. Stengel, *Who Sues Their Doctors? How Patients Handle Medical Grievances*, 24 Law & Soc'y Rev. 105, 116 (1990).

13. Carl E. Schneider, *The Practice of Autonomy: Patients, Doctors, and Medical Decisions* (Oxford University Press, 1998), 42.

14. Paul Fronstin and Sara R. Collins, *Early Experience With High-Deductible and Consumer-Driven Health Plans: Findings From the EBRI/Commonwealth Fund Consumerism in Health Care Survey*, 228 EBRI Issue Brief 1, 21 (2005).

15. Lisa M. Schwartz et al., *How Do Elderly Patients Decide Where to Go for Major Surgery?*, 331 BMJ 821 (2005).

16. John Beshears et al., "How Does Simplified Disclosure Affect Individuals' Mutual Fund Choice?" in *Explorations in the Economics of Aging*, ed. David A. Wise (University of Chicago Press, 2011), 75.

17. Sumit Agarwal et al., *The Age of Reason: Financial Decisions Over the Lifecycle* (Federal Reserve Bank of Chicago, WP 2007–05), 41, visited January 12, 2013, http://www.hss.caltech.edu/~mshum/ec106/agarwal.pdf.

18. Larry Kirsch, *Do Product Disclosures Inform and Safeguard Insurance Policy-holders?*, 20 J. Ins. Reg. 271, 273–74 (2002).

19. Jinkook Lee and Jeanne M. Hogarth, *Consumer Information Search for Home Mortgages: Who, What, How Much, and What Else?*, 9 Fin. Serv. Rev. 277, 285 (2000).

20. Schneider, *Practice of Autonomy.*

21. Musa Mayer, *Examining Myself: One Woman's Story of Breast Cancer Treatment and Recovery* (Faber and Faber, 1993).

22. Mary Alice Geier, *Cancer: What's It Doing in My Life?* (Hope Publishing, 1985), 18.

23. Penny F. Pierce, *Deciding on Breast Cancer Treatment: A Description of Decision Behavior*, 42 Nursing Res. 20 (1993).

24. Angela Fagerlin et al., *An Informed Decision? Breast Cancer Patients and Their Knowledge about Treatment*, 64 Patient Education & Counseling 303 (2006).

25. Schneider, *Practice of Autonomy.*

26. Louie Nassaney with Glenn Kolb, *I Am Not a Victim: One Man's Triumph over Fear & AIDS* (Hay House, 1990), 29.

27. Rachelle Breslow, *Who Said So?: How Our Thoughts and Beliefs Affect Our Physiology* (Celestial Arts, 1991), 15.

28. Anatole Broyard, *Intoxicated By My Illness: And Other Writings on Life and Death* (Fawcett Columbine, 1992), 39–40.

29. Michael Korda, *Man to Man: Surviving Prostate Cancer* (Random House, 1996), 101.

30. Martin, *My Prostate and Me*, 114.

31. Francis Bacon, *Aphorisms*, Bk. I, 46.

32. Richard Nisbett and Lee Ross, *Human Inference: Strategies and Shortcomings of Social Judgment* (Prentice-Hall, 1980), 41–42.

33. James Choi, David Laibson, and Brigitte C. Madrian, *Are Empowerment and Education Enough? Underdiversification in 401(k) Plans*, Brookings Papers on Economic Activity 2 (2005) 151, 192–93.

34. Yannis Bakos, Florencia Marotta-Wurgler, and David R. Trossen, *Does Anyone Read the Fine Print? Consumer Attention to Standard Form Contracts*, 43 J. Legal Stud. (forthcoming, 2014).

35. Florencia Marotta-Wurgler, *Will Increased Disclosure Help? Evaluating the Recommendations of the ALI's "Principles of the Law of Software Contracts,"* 78 U. Chi. L. Rev. 165 (2011).

36. Investment Company Institute, *Understanding Investor Preferences for Mutual Fund Information* (2006), 22.

37. Matthew A. Edwards, *Empirical and Behavioral Critiques of Mandatory Disclosure: Socio-Economics and the Quest for Truth in Lending*, 14 Cornell J. L. & Pub. Pol'y 199, 229 (2005).

38. Thomas A. Durkin and Gregory Elliehausen, *Disclosure as a Consumer Protection*, in *The Impact of Public Policy on Consumer Credit*, ed. Thomas A. Durkin and Michael E. Staten (Kluwer, 2002), 109, 129.

39. Michael Lewis, *The Big Short* (W.W. Norton, 2010).

40. Larry Kirsch, *Do Product Disclosures Inform and Safeguard Insurance Policyholders?*, 20 J. Ins. Reg. 271, 273–74 (2002).

41. E. Schneider and A. Epstein, *Use of Public Performance Reports: A Survey of Patients Undergoing Cardiac Surgery*, 279 J. Amer. Med. Assoc. 1638, 1638 (1998); M. N. Marshall et al., *The Public Release of Performance Data: What Do We Expect to Gain? A Review of the Evidence*, 283 J. Amer. Med. Assoc. 1866, 1866 (2000).

42. Arnold M. Epstein, *Rolling Down the Runway: The Challenges Ahead for Quality Report Cards*, 279 J. Amer. Med. Assoc. 1691, 1691–92 (1998).

43. Judith H. Hibbard et al., *Can Medicare Beneficiaries Make Informed Choices?*, 17 Health Affairs 181, 186 (1998).

44. James S. Lubalin and Lauren Harris-Kojetin, *What Do Consumers Want and Need to Know in Making Health Care Choices?* 56 (suppl.) Med. Care Res. Rev. 67, 91 (1999).

45. Jean M. Abraham et al., *The Effect of Quality Information on Consumer Health Plan Switching: Evidence from the Buyers Health Care Action Group*, 25 J. Health Econ. 762, 775 (2006).

46. Thomas Wilke et al., *Does Package Design Matter for Patients? The Association Between Package Design and Patients' Drug Knowledge*, 25 Pharmaceutical Med. 307, 308 (2011).

47. "Judge Posner Admits He Didn't Read Boilerplate for Home Equity Loan," *ABA Journal* (June 23, 2010), visited January 13, 2013, www.abajournal.com/news/article/judge_posner_admits_he_didnt_read_boilerplate_for_home_equity_loan/

48. Thomas Gilovich, *How We Know What Isn't So: The Fallibility of Human Reason in Everyday Life* (Free Press, 1991), 30.

49. Edwin J. Elton, Martin J. Gruber, and Jeffrey A. Busse, *Are Investors Rational? Choices among Index Funds*, 59 J. Fin. 261, 262 (2004).

50. Barry Schwartz, *The Costs of Living: How Market Freedom Erodes the Best Things in Life* (Xlibris, 2001), 29.

51. Daniel Kahneman, *Thinking, Fast and Slow* (Farrar, Straus and Giroux, 2011) 41–42.

52. James J. White, *Contracting Under Amended 2–207*, 2004 Wis. L. Rev. 723, 741 (2004).

53. "Google Terms of Service," visited January 13, 2013, http://www.google.com/accounts/TOS?hl=en.

54. Margaret Jane Radin, *Boilerplate: The Fine Print, Vanishing Rights, and the Rule of Law* (Princeton University Press, 2013), 23, 210.

55. Florencia Marotta-Wurgler, *Are "Pay Now, Terms Later" Contracts Worse for Buyers? Evidence from Software License Agreements,* 38 J. Legal Stud. 309 (2009).

56. Angela A. Hung, Aileen Heinberg, and Anne K. Yoong, *Do Risk Disclosures Affect Investment Choice?* 7 (Working Paper WR-788 Labor and Population, 2010), visited January 13, 2013, http://papers.ssrn.com/sol3/papers.cfm?abstract _id=1688038.

57. Ibid.

58. Lauren E. Willis, *Against Financial-Literacy Education,* 94 Iowa L. Rev. 197, 202 (2008).

59. *Canterbury v. Spence,* 464 F.2d 772, 780 (D.C. Cir. 1972).

60. For similar arguments, see Barry Schwartz, *The Paradox of Choice: Why More is Less* (HarperCollins, 2004); Edward C. Rosenthal, *The Era of Choice: The Ability to Choose and Its Transformation of Contemporary Life* (MIT Press, 2005).

61. Kirsch, *Product Disclosures,* (2002), 273–74.

62. The animated show *South Park* mocked this disclosure in one of its episodes. See http://osxdaily.com/2011/04/28/south-park-human-centipad/, visited January 13, 2013.

63. Omri Ben-Shahar, *One Way Contracts: Consumer Protection without Law,* 6 European Rev. Contract Law 221 (2010).

64. Eugene Bardach and Robert A. Kagan, *Going By The Book: The Problem of Regulatory Unreasonableness* (Transaction, 2002), 206.

65. Samuel P. Jacobs, "Stern Lessons for Terrorism Expert: Kennedy School Researcher Tangles with Harvard Ethics Board," *Harvard Crimson,* March 23, 2007, visited January 13, 2013, http://www.thecrimson.com/printerfriendly.aspx ?ref=517924.

66. Andrea Akkad et al., *Patients' Perceptions of Written Consent: Questionnaire Study,* 333 BMJ 1, 2 (2006).

67. Peter Neary et al., *What a Signature Adds to the Consent Process,* 22 Surg. Endoscopy 2698 (2008).

68. Katherine M. Harris, *How Do Patients Choose Physicians? Evidence from a National Survey of Enrollees in Employment-Related Health Plans,* 38 HSR: Health Services Res. 711, 716 (2003).

CHAPTER 5

1. Committee on Health Literacy, Board on Neuroscience and Behavioral Health, *Health Literacy: A Prescription to End Confusion* (National Academies Press, 2004), 61–66.

2. National Center for Education Statistics, *Literacy in Everyday Life: Results from the 2003 National Assessment of Adult Literacy* (U.S. Dept. of Education, 2007), 4.

3. Ad Hoc Committee on Health Literacy for the Council on Scientific Affairs, American Medical Association, *Health Literacy: Report of the Council on Scientific Affairs*, 281 J. Amer. Med. Assoc. 552 (1999).

4. Irwin S. Kirsch et al., *Adult Literacy in America: A First Look at the Findings of the National Adult Literacy Survey* (U.S. Dept. of Education, 2002), 82–83.

5. S. Michael Sharp, *Consent Documents for Oncology Trials: Does Anybody Read These Things?*, 27 Amer. J. Clin. Oncology 570, 570 (2004).

6. Stuart A. Grossman et al., *Are Informed Consent Forms That Describe Clinical Oncology Research Protocols Readable by Most Patients and Their Families?*, 12 J. Clin. Oncology 2211, 2212 (1994).

7. Sharp, *Consent Documents*.

8. Grossman et al., *Informed Consent Forms*.

9. Michael K. Paasche-Orlow, Holly A. Taylor, and Frederick L. Brancati, *Readability Standards For Informed-Consent Forms as Compared With Actual Readability*, 348 N. Engl. J. Med. 721, 725 (2003).

10. Mark Hochhauser, *Lost in the Fine Print: Readability of Financial Privacy Notices* (July 2001), visited January 13, 2013, http://www.privacyrights.org/ar /GLB-Reading.htm.

11. Peter Breese et al., *The Health Insurance Portability and Accountability Act and the Informed Consent Process*, 141 Ann. Int. Med. 897, 897 (2004).

12. Peter Breese and William Burman, *Readability of Notice of Privacy Forms Used by Major Health Care Institutions*, 293 J. Amer. Med. Assoc. 1593, 1593 (2005).

13. Alan M. White and Cathy Lesser Mansfield, *Literacy and Contract*, 13 Stan. L. & Pol'y Rev. 233, 239 (2002).

14. Ronald J. Mann, *"Contracting" For Credit*, 104 Mich. L. Rev. 899, 907 (2006).

15. James M. Lacko and Janis K. Pappalardo, *The Failure and Promise of Mandated Consumer Mortgage Disclosures: Evidence from Qualitative Interviews and a Controlled Experiment with Mortgage Borrowers*, 100 Amer. Econ. Rev.: Papers and Proceedings 516, 516 (2010).

16. John C. Reid et al., *Why People Don't Learn From Diabetes Literature: Influence of Text and Reader Characteristics*, 25 Patient Educ. and Counseling 31, 32 (1995).

17. *Gerhardt v. Continental Insurance Cos.* 48 N.J. 291, 225 A.2d 328 (1966). These statements are quoted in Peter Tiersma, *Legal Language* (University of Chicago Press, 1999), 220.

18. "Despite the crisis, banks still carry huge risk," *CBS News*, February 7, 2013, quoting Paul Singer, head of Elliott Associates hedge fund.

19. Lisa M. Schwartz et al., *The Role of Numeracy in Understanding the Benefit of Screening Mammography*, 127 Ann. Int. Med. 966 (1997).

20. Isaac M. Lipkus, Greg Samsa, and Barbara K. Rimer, *General Performance on a Numeracy Scale Among Highly Educated Samples*, 21 Med. Decision Making 37, 39 (2001).

21. National Center for Education Statistics, *Literacy in Everyday Life: Results from the 2003 National Assessment of Adult Literacy* (U.S. Dept. of Education, 2007), 4.

22. Justin D. Baer et al., *The Literacy of America's College Students* (American Institutes for Research, 2006), 5.

23. Judith H. Hibbard et al., *Consumer Competencies and the Use of Comparative Quality Information: It Isn't Just About Literacy*, 64 Med. Care Res. & Rev. 379, 388 (2007).

24. Schwartz et al., *Role of Numeracy*.

25. Susan Block-Lieb and Edward J. Janger, *The Myth of the Rational Borrower: Rationality, Behavioralism, and the Misguided "Reform" of Bankruptcy Law*, 84 Tex. L. Rev. 1481, 1538 (2006).

26. Karin Braunsberger, Laurie Lucas, and Dave Roach, *The Effectiveness of Credit-Card Regulation for Vulnerable Consumers*, 18 J. Services Marketing 358, 364 (2004).

27. Paul K. J. Han et al., *Conceptual Problems in Laypersons' Understanding of Individualized Cancer Risk: A Qualitative Study*, 12 Health Expectations 4 (2009).

28. Daniel Kahneman, *Thinking Fast and Slow* (Farrar, Straus & Giroux, 2011), 329.

29. Gary Klein, *Sources of Power: How People Make Decisions* (MIT Press, 1998), 24.

30. Elizabeth J. Mulligan and Reid Hastie, *Explanations Determine the Impact of Information on Financial Investment Judgments*, 18 J. Behavioral Decision Making 145, 146 (2005).

31. Donald A. Schön, *The Reflective Practitioner: How Professionals Think in Action* (Basic Books, 1983), 60.

32. Daniel E. Ho, *Fudging the Nudge: Information Disclosure and Restaurant Grading*, 122 Yale L.J. 574, 592 (2012).

33. Klein, *Sources of Power*, 157.

34. See Stephen A. Marglin, "Towards the Decolonization of the Mind," in *Dominating Knowledge*, ed. Frédérique Appfel Marglin and Stephen A. Marglin (Oxford University Press 1990), 1, 24.

35. Donald A. Schön, *The Reflective Practitioner: How Professionals Think in Action* (Basic Books, 1983), viii.

36. Gillian Rose, *Love's Work: A Reckoning with Life* (Schocken, 1997), 102–3.

37. Schön, *Reflective Practitioner*, 60.

38. Larry Kirsch, *Do Product Disclosures Inform and Safeguard Insurance Policyholders?*, 20 J. Ins. Reg. 271, 283 (2002).

39. Carl E. Schneider and Michael H. Farrell, "Information, Decisions, and the Limits of Informed Consent," in *Law and Medicine*, ed. Michael Freeman and Andrew D. E. Lewis (Oxford, 2000).

40. Nancy D. Berkman et al., *Low Health Literacy and Health Outcomes: An Updated Systematic Review*, 155 Ann. Int. Med. 97, 97 (2011).
41. Thomas Gilovich, *How We Know What Isn't So: The Fallibility of Human Reason in Everyday Life* (Free Press, 1991), 125.
42. See Susan J. Diem, John D. Lantos, and James A. Tulsky, *Cardiopulmonary Resuscitation on Television: Miracles and Misinformation*, 334 N. Engl. J. Med. 1578, 1578 (1996).
43. Gilovich, *How We Know*, 133.
44. Han et al., *Conceptual Problems*.
45. William M. Sage, *Accountability Through Information: What the Health Care Industry Can Learn from Securities Regulation* (Milbank Memorial Fund, 2000), 22.
46. Kesten Green and J. Scott Armstrong, *Evidence on the Effects of Mandatory Disclaimers in Advertising*, 31 J. Public Pol'y & Marketing, 293 (2012).
47. Truth in Lending, 73 Fed. Reg. 1676 (Jan. 9, 2008) (codified at 12 C.F.R. pt. 226).
48. Haiyang Chen and Ronald P. Volpe, *An Analysis of Personal Financial Literacy Among College Students*, 7 Fin. Serv. Rev. 107, 108, 122 (1998).
49. Debra Pogrund Stark and Jessica M. Choplin, *A Cognitive and Social Psychological Analysis of Disclosure Laws and Call for Mortgage Counseling to Prevent Predatory Lending*, 16 Psychol. Pub. Pol'y and L. 85, 98 (2010).
50. James M. Lacko and Janis K. Pappalardo, *Improving Consumer Mortgage Disclosures*, Staff Report (Federal Trade Commission Bureau of Economics, 2007), 29.
51. Angela Littwin, *Beyond Usury: A Study of Credit Card Use and Preference among Low-Income Consumers*, 86 Tex. L. Rev. 451, 497 (2008).
52. Henry T. C. Hu, *Illiteracy and Intervention: Wholesale Derivatives, Retail Mutual Funds, and the Matter of Asset Class*, 84 Geo. L.J. 2319, 2371 (1996).
53. Chen and Volpe, *Personal Financial Literacy*, 108.
54. Donna M. MacFarland, Carolyn D. Marconi, and Stephen P. Utkus, *"Money Attitudes" and Retirement Plan Design: One Size Does Not Fit All*, in *Pension Design and Structure: New Lessons from Behavioral Finance*, ed. Olivia S. Mitchell & Stephen P. Utkus (Oxford University Press, 2004), 98.
55. Mary Graham, *Democracy by Disclosure: The Rise of Technopopulism* (Brookings Institution Press, 2002), 94.
56. Ben S. Bernanke, Chairman, Fed. Reserve Bd., Address at the Federal Reserve System's Biennial Community Affairs Research Conference (Apr. 17, 2009), online at http://www.federalreserve.gov/newsevents/ speech/bernanke20090417a .htm (visited January 13, 2013).
57. Hu, *Illiteracy and Intervention*, 2371.
58. Committee on Health Literacy, Board on Neuroscience and Behavioral Health, *Health Literacy: A Prescription to End Confusion* (National Academies Press, 2004), 143.

59. Eric J. Gouvin, *Truth in Savings and the Failure of Legislative Methodology*, 62 U. Cin. L. Rev. 1281, 1314 (1994).

60. MacFarland, Marconi, and Utkus, *"Money Attitudes,"* 98.

61. Willis, *Against Financial-Literacy Education*.

CHAPTER 6

1. Barry Schwartz, *Self-Determination: The Tyranny of Freedom*, 55 Amer. Psychologist 79, 81 (2000).

2. Lauren E. Willis, *Against Financial-Literacy Education*, 94 Iowa L. Rev. 197, 228 (2008).

3. Aleecia M. McDonald and Lorrie F. Cranor, *The Cost of Reading Privacy Policies*, 4 I/S: A Journal of Law and Policy for the Information Society 543, 563–65 (2008).

4. Mary Graham, *Democracy by Disclosure: The Rise of Technopopulism* (Brookings, 2002), 95.

5. David de Meza, Bernd Irlenbusch, and Diane Reyniers, *Disclosure, Trust and Persuasion in Insurance Markets*, IZA Discussion Paper No. 5060 (2010), 1.

6. Tom Vanderbilt, "Little. Yellow. Dangerous. 'Children at Play' Signs Imperil Our Kids," *Slate* May 18, 2011, visited January 13, 2013, http://www.slate.com/id /2293460/.

7. Larry Kirsch, *Do Product Disclosures Inform and Safeguard Insurance Policyholders?*, 20 J. Ins. Reg. 271, 278 (2002).

8. Naresh K. Malhotra, *Information Load and Consumer Decision Making*, 8 J. of Consumer Res. 419, 419 (1982).

9. Douglas A. Hershey et al., *Challenges of Training Pre-Retirees to Make Sound Financial Planning Decisions*, 24 Educational Gerontology 447, 449 (1998).

10. Lynn Quincy, *Making Health Insurance Cost-Sharing Clear to Consumers: Challenges in Implementing Health Reform's Insurance Disclosure Requirements*, Commonwealth Fund pub. 1480, vol. 2 (2011).

11. Richard Rogers, *A Little Knowledge is a Dangerous Thing . . . Emerging* Miranda *Research and Professional Roles for Psychologists*, 63 Amer. Psychologist 778–79 (2008).

12. Judith H. Hibbard, Paul Slovic, and Jacquelyn J. Jewett, *Informing Consumer Decisions in Health Care: Implications from Decision-Making Research*, 75 Milbank Q. 395, 397 (1997).

13. Willis, *Against Financial-Literacy Education*, 229 n134.

14. Ronald J. Mann, *"Contracting" For Credit*, 104 Mich. L. Rev. 899, 908 (2006).

15. Dan Ariely, *Predictably Irrational: The Hidden Forces That Shape Our Decisions* (HarperCollins, 2008), 110.

16. Mann, *"Contracting" For Credit*, 908.

17. See, e.g., Kevin Larson, "The Science of Word Recognition, or How I Learned to Stop Worrying and Love the Bouma" (2004), visited January 14, 2013, www .microsoft.com/typography/ctfonts/wordrecognition.aspx.

18. Sheena S. Iyengar and Mark R. Lepper, *When Choice is Demotivating: Can One Desire Too Much of a Good Thing?*, 79 J. Personality & Soc. Psychology 995, 996 (2000).

19. Sheena S. Iyengar, Wei Jiang, and Gur Huberman, "How Much Choice is Too Much? Contributions to 401(k) Retirement Plans," in *Pension Design and Structure: New Lessons from Behavioral Finance,* ed. Olivia S. Mitchell and Stephen P. Utkus (Oxford University Press, 2004), 85.

20. Willis, *Against Financial-Literacy Education*, 229.

21. Sheena Iyengar, *The Art of Choosing* (Twelve, 2010), 195–96.

22. Yaniv Hanoch and Thomas Rice, *Can Limiting Choice Increase Social Welfare? The Elderly and Health Insurance*, 84 Milbank Q. 37 (2006).

23. Angela Hung, Aileen Heinberg, and Joanne Yoong, *Do Risk Disclosures Affect Investment Choice?* (RAND Labor and Population Working Paper No. WR-788, Sept 2010), 4, visited January 14, 2013, http://papers.ssrn.com/sol3/papers.cfm ?abstract_id=1688038.

24. Elisabeth H. Sandberg et al., *Clinicians Consistently Exceed a Typical Person's Short-Term Memory During Preoperative Teaching,* 53 Survey of Anesthesiology 131, 131 (2009).

25. William M. Sage, *Accountability Through Information: What the Health Care Industry Can Learn from Securities Regulation* (Milbank Memorial Fund, 2000), 34–35.

26. Willis, *Against Financial-Literacy Education*, 224.

27. Kirsch, *Product Disclosures*, 278.

CHAPTER 7

1. See, e.g., Robert B. Cialdini, *Influence: The Psychology of Persuasion* (rev. ed., Harper 2006); Daniel Kahneman, *Thinking Fast and Slow* (Farrar, Straus and Giroux, 2011); Dan Ariely, *Predictably Irrational: The Hidden Forces That Shape Our Decisions* (HarperCollins, 2008).

2. Richard H. Thaler and Cass R. Sunstein, *Nudge: Improving Decisions about Health, Wealth, and Happiness* (Penguin, 2009); Cass R. Sunstein, *Empirically Informed Regulation,* 78 U. Chi. L. Rev. 1349 (2011).

3. Oren Bar-Gill, *Seduction by Plastic* (Oxford University Press, 2012), 107.

4. John Ameriks, Andrew Caplin, and John Leahy, *The Absent-Minded Consumer,* (National Bureau of Economic Research Working Paper 10216, Jan 2004), 23.

5. Henry T. C. Hu, *Illiteracy and Intervention: Wholesale Derivatives, Retail Mutual Funds, and the Matter of Asset Class,* 84 Geo. L.J. 2319, 2367 (1996).

6. John Hancock Financial Services, *Insight into Participant Investment Knowledge & Behavior, 8th Defined Contribution Plan Survey* (2002), 5.

7. Dan Ariely, *Predictably Irrational: The Hidden Forces That Shape Our Decisions* (HarperCollins, 2008), 129.

8. Bar-Gill, *Seduction by Plastic*, 215–40; Stefano Della Vigna and Ulrike Malmendier, *Paying Not to Go to the Gym*, 96 Amer. Econ. Rev. 694 (2006).

9. Omri Ben-Shahar, *How Bad Are Mandatory Arbitration Terms?*, 41 Mich. J. L. Reform 777 (2008); Omri Ben-Shahar, "Arbitration and Access to Courts: An Economic Analysis," in *Regulatory Competition in Contract Law and Dispute Resolution,* ed. H. Eidenmuller (Hart, 2013), 449.

10. Gary Klein, *Streetlights and Shadows: Searching for the Keys to Adaptive Decision Making* (MIT Press, 2009), 208, 212.

11. Ibid., 223.

12. Joel Tsevat et al., *The Will to Live among HIV-Infected Patients*, 131 Ann. Int. Med. 194 (1999); Peter A. Ubel, George Loewenstein, and Christopher Jepson, *Whose Quality of Life? A Commentary Exploring Discrepancies Between Health State Evaluations of Patients and the General Public*, 12 Quality of Life Res. 599 (2003).

13. Ariely, *Predictably Irrational*, 319.

14. Barbara J. McNeil et al., *On the Elicitation of Preferences for Alternative Therapies*, 306 N. Engl. J. Med. 1259, 1261 (1982).

15. Renée R. Anspach, *Deciding Who Lives: Fateful Choices in the Intensive-Care Nursery* (University of California Press, 1993), 101.

16. Herbert A. Simon, *The Failure of Armchair Economics*, 29 Challenge 18, 21 (1986).

17. Daniel Kahneman, *Thinking Fast and Slow* (Farrar, Straus and Giroux, 2011), 87–88.

18. Elizabeth J. Mulligan and Reid Hastie, *Explanations Determine the Impact of Information on Financial Investment Judgments*, 17 J. Behavioral Decision Making 145, 146 (2005).

19. Thomas Gilovich, *How We Know What Isn't So: The Fallibility of Human Reason in Everyday Life* (Free Press, 1991), 76.

20. John C. Reid et al., *Why People Don't Learn From Diabetes Literature: Influence of Text and Reader Characteristics*, 25 Patient Education & Counseling 31, 35 (1995).

21. Lauren E. Willis, *Against Financial-Literacy Education*, 94 Iowa L. Rev. 197, 235–36 (2008).

22. Kahneman, *Thinking Fast and Slow*, 20–21. See also Steven A. Sloman, *The Empirical Case for Two Systems of Reasoning*, 119 Psychological Bull. 3 (1996).

23. Kahneman, *Thinking Fast and Slow*, 45.

24. George A. Akerlof and Robert J. Shiller, *Animal Spirits: How Human Psychology Drives the Economy and Why It Matters for Global Capitalism* (Princeton University Press, 2009), 123.

25. Bar-Gill, *Seduction by Plastic*, 21–22.
26. Baruch Fischhoff et al., *How Safe is Safe Enough? A Psychometric Study of Attitudes Toward Technological Risks and Benefits,* 9 Pol'y Sci. 127 (1978); A. Alhakmi and P. Slovic, *A Psychological Study of the Inverse Relationships Between Perceived Risk and Perceived Benefit,* 14 Risk Analysis 1085 (1994).
27. Angela A. Hung, Aileen Heinberg, and Anne K. Yoong, *Do Risk Disclosures Affect Investment Choice?* (Working Paper WR-788 Labor and Population, 2010), 7, visited January 13, 2013, http://papers.ssrn.com/sol3/papers.cfm?abstract_id =1688038.
28. Angela Fagerlin, Brian J. Zikmund-Fisher, and Peter A. Ubel, *"If I'm Better Than Average, Then I'm OK?": Comparative Information Influences Beliefs About Risk and Benefits,* 69 Patient Educ. & Counseling 140, 143 (2007).
29. Gilovich, *How We Know,* 2.
30. Richard A. Epstein, *The Neoclassical Economics of Consumer Contracts,* 92 Minn. L. Rev. 803, 808 (2008).
31. Cass R. Sunstein, *Empirically Informed Regulation,* 78 U. Chi. L. Rev. 1349 (2011).
32. Ibid., 1365–66.
33. Thomas Cooley et al., "Consumer Finance Protection," in *Regulating Wall Street: The Dodd-Frank Act and the New Architecture of Global Finance,* ed. Viral V. Acharya et al. (John Wiley and Sons, 2011), 73, 82.
34. Oren Bar-Gill, *Seduction by Contract* (Oxford, 2012).
35. Marianne Bertrand and Adair Morse, *Information Disclosure, Cognitive Biases, and Payday Borrowing,* 66 J. Fin. 1865, 1866 (2011).
36. Kahneman, *Thinking Fast and Slow,* 417.
37. Debra Pogrund Stark and Jessica M. Choplin, *A Cognitive and Social Psychological Analysis of Disclosure Laws and Call for Mortgage Counseling to Prevent Predatory Lending,* 16 Psychology, Public Pol'y, & Law 85, 89 (2010).
38. Jinkook Lee and Jeanne M. Hogarth, *Relationships Among Information Search Activities When Shopping for a Credit Card,* 34 J. Consumer Affairs 330, 333 (2000).
39. David de Meza, Bernd Irlenbusch, and Diane J. Reyniers, *Disclosure, Trust and Persuasion in Insurance Markets,* IZA Discussion Paper No. 5060 (2010), 2.
40. Ronald Mann, *Nudging from Debt: The Role of Behavioral Economics in Regulation,* (Lydian Journal 2011), visited January 14, 2013, http://www.pymnts.com /journal-bak/201/nudging-from-debt-the-role-of-behavioral-economics-in -regulation/.
41. Emir Kamenica, Sendhil Mullainathan, and Richard Thaler, *Behavioral Economics and Consumer Regulation,* 101 Amer. Econ. Rev.: Papers and Proceedings 417, 421–22 (2011).
42. Jeff Sovern, *Preventing Future Economic Crises Through Consumer Protection Law or How the Truth in Lending Act Failed the Subprime Borrowers,* 71 Ohio St. L.J. 761, 782–83 (2010).

43. See Debra Pogrund Stark and Jessica M. Choplin, *A Cognitive and Social Psychological Analysis of Disclosure Laws and Call for Mortgage Counseling to Prevent Predatory Lending*, 16 Psychology, Public Pol'y, & Law 85, 101 (2010); Ill. Dep't Fin. and Prof'l Regulation, Findings from the HB 4050 Predatory Lending Database Pilot Program 1, 3–4 (2007), visited January 14, 2013, http://nlihc.org/library/sirr/IL-2007.

44. Stark and Choplin, *Cognitive and Social Psychological Analysis*, 125.

45. Daylian M. Cain, George Loewenstein, and Don A. Moore, *The Dirt on Coming Clean: Perverse Effects of Disclosing Conflicts of Interest*, 34 J. Legal Stud. 1, 22 (2005); Sunita Sah, George Loewenstein, and Daylian M. Cain, *The Burden of Disclosure: Increased Compliance with Distrusted Advice*, 104 J. Personality & Social Psychology 289 (2013).

46. Bertrand and Morse, *Information Disclosure*, 1889–91.

47. Adair Morse, *Payday Lenders: Heroes or Villains?*, 102 J. Fin. Econ. 28, 42 (2011).

48. Victor Saliterman and Barry G. Sheckley, "Adult Learning Principles and Pension Participant Behavior," in *Pension Design and Structure: New Lessons from Behavioral Finance*, ed. Olivia S. Mitchell and Stephen P. Utkus (Oxford University Press, 2004), 221.

CHAPTER 8

1. Cass R. Sunstein, *Empirically Informed Regulation*, 78 U. Chi. L. Rev. 1349, 1369 (2011).

2. SEC Release No. 33–8861 (December 14, 2007).

3. Daniel Schwarcz, *Transparency Opaque: Understanding the Lack of Transparency in Insurance Consumer Protection*, 61 UCLA L. Rev. (forthcoming, 2014); Lynn Quincy, *Make Insurance Understandable*, Politico.com (Nov 3, 2011), visited January 13, 2013, http://www.politico.com/news/stories/1111/67548.html.

4. Plain Writing Act § 3, Pub. L. No. 111–274, 124 Stat. 2861.

5. Dodd-Frank Act § 1021, Pub. L. No. 111–203, 124 Stat. 1979, codified at 12 U.S.C. § 5511.

6. Jerry Menikoff with Edward P. Richards, *What the Doctor Didn't Say: The Hidden Truth about Medical Research* (Oxford University Press, 2006), 228.

7. Sunstein, *Empirically Informed Regulation*, 1366.

8. Ibid., 1369.

9. Michael S. Barr, Sendhil Mullainathan, and Eldar Shafir, *Behaviorally Informed Financial Services Regulation*, (New America Foundation, 2008), 9; Michael S. Barr, Sendhil Mullainathan, and Eldar Shafir, "A One Size Fits All Solution," *New York Times* (December 26, 2007), www.nytimes.com/2007/12/26/opinion/26barr.html?page.

10. http://www.consumerfinance.gov/knowbeforeyouowe/, visited January 14, 2013.

11. For an early discussion of improvement in TILA, see William N. Eskridge, Jr., *One Hundred Years of Ineptitude: The Need for Mortgage Consonant with the Economics and Psychological Dynamics of the Home Sale and Loan Transaction*, 70 Va. L. Rev. 1083 (1984).

12. Department of Treasury, *Financial Regulatory Reform: A New Foundation* (2009), 64.

13. Barr, Mullainathan, and Shafir, *Behaviorally Informed*, 7.

14. Margaret Jane Radin, *Boilerplate: The Fine Print, Vanishing Rights, and the Rule of Law* (Princeton University Press, 2012.)

15. James J. White and Robert Summers, *Uniform Commercial Code, 5th ed., 1*: 599–852 (West Group, 2006).

16. Ian Ayres and Alan Schwartz, *The No Reading Problem in Consumer Contract Law*, Stan. L. Rev. (forthcoming, 2013).

17. White House, *Consumer Data Privacy in a Networked World: A Framework for Protecting Privacy and Promoting Innovation in the Global Digital Economy* (2012), visited January 14, 2013, http://www.whitehouse.gov/sites/default/files /privacy-final.pdf.

18. Institute of Medicine, *Responsible Research: A Systems Approach to Protecting Research Participants* (National Academies Press, 2003), viii.

19. Mary Dixon-Woods et al., *Beyond "Misunderstanding": Written Information and Decisions About Taking Part in a Genetic Epidemiology Study*, 65 Soc. Sci. & Med. 2212, 2213 (2007).

20. Alan M. White and Cathy Lesser Mansfield, *Literacy and Contract*, 13 Stan. L. & Pol'y Rev. 233, 239 (2002).

21. Ibid., 242.

22. Richard Rogers, *A Little Knowledge is a Dangerous Thing . . . Emerging* Miranda *Research and Professional Roles for Psychologists*, 63 Amer. Psychologist 776, 779 (2008).

23. White and Mansfield, *Literacy and Contract*, 238–39 (2002).

24. Robert J. Levine, IRB 8 (January 1982) (letter).

25. http://en.wikipedia.org/wiki/Mastocytosis, visited January 14, 2013.

26. http://en.wikipedia.org/wiki/Mast cell, visited January 14, 2013.

27. "eBay User Agreement," eBay, April 23, 2013, pages.ebay.com/help/policies/user -agreement.html?_trksid=m40.

28. Securities and Exchange Commission, *Enhanced Disclosure and New Prospectus Delivery Option for Registered Open-End Management Investment Companies*, 17 CFR Parts 230, 232, 239, and 274 (Release Nos. 33–8861; December 14, 2007).

29. John Beshears et al., "How Does Simplified Disclosure Affect Individuals' Mutual Fund Choice?," in *Explorations in the Economics of Aging*, ed. David A. Wise (University of Chicago Press, 2011), 75.

30. Ibid.

31. *Know Before You Owe: Evolution of the Integrated TILA-RESPA Disclosures*, (2012), xxvi, visited January 14, 2013, http://files.consumerfinance.gov/f/201207 _cfpb_report_tila-respa-testing.pdf.

32. Lynn Quincy, *Making Health Insurance Cost-Sharing Clear to Consumers: Challenges in Implementing Health Reform's Insurance Disclosure Requirements*, Consumers Union Issue Brief (February 2011).

33. Ibid.

34. Schwarcz, *Transparency Opaque,* 5

35. See Eskridge, *One Hundred Years of Ineptitude*, 1166 (1984); Elizabeth Renuart and Diane E. Thompson, *The Truth, The Whole Truth, and Nothing But the Truth: Fulfilling the Promise of Truth in Lending*, 25 Yale J. on Reg. 181, 219–20 n223 (2008); Oren Bar-Gill, *The Law, Economics, and Psychology of Subprime Mortgage Contracts*, 94 Cornell L. Rev. 1073, 1078 (2009).

36. See, e.g., Jeff Sovern, *Preventing Future Economic Crises through Consumer Protection Law or How the Truth in Lending Act Failed the Subprime Borrowers*, 71 Ohio St. L. J. 761 (2010); James M. Lacko and Janis K. Pappalardo, *Improving Consumer Mortgage Disclosures: An Empirical Assessment of Current and Prototype Disclosure Forms* (Federal Trade Commission, Bureau of Economics Staff Report, 2007); see also *Design and Testing of Effective Truth in Lending Disclosures: Findings from Experimental Study*, visited January 14, 2013, http://www.federalreserve.gov/newsevents/press/bcreg/bcreg20081218a8.pdf.

37. Andrew Martin, "Prepaid, but not Prepared for Debit Card Fees," *New York Times* (Oct 5, 2009), visited January 14, 2013, http://www.nytimes.com/2009/10/06/your-money/06prepay.html?hp.

38. Julia Marlowe and Martina Rojo, *Consumer Problems with Prepaid Telephone Cards*, 51 Consumer Ints. Ann. 126, 131 (2005).

39. Attorney General Pam Bondi News Release, visited January 14, 2013, http://www.myfloridalegal.com/newsrel.nsf/newsreleases/7AD2F1581F3BB2A485257895004D18D5.

40. Smart disclosure builds on the idea of "RECAP" developed in Richard H. Thaler and Cass R. Sunstein, *Nudge: Improving Decisions about Health, Wealth, and Happiness* (Penguin, 2009).

41. Cass Sunstein, *Informing Consumers through Smart Disclosure*, White House Office of Management and Budget Blog, March 30, 2012, visited January 14, 2013, http://www.whitehouse.gov/blog/2012/03/30/informing-consumers-through-smart-disclosure.

42. See Oren Bar-Gill and Franco Ferrari, *Informing Consumers about Themselves*, 3 Erasmus L. Rev. 93 (2010); Emir Kamenica, Sendhil Mullainathan, and Richard Thaler, *Helping Consumers Know Themselves*, 101 Amer. Econ. Rev.: Papers and Proceedings 417 (2011).

43. Ariel Porat and Lior J. Strahilevitz, *Personalizing Default Rules and Disclosure with Big Data*, 112 Mich. L. Rev. (forthcoming, 2014).

44. Bryan Bollinger, Phillip Leslie, and Alan Sorensen, *Calorie Posting in Chain Restaurants*, 3 Amer. Econ. J.: Econ. Pol'y 91, 91 (2011). See also C. A. Roberto et al., *Evaluating the Impact of Menu Labeling on Food Choices and Intake*, 100 Amer. J. Pub. Health 312, 312 (2010).

45. Gary Jones and Miles Richardson, *An Objective Examination of Consumer Perception of Nutrition Information Based on Healthiness Ratings and Eye Movements*, 10 Pub. Health Nutrition 238, 238 (2007).

46. Gill Cowburn and Lynn Stockley, *Consumer Understanding and Use of Nutrition Labeling: A Systematic Review*, 8 Pub. Health Nutrition 21, 23 (2005).

47. Mary Margaret Huizinga et al., *Literacy, Numeracy, and Portion-Size Estimation Skills*, 36 Amer. J. Preventive Med. 324, 326 (2009); Russell L. Rothman et al., *Patient Understanding of Food Labels: The Role of Literacy and Numeracy*, 31 Amer. J. Preventive Med. 391, 393 (2006).

48. L. J. Harnack et al., *Effect of Calorie Labeling and Value Size Pricing on Fast Food Meal Choices: Results from an Experimental Trial*, 5 Int'l J. Behavioral Nutrition & Physical Activity 63, 63 (2008).

49. Brian Elbel et al., *Calorie Labeling and Food Choices: A First Look at the Effects on Low Income People in New York City*, 28 Health Affairs 1110, 1110–11 (2009); Julie S. Downs, George Loewenstein, and Jessica Wisdom, *The Psychology of Food Consumption: Strategies for Promoting Healthier Food Choices*, 99 Amer. Econ. Rev. 159, 159–60 (2009).

50. Brenda M. Derby and Alan S. Levy, "Do Food Labels Work?," in *Handbook of Marketing and Society*, ed. Paul N. Bloom and Gregory T. Gundlach, (Sage, 2001) 372, 389; Daniel S. Putler and Elizabeth Frazao, "Assessing the Effects of Nutrition Education Programs on the Consumption and Composition of Fat Intake," in *Economics of Food Safety*, ed. Julie A. Casell, (Elsevier Science, 1991), 247.

51. Kiyah J. Duffey and Barry M. Popkin, *Energy Density, Portion Size, and Eating Occasions: Contributions to Increased Energy Intake in the United States, 1977–2006*, 8(6) PLoS Med 1 (2011).

CHAPTER 9

1. Louis Brandeis, *Other People's Money and How Bankers Use It* (1914), 103.

2. "Geithner: New Bureau to Focus on Improved Disclosures," http://m.foxbusiness.com/quickPage.html?page=19453&content=42943554&pageNum=-1.

3. Richard Cordray, "CFPB Helping Fix Mortgage Industry," Politico.com, February 13, 2012, http://www.politico.com/news/stories/0212/72769_Page2.html #ixzz1mIKy5uMH.

4. H. R. Res. 1609 (2010).

5. Statement of Representative Rick Lazio, Chairman of Subcommittee on Housing and Community Opportunity, July 22 1998, http://commdocs.house.gov/committees/bank/hba50286.000/hba50286_0.htm.

6. James Q. Wilson, *Bureaucracy: What Governments Agencies Do and Why They Do It* (Basic Books, 1989), 341.

7. Eugene Bardach and Robert A. Kagan, *Going By the Book: The Problem of Regulatory Unreasonableness* (Transaction, 2002), 23.

8. 611 P.2d 902 (Cal., 1980).

9. In the United States, over 80 percent of women between the ages of eighteen and forty-four report having had a Pap smear within the last three years. http://www.cdc.gov/cancer/cervical/statistics/screening.htm.

10. *In the Matter of International Harvester Company*, 104 F.T.C. 949 (1984).

11. Jeremy Sugarman et al., *The Cost of Ethics Legislation: A Look at the Patient Self-Determination Act*, 3 Kennedy Instit. Ethics J. 387, 389 (1993).

12. Mark A. Hall, *Making Medical Spending Decisions: The Law, Ethics, and Economics of Rationing Mechanisms* (Oxford University Press, 1997), 198; Martin Grunderson, *Eliminating Conflicts of Interests in Managed Care Organizations through Disclosure and Consent*, 25 J. L. Med. & Ethics 192, 195 (1997).

13. *Citizens United v. Federal Election Commission*, 558 U.S. 310 (2010).

14. Cass Sunstein and Richard Thaler, *Libertarian Paternalism*, 70 U. Chi. L. Rev. 1159, 1160 (2003); Richard Thaler and Cass Sunstein, *Nudge: Improving Decisions about Health, Wealth, and Happiness* (Penguin, 2009), 5–14.

15. Robert Pear, "U.S. to Force Drug Firm to Report Money Paid to Doctors," *New York Times*, January 16, 2002.

16. Statement of Robert F. Elliott, president, Household Finance Company, in *Re-examining Truth-in-Lending: Do Borrowers Actually Use Disclosures?* 52 Consumer Fin. L. Q. Rep. 3, 7 (1998).

17. Lauren E. Willis, *Against Financial-Literacy Education*, 94 Iowa L. Rev. 197, 265 (2008).

18. Robert A. Hillman and Maureen O'Rourke, *Defending Disclosure in Software Contracting*, 78 U. Chi. L. Rev. 95 (2011).

19. Ilene Albala et al., *The Evolution of Consent Forms for Research: A Quarter Century of Changes*, 32 IRB: Ethics & Human Research 7 (May/June, 2010).

20. *Wyeth v. Levine*, 555 U.S. 555 (2009).

CHAPTER 10

1. W. Kip Viscusi, *Individual Rationality, Hazard Warnings, and the Foundations of Tort Law*, 48 Rutgers L. Rev. 625, 628 (1996)

2. U.S. Department of Education, Office of Postsecondary Education, *The Handbook for Campus Safety and Security Reporting* (2011).

3. U.S. Department of Education, Office of Postsecondary Education, *The Handbook for Campus Crime Reporting* (2005), 1.

4. Sara Lipka, "Do Crime Statistics Keep Students Safe?," *Chron. Higher Educ.*, Jan. 30, 2009.

5. Ibid.

6. See, e.g., "Univ. of Mich., Annual Security Report & Annual Fire Safety Report (2012–2013)," http://www.umich.edu/~safety/pdf/annual_report_2012.pdf.

7. Michael M. Greenfield, *Consumer Transactions*, 5th ed. (Foundation Press, 2009), 185.

8. Edward L. Rubin, *Legislative Methodology: Some Lessons from the Truth-in-Lending Act*, 80 Geo. L.J. 233, 236–37 (1991).

9. Archon Fung et al., *Full Disclosure: The Perils and Promise of Transparency* (Cambridge University Press, 2008), 82.

10. Ginger Zhe Jin and Philip Leslie, *The Effect of Information on Product Quality: Evidence from Restaurant Hygiene Grade Cards*, 118 Q. J. Econ. 409 (2003).

11. Omri Ben-Shahar and Carl E. Schneider, *The Failure of Mandated Disclosure*, 159 U. Penn. L. Rev. 647, 743–48 (2011).

12. Daniel E. Ho, *Fudging the Nudge: Information Disclosure and Restaurant Grading*, 122 Yale L.J. 574 (2012).

13. Ibid.

14. Ibid.

15. *Canterbury v. Spence*, 464 F.2d 772, 781–88 (D.C. Cir. 1972).

16. The court quoted this sentence from Jon R. Waltz and Thomas W. Scheuneman, *Informed Consent for Therapy*, 64 Nw. U. L. Rev. 628, 640 (1970).

17. "Common and Rare Side Effects for Aspirin Oral," WebMD, visited Nov. 15, 2010, www.webmd.com/drugs/drug-1082-aspirin.aspx?drugid=1082&drugname =aspirin&source=1&pagenumber=6.

18. See Byron Cryer, *NSAID-Associated Deaths: The Rise and Fall of NSAID-Associated GI Mortality*, 100 Am. J. Gastroenterology 1694, 1694 (2005).

19. Ibid.

20. Thomas O. Stair et al., *Variation in Institutional Review Board Responses to a Standard Protocol for a Multicenter Clinical Trial*, 8 Academic Emergency Medicine 636, 638 (2001).

21. Lee A. Green et al., *IRB and Methodological Issues: Impact of Institutional Review Board Practice Variation on Observational Health Services Research*, 41 HSR: Health Services Research 214, 221 (2006).

22. Jerry Goldman and Martin D. Katz, *Inconsistency and Institutional Review Boards*, 248 JAMA 197 (1982).

23. 225 Ill. Comp. Stat. Ann. 410/3B-12(a) (West 2007).

24. Dave Wendler and Jonathan Rackoff, *Consent for Continuing Research Participation: What Is It and When Should It Be Obtained?*, IRB: Ethics & Human Res., May–June 2002, 1, 1.

25. Tim Smits and Vera Hoorens, *How Probable is Probably? It Depends on Whom You're Talking About*, 18 J. Behav. Decision Making 83, 84 (2005).

26. Kimberley Koons Woloshin et al., *Patients' Interpretation of Qualitative Probability Statements*, 3 Archives Fam. Med. 961, 965 (1994).

27. Dianne C. Berry et al., *Patients' Understanding of Risk Associated with Medication Use: Impact of European Commission Guidelines and Other Risk Scales*, 26 Drug Safety 1, 2 (2003).

28. David A. Grimes and Gillian R. Snively, *Patients' Understanding of Medical Risks: Implications for Genetic Counseling*, 93 Obstetrics & Gynecology 910, 912–13 (1999).

29. Peter Knapp et al., *Communicating the Risk of Side Effects to Patients: An Evaluation of UK Regulatory Recommendations*, 32 Drug Safety 837, 838–39 (2009).

30. Richard Rogers, *A Little Knowledge is a Dangerous Thing . . . Emerging* Miranda *Research and Professional Roles For Psychologists*, 63 Am. Psychologist 776, 778–79 (2008).

31. Peter A. Ubel, *Truth in the Most Optimistic Way*, 134 Ann. Int. Med. 1142, 1143 (2001).

32. Tracy M. Robinson et al., *Patient-Oncologist Communication in Advanced Cancer: Predictors of Patient Perception of Prognosis*, 16 Supportive Care Cancer 1049, 1050 (2008).

33. Lynn Quincy, *Making Health Insurance Cost-Sharing Clear to Consumers: Challenges in Implementing Health Reform's Insurance Disclosure Requirements*, Consumers Union Issue Brief 4–6 (February 2011).

34. University of Michigan, "Protecting Consumer Privacy 3.3," www.uofmhealth .org/patient+and+visitor+guide/hipaa.

35. U.S. Federal Trade Commission, *Protecting Consumer Privacy in an Era of Rapid Change* (FTC Report, March 2012).

36. Richard A. Leo, *Questioning the Relevance of* Miranda *in the Twenty-First Century*, 99 Mich. L Rev. 1000, 1009–10 (2000).

37. Jessica Silver-Greenberg, "Don't Buy Too Much Insurance," *Wall Street Journal* (Oct. 8, 2011).

38. Susan Block-Lieb and Edward J. Janger, *The Myth of the Rational Borrower: Rationality, Behavioralism, and the Misguided "Reform" of Bankruptcy Law*, 84 Tex. L. Rev. 1481, 1560 (2006).

39. Truls Østbye et al., *Is There Time for Management of Patients With Chronic Diseases in Primary Care?*, 3 Ann. Fam. Med. 209, 212 (2005). See also Kimberly S. H. Yarnall et al., *Primary Care: Is There Enough Time for Prevention?*, 93 Am. J. Pub. Health 635, 637 (2003).

40. Dianne C. Berry et al., *Patients' Understanding of Risk Associated with Medication Use: Impact of European Commission Guidelines and Other Risk Scales*, 26 Drug Safety 1, 2, 54–55 (2003).

41. Neil Carrigan et al., *Adequacy of Patient Information on Adverse Effects: An Assessment of Patient Information Leaflets in the UK*, 31 Drug Safety 305, 306–7 (2008).

42. Mark A. Hall, *The Theory and Practice of Disclosing HMO Physician Incentives*, 65(4) Law & Contemp. Probs. 207, 227 (2002).

43. Lawrence D. Brown, *Management by Objection?: Public Policies to Protect Choice in Health Plans*, 56 Med. Care Res. & Rev. 145, 161 (Supp. 1 1999), quoting Paul Lengerin, president, New Jersey HMO Association.

44. *Kohn v. American Metal Climax*, Inc., 322 F. Supp. 1331, 1362–53 (E.D. Pa. 1971).
45. Lauren E. Willis, *Decisionmaking and the Limits of Disclosure: The Problem of Predatory Lending: Price*, 65 Md. L. Rev. 707, 790 (2006).
46. *In re Martinez*, 266 BR 523 (Bkrtcy. S. D. Fla., 2001).
47. *Gutierrez v. Wells Fargo Bank*, 730 F. Supp. 2d. 1080 (N.D. Cal. 2010).
48. Financial Services Regulatory Relief Act, 15 U.S.C. § 1692g(b) (2006).
49. Robert A. Prentice, *Moral Equilibrium: Stock Brokers and the Limits of Disclosure*, 2011 Wis. L. Rev. 1059, 1088–89.
50. Kevin P. Weinfurt et al., *Disclosing Conflicts of Interest in Clinical Research: Views of Institutional Review Boards, Conflict of Interest Committees, and Investigators*, 34 J. L. Med. Ethics 581, 583 (2006).
51. Kevin P. Weinfurt et al., *Disclosure of Financial Relationships to Participants in Clinical Research*, 361 N. Engl. J. Med. 916, 918 (2009).
52. Christine Grady et al., *The Limits of Disclosure: What Research Subjects Want to Know about Investigator Financial Interests*, 34 J. L. Med. Ethics 592, 597 (2006).
53. Weinfurt et al., *Disclosing Conflicts of Interest*, 590.
54. Mark A. Hall et al., *How Disclosing HMO Physician Incentives Affects Trust*, 21 Health Affairs 197, 203–5 (2002).
55. Richard S. Saver, *Medical Research Oversight From the Corporate Governance Perspective: Comparing Institutional Review Boards and Corporate Boards*, 46 Wm. & Mary L. Rev. 619, 717 (2004).
56. Weinfurt et al., *Disclosure of Financial Relationships*, 917.
57. Grady et al., *Limits of Disclosure*, 598.
58. Stacy W. Gray et al., *Attitudes Toward Research Participation and Investigator Conflicts of Interest Among Advanced Cancer Patients Participating in Early Phase Clinical Trials*, 25 J. Clin. Onc. 3488, 3492 (2007).
59. Daylian M. Cain et al., *The Dirt on Coming Clean: Perverse Effects of Disclosing Conflicts of Interest*, 34 J Legal Stud. 1 (2005).
60. Robert A. Prentice, *Moral Equilibrium: Stock Brokers and the Limits of Disclosure*, 2011 Wis. L. Rev. 1059, 1073 (2011).
61. David de Meza et al., *Disclosure, Trust and Persuasion in Insurance Markets*, IZA Discussion Paper No. 5060 (2010), 3.
62. Cain et al., *Dirt on Coming Clean*.
63. Sunita Sah, George Loewenstein, and Daylian M. Cain, *How Doctors' Disclosures Increase Patient Anxiety* (unpublished manuscript 2011).
64. Michael S. Barr, Sendhil Mullainathan, and Eldar Shafir, *Behaviorally Informed Financial Services Regulation* (New America Foundation, 2008), 7.

CHAPTER 11

1. Stephen Breyer, *Regulation and its Reform* (Harvard University Press 1984), 161.
2. Restatement (Second) of Torts §402A cmt. j. Recognizing that a warning may not be seen or may be disregarded, the Restatement (Third) of Torts seeks to

reform this rule. Restatement (Third) of Torts: Products Liability § 2 cmt. 1, (reporter's note on cmt. 1), (2008).

3. Steven Waldman, "Do Warning Labels Work?," *Newsweek*, July 18, 1988, 40.

4. Howard Latin, *"Good" Warning, Bad Products, and Cognitive Limitations*, 41 UCLA L. Rev. 1193, 1218 (1994).

5. *Verna Emery v. American General Finance, Inc.* 71 F.3d 1343, 1347–48 (7th Cir. 1995).

6. Ibid., 1350 (Coffey, J., dissenting).

7. Robert A. Hillman, "Online Boilerplate: Would Mandatory Web Site Disclosure of e-Standard Terms Backfire?," in *Boilerplate: Foundations of Market Contracts*, ed. Omri Ben-Shahar (Cambridge University Press 2006), 83–94.

8. *Rienche v. Cingular Wireless*, 2006 WL 3827477 (W. D. Wash.). See also *Williams v. First Gov't Mortgage Investors*, 225 F.3d 738, 749 (D. C. Cir., 2000).

9. M. Todd Henderson, Alan D. Jagolinzer, and Karl A. Muller, *Strategic Disclosure of 10b5-1 Trading Plans* (University of Chicago Law School, Law and Economics Research Paper Series 05/2008).

10. Lauren E. Willis, *Decision Making and the Limits of Disclosure: The Problem of Predatory Lending*: Price, 65 Md, L. Rev. 707, 794–95 (2006).

11. Victoria Groon and M. Ryan Calo, *Reversing the Privacy Paradox: An Experimental Study* (mimeo., Stanford Law School, 2011); Yue Pan and George M. Zinkhan, *Exploring the Impact of Online Privacy Disclosures on Consumer Trust*, 82 J. Retailing 331–38 (2006).

12. Sara Lipka, "Do Crime Statistics Keep Students Safe?," *Chron. Higher Educ.*, Jan. 30, 2009.

13. Daniel E. Ho, *Fudging the Nudge: Information Disclosure and Restaurant Grading*, 122 Yale L.J. 574 (2012).

14. *ProCD v. Zeidenberg*, 86 F.3d 1447 (7th Cir. 1996).

15. Omri Ben-Shahar and Eric Posner, *The Right to Withdraw in Contract Law*, 40 J. Legal Stud. 115 (2011).

16. ALI Principles of the Law of Software Contracts (2010), 130–31.

17. U.S. Department of Housing and Urban Development and U.S. Department of Treasury, *Recommendation to Curb Predatory Home Mortgage Lending* (2000), 67, visited August 31, 2013, http://archives.hud.gov/reports/treasrpt.pdf.

18. Richard Craswell, *Taking Information Seriously: Misrepresentation and Nondisclosure in Contract Law and Elsewhere*, 92 Va. L. Rev. 565, 584 (2006).

19. Douglas A. Hershey et al., *Challenges of Training Pre-Retirees to Make Sound Financial Planning Decisions*, 24 Educ. Gerontology 447, 468 (1998).

20. Susan Feng Lu, *Multitasking, Information Disclosures and Product Quality: Evidence from Nursing Homes*, 21 J. Econ. Management Strategy 673 (2012).

21. Leemore Dafny and David Dranove, *Do Report Cards Tell Consumers Anything They Don't Already Know? The Case of Medicare HMOs*, 39 RAND J. Econ. 790 (2008).

22. Frank H. Easterbrook and Daniel R. Fischel, *Mandatory Disclosure and the Protection of Investors*, 70 Va. L. Rev. 669, 671 (1984).

23. *Dalton v. Bob Neill Pontiac*, 476 F. Supp. 789 (M.D. N.C.1979).

24. Mark Petit, Jr., *Representing Consumer Defendants in Debt Collection Actions: The Disclosure Defense Game*, 59 Tex. L. Rev. 255 (1981). See also *Re-Examining Truth in Lending: Do Borrowers Actually Use Consumer Disclosures?* 52 Consumer Fin. L. Q. Rep. 3 (1998).

25. Christine Haughney, "After Bust, Using '60s Law to Get Out of Condo Deals," *New York Times*, October 20, 2010.

26. *Wilson v. Allied Loans, Inc.*, 448 F. Supp. 1020, 1022–23 (D. S.C. 1978).

27. David Klein, *Societal Influences on Child Accidents*, 12 Accident Analysis & Prevention 275 (1980).

28. Kenneth McNeil et al., *Market Discrimination Against the Poor and the Impact of Consumer Disclosure Laws: The Used Car Industry*, 13 Law & Soc'y Rev. 695, 699 (1979).

29. Angela Fagerlin et al., *Patient Education Material about the Treatment of Early-Stage Prostate Cancer: A Critical Review*, 140 Ann. Int. Med. 721 (2004).

30. Stuart A. Grossman et al., *Are Informed Consent Forms That Describe Clinical Oncology Research Protocols Readable by Most Patients and Their Families?*, 12 J. Clin. Onc. 2211, 2212 (1994).

31. David Dranove et al., *Is More Information Better? The Effects of "Report Cards" on Health Care Providers*, 111 J. Pol. Econ. 555 (2003).

32. "Comcast Agreement for Residential Services," § 13 (October 2007).

33. Keith Humphreys et al., *The Cost of Institutional Review Board Procedures in Multicenter Observational Research* 139 Ann. Int. Med. 77 (2003).

34. Rory Collins et al., "Ethics of Clinical Trials," in *Introducing New Treatments for Cancer: Practical, Ethical, and Legal Problems,* ed. C.J. Williams (Wiley, 1992), 54; Simon N. Whitney and Carl E. Schneider, *Viewpoint: A Method to Estimate the Cost in Lives of Ethics Board Review of Biomedical Research*, 269 J. Int. Med. 396 (2011).

35. Ian Roberts et al., *Effect of Consent Rituals on Mortality in Emergency Care Research*, 377 Lancet 1071, 1071 (2011). In addition, the delay "obscure[d] a real treatment benefit from the administration of a time-critical treatment."

36. See Carl E. Schneider, *The Censor's Hand: The Misregulation of Human-Subject Research* (MIT Press 2014).

CHAPTER 12

1. See Alan Schwartz and Louis L. Wilde, *Intervening in Markets on the Basis of Imperfect Information: A Legal and Economic Analysis*, 127 U. Pa. L. Rev. 630 (1979); George L. Priest, *A Theory of the Consumer Product Warranty*, 90 Yale

L.J. 1297 (1981). But see Clayton P. Gillette, *Rolling Contracts as an Agency Problem*, 2004 Wis. L. Rev. 679 (2004).

2. Richard H. Thaler and Cass R. Sunstein, *Nudge: Improving Decisions About Health, Wealth, and Happiness*, (Penguin, 2009), 81–100.

3. Michael Barr, Sendhil Mullainathan, and Eldar Shafir, "A One-Size-Fits-All Solution," *New York Times*, December 26, 2007, visited January 11, 2013, www .nytimes.com/2007/12/26/opinion/26barr.html?page.

4. Carl E. Schneider, *The Practice of Autonomy: Patients, Doctors, and Medical Decisions* (Oxford University Press, 1998), chap. 6; Carl E. Schneider, *The Channelling Function in Family Law*, 20 Hofstra L. Rev. 495 (1992).

5. Michael S. Barr, Sendhil Mullainathan, and Eldar Shafir, *Behaviorally Informed Financial Services Regulation* (New America Foundation, 2008), 7.

6. Federal Deposit Insurance Corporation, *FDIC Study of Bank Overdraft Programs* (Nov. 2008), visited September 2, 2013, http://www.fdic.gov/bank/analytical/over draft/FDIC138_Report_Final_v508.pdf.

7. Lauren E. Willis, *When Nudges Fail: Slippery Defaults*, 80 U. Chi. L. Rev. 1155, 1185 (2013).

8. Margaret Jane Radin, *Boilerplate: The Fine Print, Vanishing Rights, and the Rule of Law* (Princeton University Press, 2013).

INDEX